WHO SAYS YOU CAN'T?
YOU DO

DANIEL CHIDIAC

DC GROUP GLOBAL

Who Says You Can't? YOU DO is stimulating and, regardless of one's success, perceived and otherwise, assists in determining how to engineer what we want in life and from life. I found Daniel's philosophy unique. I recommend that everyone, regardless of their status in life, would gain much benefit from reading this book.

Professor Geoffrey Edelsten
Medical entrepreneur and author of Enigma

Making my way through a lifetime of self-help books, finally a text which executes practical use of how to apply the switch to an intelligent and positive lifestyle. Daniel's enthusiasm leaps out of the pages like he is personally behind your cause. Compelling reading!

Helen Kapalos
Senior news presenter, Network Ten

Daniel is someone who amazes you with his personal experiences and knowledge. Don't let his age fool you: Daniel possesses the clear and positive understanding of how the world works, and the effects that certain behaviour can have on a person's self esteem. His passion and thoughtful commentary should be shared with everyone.

Ahron Young
Bureau chief, Sky News

Daniel has uncanny intuition of the core issues driving the challenges his clients face. He possesses the skill to gently guide them to a new and empowering perspective. His intelligence and vibe is contagious. Daniel has the capacity to understand and respect each person's situation, yet at the same time he challenges them to move beyond their obstacles and achieve what they want in life.

Toby O'Brien
Senior psychologist, Sydney, Australia

His [Daniel's] encouragement and strategies to push past known limits are second to none, truly genius. If only the world had more people like Daniel in it.

Angela Jacobsen
Celebrity nanny and author of Baby Love: Angela Jacobsen's A to Z

Daniel understands people of any age group. In my experience, he can easily connect with the youth. He knows what they need to achieve. His strategies transform lives.

Nick Bracks
Media figure and owner of underBracks

ACKNOWLEDGEMENTS

How does someone who has been emotionally touched by so many people in life ever have the words to express how they feel? These words are like a grain of sand in an ocean compared to the enormity of the gratitude I feel towards these amazing people.

I dedicate this book to my unconditionally loving mother and father. Thank you for always encouraging me to be the best person I can be. Your belief and faith have driven me to levels I once dreamed about.

To my brother and mentor Matthew, I appreciate the life chats and support you have given me throughout my life. We are in this together.

To my sister Jeannie, thank you for giving me unforgettable Saturdays with my two beautiful nephews, Zac and Adam. To raise children the way you have says it all about the qualities you attain.

To my second mother, Aunty Helen, I would definitely not be where I am today without you. I don't need to explain; you know how much you mean to me.

To my Nan and Aunty Adele, thank you for the support you continue to give me throughout my life. And to my grandfather, even though it has been many years since your passing, your spirit continues to inspire me.

I would also like to thank all my friends who have been there through thick and thin. You know who you are.

To the rest of my family, thank you for always being there. Our family is so special because of the morals we have been raised to value. Let's never forget them.

I would also like to thank all the people who said, 'No you can't'. You have been the fuel that drives me to prove that I can.

Lastly, to all of you who want to dump the word 'can't' and go on a journey that will empower your life forever, I salute you for having the courage to master your life.

I believe the true meaning of our experiences is not just to learn, but to teach others what we have learnt.

Daniel Chidiac

CONTENTS

INTRODUCTION

'There are powers inside of you which, if you could discover and use, would make you everything you ever dreamed or imagined you could become.'
Orison Swett Marden

Why do you act the way you do? Why are some highly motivated while others would almost be in tears for having to get up and get the TV remote? What makes the difference in people's lives? How do you change your approach and outlook when the world seems to be crashing down around you? How do you create your life the way you want it? What are the strategies that have worked for the most successful people in history? How do you build a relationship with yourself to a point of trust, which will ensure you achieve what you set out for? The burning desire to search for answers has become my life's passion and has granted me an infinite source of intelligence and wisdom that waits patiently within every human. I am committed to regaining that fighting spirit which has been diminished over time and through experience, for so many individuals.

It's obvious that we all have visions as to what we wish our life would be, but very few of us ever get to experience it. Why? Could it be reluctance to search deeper? Could it merely be not knowing how? Could it be psychological or emotional barriers that prevent our true powers being displayed? The sad reality is that most people will live out their lives, dreaming about another life that seems out of reach. The hope and faith in their own ability will be clouded by the stress and worry of everyday life.

'Where there is no vision, the people perish.'
Proverbs 29:18

Not so long ago, I found myself in one of life's uncertain events. I was in my room on my knees, experiencing the physical and emotional effects after a big weekend on drugs. I had no job, no sense of direction, and had lost all hope in my ability to shape my destiny. I felt helpless to myself, and the world. Just like everyone else, I wanted my life to mean something; to have the ability to make a difference in people's lives and live by a purpose that inspired my every move; to fulfil my own desires, contribute to society, and wake up in the morning actually looking forward to the day!

And since that point, when I felt like a failure, I have embarked on a journey to find **why some people are living an extraordinary life, while others are never really fulfilled?** Through this journey I have modelled the most successful people known to man, travelled overseas to meet with leaders who have the strongest mindsets on the planet, interacted with exceptional achievers, coached people from all the around the globe, from professional athletes to TV personalities, but most importantly I have delved deeply into the human mind and emotion. And let me assure you, all the fulfilled individuals I have met, live with similar attributes. Have you ever wondered why only a few people are living their dream, but the vast majority are not? Those people who live a successful life, and by successful I mean fulfilled, think in a similar way, feel in a certain way, and act according to those patterns. Yes, they are very different in many ways, but the core nature of their existence is very similar. Surprisingly, I also discovered that they, too, had to learn and practise those patterns and principles.

One important aspect that I learnt, is that every experience happens for a reason: to lead us to a point where we are to make a decision, which will ultimately determine how we live out the rest of our life. Wherever you are in your life, whatever your achievements are, or whatever you have set up to conquer, you are reading this book to make that very decision. One that will give you a fulfilment that you never knew existed; one that will drive you to that level you want to reach; one that will obtain that healthy lifestyle you dream about; attract that person you have searched for your whole life, or exceed the relationship you are in. One that will guide you to achieve things you once thought impossible, and master your financial state. One that will give you control of your emotions, break fears you thought would last forever, and one that forces you to wake up every day with an outlook on life that guides every step you take. One decision that ensures you hit the targets you set out to achieve.

Now, as much as this book is about how to make that crucial decision, it's also to create direction in your life, so that every decision will be made with the knowledge and strategies that are certain to elevate you to a level that others will speak about forever. It doesn't matter what level you currently consider yourself to be at, there is always room for growth.

Just like any journey, this book contains steps…

The 1ˢᵗ Step: Self Discovery: The Knowledge To Empower Your Life Forever will do just that. Everyone I have come in contact with has shown their interest in going through a self-discovery, but has said that they wouldn't know where to start. This step is the most crucial in forming a lasting understanding of yourself and enhancing the ability to create change in an instant.

The 2ⁿᵈ Step: Energy: That Fundamental Force explains how to properly use that vast energy within your being. We all know that the more energy we direct towards something, the quicker it comes about. Most people expend all their energy on things that are actually destroying their life rather then enriching it. This is the ultimate guide to distinguish between the two, and provide the knowledge that will raise your awareness for ever.

The 3ʳᵈ Step: The System Of Achievement is by far the foreground of anything you set out to achieve. I would never include anything in this book that was not practised by me, worked on by my clients or anything different to what the greatest in history have used. The detailed strategy in this section will give you the arsenal to excel. It will show you in a step-by-step process how to overcome any challenge in business, help you find what you are passionate about and create the *clarity* and *emotional charge* that is needed to succeed.

The 4ᵗʰ Step: Steer Your Relation-SHIPS will show you how to take immediate control of your relationship situation. Is your ship sailing smoothly, rockily, or is it yet to set sail? Whether you are currently struggling in your relationship and want to let go, or striving to enhance it, this is your guide. It has also been designed for those who have been looking for their dream partner, but are unsure how to attract him or her.

The 5th Step: To A Healthy Physical Existence gives you the mindset and strategy to take charge of your health. We can all agree that our health is definitely one of the most important things in life. If it isn't to you, then you probably need to read this section more than anyone. Without a healthy body, your life is not successful, period. I am qualified in Personal Training and have used my knowledge from previous clients to show the most effective ways to attain that body you want, but more importantly, the emotion of feeling great about yourself. There is also detailed information about how the mind affects your body in every way imaginable.

The 6th Step: Awaken Your Mind, Unchain Your Heart enforces the magnitude of being consciously awakened, self-aware, and enlightened to the world around you. This journey through your emotional state will scientifically and morally prove how we are all one in essence. It looks at how your actions not only affect your own life, but the world at large. Walk with me as I go on my spiritual journey through Thailand to meet and stay with one of the most respected monks in the country. This step takes you through the vast influence we have on youth, from our children, nephews and nieces, to the kid on the street! Nothing drives you more than being awakened to your role in this world.

The 7th Step: Finding Fulfilment is the ultimate advantage one can have. No life is successful without fulfilment. Do not be mistaken: a great achiever is not always fulfilled. Success is fulfilment in essence. Find out what makes us truly happy and knock down the social myth that has influenced our heart to believe that happiness is synthetic. That system has failed many throughout history, so don't allow yourself to be fooled any longer. True fulfilment does exist!

In saying all this, it would be absurd to attempt to minimise the enormity of the life changing content in this book. I don't want any aspect of this journey to be tainted by an introduction that attempts to sum its power up in a few paragraphs. While this is a fun and interactive read, it does not sugar-coat anything. It is real, raw and direct in its approach to bring out the absolute greatest qualities you have always had within you. Be ready to be intrigued, fascinated and amazed. Not by this book, but by your own power.

'Man's mind, stretched by a new idea, never goes back to its old dimensions.'
Oliver Wendell Holmes

Before I turned my tide

'The ultimate measure of a man is not where he stands in moments of comfort, but where he stands at times of challenge and controversy.'
Martin Luther King Jr.

Growing up as a child I always dreamed of a better life. I wasn't as unfortunate as others, but I had a common want: to escape the world as I knew it, and what surrounded me every day. I remember thinking big from a young age, yet there always seemed something that prevented me from believing it would ever be my reality. As most kids do, I would watch people on TV, listen to singers, or see businessmen and wish I could achieve like that. My parents always attempted to create a happy environment for me and were always supportive, although kids see things in a different way to how their parents hope at times.

My father was a man that could be on either side of the equation. He could be extremely hard on one hand, and yet the most loving person I know on the other. Through his hard side he taught me a lot, though, and one major thing was that giving up just doesn't cut it. Second was never good enough and he expected the most out of everything I committed to. It was tough to handle at times, yet I now see the massive effect those teachings had on where I am today. His 'never give up' attitude is something that will stay cemented in me forever. As for my mother, she never had a doubt or really questioned me. My parents didn't have much money when I was growing up, and that was difficult to watch. My parents are both unconditionally loving people, and for that I am ever indebted. For some reason, though, I still didn't like to hang around, or abide by the rules.

*'It's not what you own in this world, it's what legacy you leave behind
that matters.'*
My mother

I began to find comfort in my grandfather and my aunty. When my parents moved from my grandparents' home, I decided to stay put rather than move with them. I looked up to my grandfather as a role model because of his strong connection with his family and, among so much money and external respect, he had a sense of fulfilment. He seemed at peace with the world and used his strong mind to deal with all his family's issues. On a daily basis he would go down to the local church and still serve as an altar boy. That was such an awakening; being young, I had a misconception of what it was like to be successful. I equated success to money, only to grow up and appreciate that he was really rich, abundant in all areas, not only in the monetary sense.

One of the hardest moments of my life was when my grandfather was diagnosed with cancer. As a twelve year old I would kneel in the shower, crying and praying to God to cure him. Without realising it at the time, I was trying to cure myself of the emotional pain and suffering I was about to endure. After three long years, my grandfather finally gave up his battle with cancer. As expected, my battle in life was just beginning. The world around me seemed to crumble. The rock of the family was gone, and a deep sense of loss would follow me for many years to come.

Living in a working class suburb of Melbourne, I thought my opportunities were limited. Anger towards the world really started to build up. I chose to run instead of facing it. I began losing all sense of direction, and became a child who would go out just to cause problems. Nearly getting kicked out of school, getting into vicious fights and having little respect for the world were becoming my way of life.

My friends at the time seemed to show me a lot of love. We would hang out in the backstreets all night just thinking how we would get our next laugh. That laugh didn't really have many boundaries and would go against authority. I was on a one-way road to self-destruction. I knew all along that what I was doing wasn't a true reflection of who I really was, but I was living the way I thought I had to. I guess it was for attention, acceptance, praise, recognition, selfish satisfaction, and every other feeling that leads to unhappiness.

'There can be no happiness if the things we believe in are different from the things we do.'
Freya Stark

There was a bridge near my house that I used to look over and reflect. I was only about fourteen at the time, but I would analyse the cars as they drove past. I was fascinated by the fact that everyone seemed to be in their own worlds, driving to their own destination, yet we are all part of the same 'big world.' I would see someone driving a Mercedes Benz, and shortly after someone else drive past in an old Toyota, and try to figure out why the tables weren't turned. Why did this woman get to drive a car like that, and the other guy didn't? Was it by chance? Then I would refer back to 'but we are in the same world.' I even remember questioning whether the person in the Mercedes was really happy and whether the other guy was sad. I was intrigued with human emotion, the different ways of life, but more importantly, with answers. At the time it had no real effect on myself, it would only help to reflect on others, but the interest always remained. I always felt that I was here to affect the world. Little did I know I was doing it all along with my actions, but I guess that's a common trait with most people these days.

A few years went by and not much had changed. I met a girl who would become my girlfriend for three years, and I based my happiness around her presence. Things were great at the start, then just seemed to crumble, much like most events that were taking place in my life. We would fight, and things turned into a real disaster. I found out that she was cheating on me. Even though our relationship was on the rocks, this event sent me to a real emptiness once again. It's become apparent that most of us who aren't self-aware don't feel the impact of our actions until they come around and knock on our door.

I couldn't eat or sleep, my whole day and every ounce of energy revolved around reminding me of this deep pain I was experiencing. I felt as if she hadn't finished in my life yet, and told myself that I needed her in order to live. We got back together, and after a while the feelings started to fade. I believe it was my lies telling me that I needed the comfort of knowing that she still loved me. I now realise it was a selfish act that I thought was protecting me. Making the decision to leave was the hardest one I've ever had to make, and was a real test of strength. I just knew there were things I had to do in life first, and I needed to do them on my own. Looking back, I don't really ever think I was in love with who she was, but in love with filling my emotional gaps with her presence.

After losing all contact with my ex-girlfriend, I lost contact with what I believed was happiness. Once again, I began to look for external things to complete me. All along, I didn't realise I was doing it for that reason, but more importantly I was blinded to the fact that complete happiness can only be attained within one's self. So off I went, on another journey to outside happiness.

I began to live a party lifestyle. Took up smoking, was drinking heavily, and began experimenting with drugs. I just lived for the weekends. I was doing a Commerce degree at university, but I knew that was not what I wanted out of life. Sitting in a lecture one day with about 300 other students, my mind was racing. All I could think about was how I would be competing with these other people for a job that I didn't even want. I knew I had two options right there: stay and live a life I'd never be happy with, or take the leap of faith straight into the unknown without having a clue as to what I wanted to do.

I stood up, picked up my books, walked out, and never looked back. As most parents do, mine wanted me to finish the degree, but I just knew that I didn't want to live my life by what social expectation deems appropriate, so I decided to take the risk. The main point, however, was that I didn't have a clear vision as to what I really wanted out of life, I just knew I didn't want to be where I was. I started working for a marketing company, left that, then got a full-time sales job. I had an uncanny ability to excel in both occupations and was promoted as the youngest sales coach in the company, even though I had only been there for six months. But there was only one thing: it didn't fulfil me!

During this time I partnered with my brother and we began a clothing importing business. Still unsure as to what my true passion in life was, I can honestly admit that I was never 100 per cent committed. I worked at it, but it was only to try and generate money, because that's where I thought happiness lay. With another one of my assumptions about life's greatness gone, I was exhausting all avenues, and the truth was close to showing itself once again. This time it would have no mercy.

I was close to nineteen at the time, flying over to Italy and reading books on negotiation. Not something the average teenager does, so I definitely have no regrets. While looking out of the plane window, I would think about where my life was headed. **What is all of this? What does it all mean? What I am doing here?** I wouldn't give these questions too much energy as I thought my time needed to be better spent. I now see that that belief was far from the truth. Instead of answering those questions, I would mentally re-enact the scenario of me walking into the boardroom, surrounded by international businessmen, trying to get the best deal. I was nervous, anxious, but amazingly excited at the same time. I knew that I was never going to live a life that was less than what I knew I deserved. I was never willing to settle or accept that I couldn't be my own boss, or live that dream life.

By the age of twenty-one I had been to Europe five times for the business. I always put on a happy face and told people about it, which gave me some satisfaction. I thought I had found happiness by attempting to portray this great lifestyle I made out I was living. Every time someone asked me how I was, I would say 'loving life'. What these people didn't know, is by that stage, I was addicted to drugs, couldn't make a relationship work, I was broke, mentally, emotionally and spiritually spent, and had no sense of direction. I would hang out all night smoking dope just to try and cloud the confusion of my inner self. It's like putting a thousand bandaids over a fresh wound. It doesn't matter how many you put on top, the wound is still there and as fresh as always. On the outside, everything seemed perfect, because I was pretty good at hiding it.

Who knew all along? I did. I was lying to myself, and being me, **I had the ability to know my own truth — a gift we all have.**

I knew I was lost and would call out to a God I didn't even really feel or understand to light up the path for me and show me the right direction. Did I ever doubt God's presence? Of course I did, especially at the times when I was so low. But who was I to turn to? I had already invested all of my energy into things that I thought would make me happy.

People began to come into my life and I would hear them talk about a real happiness. I guess they were always there; my mind just chose to take some notice of them now. I repeat, I would 'hear' them, because in order for me to be really interested, I would have listened, and I didn't. I couldn't imagine such fulfilment without what I had thought appropriate to fill it, so I would reject them just as quickly. I would argue and come up with so many different excuses and get frustrated as they would throw my lies back at me with the question, 'Well, are you really happy?' Funnily enough, I would say yes. Every time I said it, I knew I was lying, and it would have even more of a detrimental effect on my life. I was scared to venture out of my fear, as weird as that sounds. I felt my truth arising more, that deep voice inside. But I didn't act upon it, because I guess I didn't have the faith that it could change my life. Even though I always knew I was a good person deep down, I would keep doing things against that belief, and it would confuse me even more.

Things were arising that would make me question everything I was doing. The hardest part was questioning those actions I had previously done subconsciously. One particular night I hit what I thought was my lowest point. After having another big weekend on a cocktail of drugs, I hadn't slept for forty-eight hours. I was mentally and physically exhausted. This was no ordinary 'come down'. No words can ever describe the feeling of emptiness. I thought this was it, the end of any little hope I had tried to hold on to. I was wishing the ground would just open up and swallow me. Standing in my bedroom, feeling numb to everything around me, and having thoughts that it would be easier if I were dead, I felt as if there was nowhere to turn. A deep sadness and fear came over me, like a child locked in a dark room, but a thousand times worse. I broke down, got on my knees, and screamed out to God, saying 'Where the hell are you now?' I was so low that I felt I had to reach up to touch the bottom. Choked up and tears blurring my sight, I stood up only to be facing myself in the mirror. Through the tears, I looked deformed, until I wiped them away. My face became clearer and the most overwhelming feeling came over me. Such an awakening and enlightening experience that it would **change my life forever**. I stood there staring at myself for twenty minutes. I finally realised the person I had wanted to be my whole life was looking straight back at me. And so OUR JOURNEY BEGINS...

Your personal contract:

I ....

Declare that I must master my life in every area. I will no longer settle for a life that is less than what I know I deserve. I have had enough experience to know one side of life, and now it's my **time to shine**. I will commit myself to enrich the quality of my life from what it is now. I will persist under any circumstance to act upon the tasks in this book, which are going to empower me forever. I will not leave any task undone, relentlessly work to empower my life, and push beyond my known limits.

I AM responsible for shaping my destiny, and entrust my ability to see this book through. I understand that the only way to real success is by having a great State Of Mind, and I'm willing to vigorously work to create and enhance it. I am ready to LIVE MY LIFE in the never-ending cycle of self-growth and use the unlimited power within my being.

I am ready to attain a burning desire, compelling visions, and a passion for life that sits well above all else.

Sign:..Date: ....

1ˢᵀ STEP

SELF DISCOVERY:
THE KNOWLEDGE TO
EMPOWER YOUR LIFE
FOREVER

I

ABSOLUTE POWER OF QUESTIONING

'The definition of insanity is doing the same thing over and over
again and expecting different results.'
Albert Einstein

Great questions = great answers

Regardless of your age, if you are breathing, then you are always
ready for change. It might be in a relationship, career, an old habit,
anger issue, or something that is really affecting your life. I want
you to ask yourself, **'Everything I have come to know in the last
eighteen, twenty-two, forty-five or even sixty-five years, what
impact has it had in this particular area of my life? Am I happy
where I am? Have I attained fulfilment? Do I feel lost and
confused?'**

Now think back to how many times you have asked yourself those
same questions. Do you see a pattern with your previous answers
and your current ones? Unfortunately, most continue on that
circular train track their whole life and are never able to implement
real change. Firstly, they don't build the belief system because
they remind themselves of why they think they can't change; and
secondly, some people just don't know how to approach it. It's
evident that we are always obtaining knowledge in this life, but
learning requires rapid action. You could watch someone change a

car tyre twenty times over, but unless you get down and do it, your knowledge is never tested, nor will you learn. It seems a lot of us believe we are taking appropriate action yet still feel as if we have failed. This is why we must direct that energy in a way that is going to be effective and implement lasting change.

Society has made us believe that if we 'change' then we are not being true to ourselves. Even our friends will have a dig at us and say things like, 'You've changed,' in a tone that makes us feel pain. There are two things that are neglected in this lie. They are: change is extremely powerful, but more importantly, it's *inevitable*. Nothing remains the same. Every new moment, you are a new person, even physically. Not one single cell in your body has remained the same. This means we are always 'becoming'. But what you are becoming depends on you. The challenge is that most people aren't becoming what they want.

Essentially, something must change in order to grow, right? Whether it is financially, physically, emotionally or mentally, the same rule applies. **Proper questioning is definitely the basis for directing change towards our immediate growth.** It allows us to broaden the way we think and stop being narrow minded by creating a belief that 'there is only one option'. We are asking questions to ourselves; however, we usually ask ones that result in answers that are of no real benefit and cause us to feel the same way.

That usually results in creating the same experiences. **Stay away** from such questions…

Why can't I do that?

Why am I so unlucky?

Why does this always happen to me?

Why are all girls/guys the same?

All people with money have screwed someone over to get there, right?

Why can't I enjoy life like others?

Why am I the only one faced with so many challenges in life?

When you change the way you think, you change the way you feel. When you change the way you feel, you change the way you act. When you change the way you act, you change your life. It starts by changing the way you…?

Who am I?

'An unquestioned mind is the world of suffering.'
Byron Katie

We need to ask questions that spurt growth and prevent us from feeling as if we are insignificant and worthless. It's very important to ask and reflect on the question 'Who am I?' before anything else. This may seem a daunting question when first glanced at; however probing deeper will surely unravel the truth.

Not fully acknowledging the answer may really cloud what you **really** want, and deter you from ever experiencing a 'great' life. Ask what type of person you are deep down, regardless of some decisions you have made in the past. Let's give some examples, but just note, that the answers are **away from experience for now, but more to the point of who you know you really are, deep within your heart.** Take a few seconds to think as you go through each question.

Am I a loving person?

Am I respectful?

Am I compassionate?

Am I generous and sharing?

Am I an honest person?

Am I grateful?

After going through those questions, did your mind automatically begin to remind you of times that you **weren't** that person? If that was the case, it's because your mind is still conditioned to looking at experiences, and especially yourself, in the worst possible way. If you are human, then I'm sure there have been times in your life when these positive attributes haven't been displayed. I'm definitely guilty of that, but it doesn't alter the fact that we are not that person deep down. Realistically, if we were stuck with choices and some of the actions we have taken in life, I'm certain that most wouldn't even be reading this right now. So don't deliberately remember the times you weren't, be intelligent and focus on the times you did display these qualities. Now, run through the questions again, but in addition ask this: '**When was a time that I did display this quality?**' After you do, come back and read on...

The more you focus on being that great person, the more invigorated and energetic you feel. Did you feel proud of yourself when you went back to that moment? How did it compare to focusing on not being that person? Reminding yourself of these essential values to gain fulfilment will give you incentive to use them more often.

If you truly don't think you are that person, ask yourself, 'How can I be?' and you will instantly be flooded with ideas. Further to that, if you don't want to be that person, then unfortunately that's the reason you are unfulfilled in the first place, and never experiencing the true essence of life. In my opinion, that is a very sad life to live, and one I wouldn't trade with for all the money in the world. **The challenge isn't knowing who we are as a person, it's having the courage to act like it.**

It seems that we are almost separated into two parts. One part is the 'Me' and the other is the 'I'. The 'Me' seems to be all the social tags we adopt. For example, it is my duty to be a friend, a son, a life coach, a mentor, a brother, and so on. It so happens that I am all these things, but weirdly enough, when I'm all alone and away from these duties, I find myself not being any of them. That's when I finally discover that the 'I' is who I really am. It's those qualities within me, that diversity and ability to be everything, and at times, nothing. There are also times when we feel alienated from the world, and that's because people won't always understand the 'I' part to our life. But they don't have to, we do. It's not until we are aligned with who we really are as person, not who society brands us as being, that we will be eternally happy and live passionately every moment.

I invite you to do the next task, which is life transforming:

Task

1. Take five minutes and really reflect on those 'Am I' questions. Make sure you don't rob yourself of this opportunity. These are life-changing exercises. Write these down. **Do not** go onto Task 2 until you have completed this one.

2. Now swap the 'Am' and the 'I' around. It should now read 'I Am' followed by the quality. Write them down.

3. Next take another few minutes and reflect on the new list you have written down. Close your eyes and repeat them in your mind or say them out loud. Just make sure all your focus is on those qualities that have the power to change your life. It's usually not being sure of who we are that causes so much confusion when it's time to make a decision in our life. This creates clarity.

If you're in a public place and you don't really want to scream how great you are, I suggest you do it in your mind for now. And don't forget: **FFF (Full Focus on Feeling).**

I don't even need to know you to know that you're a big softy deep down. By reaffirming those statements, you align yourself with who you really are. It's a very important key to finding happiness or success on any level. If completed correctly, that exercise was surely invigorating and fulfilling. See how quickly it is to fill ourselves up once we focus all our energy on the qualities of life? That exercise can be done during any issue that we are facing to gain a clear consciousness, and I highly advise it is done on a daily basis for a while, especially in the morning. I would never suggest something here that I don't personally do, and didn't use for others. I have used this on some of the most successful and fulfilled people I know and it adds massive value to their life.

The qualities mentioned above are just some examples; I'm sure you can think of more. You must start with 'I AM', followed by a quality. Now that you covered some qualities that reflect who you **really** are, it allows you to properly assess decisions you make on a constant basis.

I've also come to the conclusion that all human beings have the same true essence, regardless of our religious background, social status, or past decisions. I have spoken to people from all walks of life, even some hard criminals, and never had anyone refuse, after enough probing, to finally admit that they are all those great qualities deep down. We are human and such qualities have been in us since birth, hence it is our true essence. Have you ever noticed that's why babies bring so much joy to the people around them? Like when you go to someone's house and everyone runs up to the baby. We nearly get into arguments over who's going to hold it first. It's amazing, and that's because they just are who they are, pure and love. They have not been restricted by social myth, and ego has yet to take control over their life. You must understand that your truth will never go away, and will always be there to correct you when you feel otherwise. It is also accessible for growth and learning; hence we can relate who we really are to any situation and decision we make.

I must ask you this question: Are you really being who you know you are? Nearly everyone I have asked this question of has become defensive and answered with, 'of course I am'. In my opinion and through my own experience, most times we are acting how we think we have to, not the way we truly want to. We think about what others are thinking about us. What are they going to think when I do this? What are they looking at? What makes them laugh? How do I have to be to fit in? What can I do to impress them? We have thoughts like, 'Oh my God, they are all looking at me, straighten up, no, don't look down, look up, look cool,' and so on. We do this when we walk down the street, go for a run, while visiting the beach, or socialising. It's usually a subconscious reaction because we have repeated it throughout our life. If you say that you don't care about what others think, or the effect they have on your life, then that is an outright lie. If you didn't care what others thought, you would be walking around the streets naked. And I know I'm not alone with drifting off at some points and wondering what my funeral would be like. Come on; tell me that hasn't crossed your mind? What would people say about me? Would they cry? Would I be missed? How would they remember me?

We have always cared what other people think; it's human nature. It's obvious that people are going to remember whatever legacy we leave behind. In order to leave a legacy, we must be our legacy now. The greatest legacy we can live and leave behind is to be who we really are. Doing this allows your true destiny to be displayed. If you don't know who you are, how can you make yourself happy? So are we being who we really are, or who we feel we have to be? It's a fine line, but with a bit of thought you will be able to distinguish. Finding this distinction allows progress to soar.

People will remember who you are, not what you have.

Keep on probing

'Each man is questioned by life; and he can only answer to life by answering for his own life; to life he can only respond by being responsible.'
Viktor Frankl

Other important questions should arise about current decisions you are making in life. We must be able to clearly identify other options in order to change an old habit. Asking questions, then more probing questions, until you reach an answer that is beneficial is the key. Do not just stop at one, but ask yourself as many as you have to. In the beginning of my change, I began questioning everything about my life. I remember my friend asked me once if I was lost because I was walking around the house in a daze. My reply was that I'm actually finding answers, which is the opposite of being lost. Initially you might feel a bit uncomfortable with some answers because your ego tries to stand in the way of getting the real truth out. Ask as many as you have to.

We never stop questioning, however, we must ask questions that are going to help us. Just note that it's easy to tell a lie, but it feels like hell when we live a lie. You will know when you are lying to yourself because the answer will not satisfy you, and the same feeling of un-fulfilment will continue to arise. This now leads us to our next set of questions, keeping in mind that you should definitely add to the list…

Does a loving person really judge others?

If I'm respectful, am I respecting myself enough to make change?

Do the things that I'm doing now reflect the real person I am?

Am I truthful to myself when a certain situation arises?

When things seem distorted, am I grateful for being alive and having the opportunity to persist again?

Do I allocate some time for me, even if it's fifteen minutes a day, to really focus on how to improve my life?

Do I usually focus on the worst in life rather than the best things about it?

When I was taking drugs every day for three years, I built some distorted beliefs around the whole concept. I tried to make myself believe that drugs contributed to my happiness, and that it was a time for socialising. Obviously not the truth, but I would refuse to probe deeper in order to get the real answer. I did this because I thought I found comfort in doing it. In a way, I did for that brief moment; but that was only because it made me think the world, as I'd come to know it, was still intact. Along with the fear of going into the unknown, I also hadn't come to the understanding that the world only seemed the way it did because I had made it that way. I didn't allow myself to see the truth, until I went through a deep process of questioning. I began to ask myself, does taking drugs really make me happy? I would answer with 'maybe'. Still not a stable answer, so I asked again. If it makes me happy for a couple of hours, but I hate the rest of the week, is that really happiness? No.

Then another one: is taking drugs stopping me from getting what I really want out of life? I want to achieve, I want a great relationship, and I want to be healthy, so yes, it's preventing me from ever getting those things.

Is it really socialising when I'm destroying my whole life in the process? No. What can I do instead? I want to build a better relationship with my family, so I could start hanging out with them.

That's what I did — started spending more time with my family and I loved it. The same went with my relationships, people I knew, situations I would put myself into, and my job. I questioned everything about my life, and I would always refer back to who I knew I really was. None of them weighed up, so I knew I had to start making massive changes. I was now dealing with answers that were going to benefit every step I was taking. Did I go and change everything instantly and my life was just covered with roses? Of course not. The questions kept coming, still do today, and will until the day I'm gone.

You must remain strong throughout the process and you can do this by weighing up your answers (new beliefs), compared to the old lies. It even reaches a point where you should be so disgusted with your old way that it turns into good frustration.

Physically scream at yourself in the mirror if you feel the urge. I would personally repeat again and again, 'That life is destroying you, you're not going back under any circumstance, do you understand? YES'. Then I would I repeat, 'You're living a better life, you're living a better life,' and so forth. Something I highly recommend if you find yourself battling the old habit. Say it with as much **power** as you can, so it feels like you just got a baseball bat and hit those old beliefs out of the park. Also feel free to tell people about your change. I remember the day I stopped smoking I went and told as many people as I possibly could. I made myself feel extreme pleasure and pride every time I did. I knew that if I began the habit again, everyone would consider me weak, but more importantly, I would. I enforced the belief that if I started smoking again I would not be successful in life and every time it came to mind I began to imagine the chemicals eating away at my body. Further to that, the thought would make me nearly physically throw up. Sounds extreme, but when you think of the extreme effects it has on your health, it sounds like a pretty good substitute. The question is: how much do you want change?

If I told you that you could change the direction of your life to be more fulfilling right now, would you? If the answer is yes, then you acknowledge that there are areas of your life that you feel you are personally destroying. No one really wants to destroy their own life. Even though they might be doing just that doesn't mean it's what they want…

Am I attracting what I want?

It seems when most people question, they don't go deep enough. They deliberately ignore the answers that will serve them.

We are ready to move on to our next set of questions, which will enable us to clearly see what we want. We need to ask questions that will criticise our thinking patterns and the self beliefs we have continually built, so we can come up with a strategic plan to implement life-changing replacements. If we don't question, we don't get answers, and hence will not get what we want. The examples below are broad, but as we progress in further tasks they will become more specific.

Do I want to own my own business?

Do I want a girl/guy that I would like to spend my life with?

Do I want to be healthy and fit?

Do I want a better relationship with my family?

Now the next step…

What would I have to do to attract that particular person?

Would they want to be with someone who had unstable answers in the 'keep on probing' questions we previously went through?

Do people achieve when they remind themselves how lazy they are?

Can I live a healthy life by flooding my liver with alcohol?

Am I affecting my children or family by smoking, which could cause a terminal illness?

Is the mindset that I'm approaching life with ever going to allow me to make change in my life?

Are the same experiences and feelings ever going to change if I continue to think, speak, and act the same way?

If my answers were unstable in some of the questions in the 'Keep on probing' section, how is that affecting me getting the most out of life, and how is it affecting the people I love the most?

Don't ask how life is treating you; ask how you are treating life! Once this is focused on, you will soon see you are not the victim of an unloved destiny, but rather the creator just as equally. You must think of where you are today, and say whether **who you really are** balances out with what situations you are in. Then you must take sole accountability for all your actions that have caused you to be in this situation, as no one thinks, speaks, or ultimately makes decisions for you. The more we blame our situations on others and external events, the more we remove ourselves from ever experiencing the change we so desperately desire. Once we take responsibility, we are able to determine an action plan to obtain what we really want.

If you drive a car, you would know how it feels at times to be a passenger. You may be on the highway, speeding around bends, and all of a sudden you begin to feel a **lack of control**. The driver doesn't know what you're scared of, because to them they are driving normally. When you live in excuses, it seems as though everyone and everything else is in control of your life. **When we feel that we are not in control, we experience fear.**

If we are not in the cycle of self-growth, then we are taking part in self-destruction. Taking accountability means to 'own' your life, and ask 'What can I do differently?'

We must question everything about our life. Massive change comes through deep questioning so you must refuse to stop asking until an answer aligns with your truth. When you are unsure about something, or feeling stressed and worried, you should question until you get to its core. It's okay to take advice from those who clearly demonstrate an ability to have a positive effect on your life, but don't **only** believe what everyone else has to say. Many friends and family will feed your victimisation because they love you. You ultimately know what is best for you, and you can't escape it. Once we take care of us, everyone else reaps the benefits as well.

Questions for solutions

It takes One Moment to change your course of direction, One Decision that makes you step up to the greatness you deserve, and only One Life to make it happen.

When I tell people only a mere two years before this book was released, I was smoking dope in backstreets all night with no sense of direction, you could only imagine their reaction. Further to that, only eight months later, I began coaching strong social figures twice my age, TV and radio personalities, athletes, and people all over the world. In no way am I saying this to toot my own horn, but I say it in the hope that you will realise the enormity of human capacity, which can evidently change your own life. People began emailing from countries such as Columbia, England, USA, Brazil, South Africa, India and Ghana, thanking me for being their 'guru', 'philosopher', or 'master trainer'. I seemed to have attracted many titles, but I wanted to avoid all of them. I didn't like to think that these people, who are skilled in so many areas that I'm not, consider me the expert of their life. They were the only expert of their life, and ultimately the only ones who had the power to enhance it. I was just a guy following his passion who thrived on helping people find what is great in them.

Some of these individuals had achieved great things. I especially wanted to avoid the title of 'trainer'. A trainer is someone who usually teaches you new things. A coach is someone who helps drag out the great qualities in you, and create empowering strategies to get the results you want. And if life/success coaches are doing their job properly, they will be unswerving in their approach to tell you the truth, no matter how much it may hurt or how bold it sounds at the time. Everyone needs that at some points in their life, even me. I guess that's why even the richest and most powerful people in the world still have coaches.

It doesn't mean the coach is more intelligent than them, or is skilled in the same areas they are. I can guarantee you that if I needed to build a house, I wouldn't be getting up there with a hammer and nails. I would call the experts, because they are great at what they do. However, no matter what the background of this diverse collection of people contacting me, nearly all of them asked me the same initial question. They all asked *'What were the fundamental aspects of your change?'* My answer was that I relentlessly committed to answering the following five questions. Obviously it doesn't stop there, as there is a lot more to changing your life, but these have the power to alter its direction in an instant.

As you go through each of these questions, focus on them individually for a few moments. Don't rush, but really focus on finding answers. They are life changing:

1. What drives you every day and what is the basis of your decisions?

2. What are you going to do today, that was different to yesterday, which will ultimately shape who you are tomorrow?

3. What are the life-changing decisions you are committed to making today that will produce the results you so desperately want?

4. What's at least one thing that you can change about your life right now, which will prevent a lifetime of pain and generate a never ending supply of pleasure?

If you don't think you really have a clear indication of what the answers are, think harder and implement some now. You must be specific. For the first question, examples would be: wanting to give your children the best life you possibly can; to be the best person you know how to be; having that feeling of being in charge of your life; contributing to others; that feeling of success; feeling healthy and fit; holding up that trophy; and many more. Those **feelings**

must drive you, because emotion precedes action. If you refer back to those feelings, you will soon get a whole different range of emotions in which to base your decisions.

This is the fifth question where great solutions are based…

5. How can I…?

- be healthy and fit?
- attract that person of my dreams?
- get that **rush** in life?
- experience different emotions?
- push myself that extra mile?
- get that car?
- take control over my life?

When the question 'How can I…?' is asked, it allows us to broaden our options. Inspiration is noticed everywhere, even in places that would once seem normal daily activities, like going for a walk, shopping at the mall, or driving to work. In an amazing way, signs begin jumping out everywhere. It doesn't mean they were never there, but now **your mind is subject to taking notice of them.** You have enlarged the picture frame, so it increases the space for more pictures. The solutions may not be perfect instantly, but by asking this question, you will continue to come up with diverse answers.

All successful people dedicate their life to finding solutions. This one question allows for responses that will benefit your current situation, rather than asking, 'Why can't I…?' which continually reaffirms to yourself why you can't create that life you desire. 'How can I…?' forces you to come up with answers that will drive you.

Let's now take a step into the 'Zone' that most of us find ourselves in, especially after a deep process of questioning. Being able to shift our mindset in a heartbeat when in this zone is essential for creating a life worth dreaming about…

2

UNCOMFORTABLE IN THE 'COMFORT ZONE'

'Somewhere in the archives of crudest instinct is recorded the truth that it is better to be endangered and free than captive and comfortable.'
Tom Robbins

Are we really comfortable where we are in life, or are we just settling because we don't believe we can get any better? Most people I have met try to portray that they are comfortable, yet once they really open up it seems there are many things that they wish they could achieve or attain. It's then evident by their constant disappointment that they are quite uncomfortable. Every time someone asked me how I was, I would reply with the words 'not bad' or 'okay'. For a long time I thought I was lying to myself, until I finally had the feeling of being great. Life is made up of decisions we make, and accepting a 'not bad' or even 'okay' life is the case for most. People rarely admit when they aren't doing too well, and believe that they can take cover behind lying to others and themselves. There is one fact we have to acknowledge: **we can't run and we can't hide from ourselves, because everywhere we go, we're there**.

The hard reality is that most people aren't truly happy with where they are in life. They submit to beliefs that have made them feel that it is the most they can be, and accept a life that never fulfils them. It's quite upsetting because I know the exact feeling, and I also know how it feels to be on the other side. This is one of the main reasons for dedicating my life to sharing it. The first thing I would say is that facing it, rather than running, is the first step towards change. The questions we asked in the last chapter are a great start. They all lead us to a point of *acknowledgement*. We seem to be blinded to the powerful part of that word which is 'ac**knowledge**ment'. We can have all the knowledge in the world, have ten university degrees, travelled the globe, or know how to speak five different languages, but if we don't have true knowledge of ourselves, we will never create the life we want.

Coming to realisations of where you are in life due to past events, decisions you are making now, and how it can affect what you create next is the greatest knowledge you can obtain. It allows you to truly come to the understanding that your life has always been controlled by you. Taking accountability for the state you find yourself in will allow you to make the changes needed to drive your life to a new level.

What's wrong?

As you progress through your self-discovery, you will realise that rather than seeing previous beliefs and decisions as wrong, they actually promote massive progress. It's like stacking Lego blocks together as you begin to come to new realisations on a constant basis. Your beliefs advance from one another and assist each other in growing. You will use all your new knowledge as a means to make sense of new beliefs that show themselves, rather than previously being unsure and using lies as a base to cover the truth.

Many people consider their previous thoughts and actions as being 'wrong'. I'm sure you have realised that no one is perfect — if we were, then we wouldn't know the difference between living an ordinary life compared to a great life. That's the beauty of it. When we live and experience, we are able to distinguish the two, so what's right and what's wrong? I don't care how bad you might think something you have done is, you cannot go back and change it.

If we consider something we have done as being wrong, then we must be able to acknowledge the opposite. In other words, there is information that has taught you how to do it differently the next time. What you choose to learn from that is up to you alone. The more you ignore and disregard your ability to reason with yourself, the more energy you are putting towards a life you don't want to live. It's up to you to learn along the journey, and that's what we are all on, a journey of self-growth. No one is going to just come along and drop fulfilment in your lap. If that were the case my vision in life for others would be a lot easier to bring about.

So does making a so-called 'mistake' along the way mean you are back to where you started? The intelligent answer is obviously 'no' but few ever answer intelligently. Why do so many people become disheartened on their journey to create an extraordinary life? They rarely look at the progress they have made, but will always notice what's 'wrong'.

Something that is deemed 'negative' is also a great positive if you look hard enough. These things have an important role to play. In order for us now to be able to distinguish that a thought is negative, we must be able to identify the flip side. We can now act on it, and don't have to submit to the belief that it's just the way it is. Through such awareness it will allow you to put a **strategy** in place to eliminate it. Another way of looking at negativity is that it reminds you that you are making progress. Seeing that most people surrender to negative perceptions subconsciously, by being consciously aware that they are 'negative', you are becoming more emotionally intelligent. You are using your mind to distinguish and correct, rather than just accept! Instead of beating yourself up over thinking or acting negatively, take them as a chance to learn and implement change.

The logic in unlogic

You've heard it all before: the logical and illogical side. Becoming aware, and being able to compare the two to your benefit, is your greatest asset to strengthen your success. We should use the logical side as our defence mechanism against those decisions that are leading us towards feelings that don't really fulfil us. It will prevent you from being in situations where you question the same thing one hundred times over, even though you are already aware of the answer that is beneficial. You will recognise in time that it will be hard not to make a decision without assessing it, and finding answers that spur growth. Choosing your true side of logic will become quite natural.

I once found myself in a situation where I was helping out someone who was having a reaction on drugs that caused him to believe he had no control over himself. After walking through the feelings with him, and trying to calm him down the best way I knew how, we began to get into a brief chat. He was still at the height of the drug, so I knew I had to take massive action. I asked him if he needed some fresh air. He told me that he would probably do something very stupid and jump off the balcony.

Knowing that this battle of control was going on in his mind, I took an approach. I began to explain that he just proved to me that he was much better and was making progress. Being confused and 'rushing' at the same time, he was convinced he was still at its worst. I said that if he had no control over himself then he wouldn't have told me he would jump off the balcony; he would have just done it. That by being aware that he 'might' do something 'stupid', he logically understands he has a choice, and is far more in control then he currently believes. It worked wonders, and within minutes he started to snap out of it. By being able to compare the logical side to the illogical, he had control over the way he felt, and the decisions he was going to make.

He thanked me later, and said that he felt that he had no control over what was happening, and just by making him aware that he did, he started to fight that belief. When I explained that he would have just jumped off, his control became evident to him.

I would just like to bring up the point of everyday life, and how this could be of relevance, if you haven't already noticed. We make ourselves believe we have no control over the way we feel, or what decisions we make, as we are always quick to throw the blame on someone or something else. We will blame it all on people around us, certain situations, or even drugs! Are they really the challenge, or is it that you are just unaware that you have always been in full control of your own emotional state? We choose to let people and situations take our happiness. We willingly submit and hand it over to them. Realistically, a situation just 'is', which means it's up for whatever you wish to attach to it. That's why so many people can have completely different views on exactly the same situation. We must look at it intelligently and let our initial knee jerk reaction and common sense be good guides. We know the truth initially, yet sometimes we are good at talking ourselves out of it. The control has always been there for your life; sometimes you just choose not to use it.

By being able to differentiate between right and wrong, negative and positive, or the logical and illogical, we can use it to our benefit. In order to grow, we must take action on our knowledge. If we refuse to, we are eventually forced to reach a…

Point of awareness (POA)

'Don't judge each day by the harvest you reap but by the seeds you plant.'
Robert Louis Stevenson

I'm sure we have all reached points in our life where we felt as if there was nowhere to turn. Some of us have even hit points where our whole life, not just one aspect, is distorted. It then seems as if we are truly lost on this journey we call life. It's a feeling of hopelessness, of desperation, and no sense of direction. If you are at this point in your life in one or all areas, I would like to explain that you are actually at a great spot! Yes, that's right, a great spot. I know you're probably swearing at the book and thinking I'm a madman, but just hear this out.

You are on a journey and you have been walking for days. Along the way you have felt a sense of unfamiliarity, yet you have continued to walk anyway. You're walking along singing, and all of a sudden you STOP! It's just hit you. You finally realise that you have been going a different way this whole time. A **point of awareness** has just shown itself. Thoughts start rushing through your mind, questions begin to appear, and panic takes over your emotional state. Then you snap out of it and recognise that you'd better pull yourself together. If you don't think about your previous steps as a means to gather knowledge to get back on track, then you will sit there and die of thirst. All of a sudden that point starts to become a really good one, because **if you never had that feeling of being lost, who knows where you would have ended up.** Even when we are looking at those previous steps, we stop thinking back and cursing ourselves over taking them, because we know it's just making things worse. We are now going to start using the information we obtained from those past steps to help us back on our intended journey. But more importantly to arrive at that desired destination.

> 'When one door closes, another opens; but we often look so long and so regretfully upon the closed door that we do not see the one which has opened for us.'
> *Alexander Graham Bell*

I would like to illustrate using a graph, to visually put this across as much as I can.

When you feel like you are declining in life, it may just be the complete opposite. You have actually advanced to a stage where you recognise how you must change in order to grow. Most people in society call a point of awareness, rock bottom. I refrain from using the metaphor 'rock bottom' because to me it is false. I believe you have actually gone up at these points, because without them you wouldn't make the crucial decisions that change your life forever. It's as if you have prevented yourself from going deeper into your confusion and experiencing more pain. Usually the most valuable information can be gathered from times that seem the most hopeless or distressing. I guess it's some greater force telling us that we need to wake up. A point of awareness forces you to reassess every step you took. And if you learn from this experience, it also reminds you to carefully assess future steps that are taken.

Why is it that people usually find true direction in life at a time that seems the most confusing? My opinion is that when all roads seem to be blocked, there is only one way, and that is THROUGH!

3

THE CERTAINTY OF APPRECIATION

Don't hate, appreciate!

'There was once a man who was complaining about only having one pair of shoes, until he met a man with only one leg.'
My grandfather

In a hotel elevator in Paris, I was faced with a question that warranted an immediate answer. I was smiling from ear to ear and began laughing to myself in joy. I was having such an overwhelming moment of appreciation that it caused me to forget that someone was in there with me. This woman turned around to me and said 'Why are you so happy?' as if it was a rare sight. And I guess in some sense it is quite rare. Without hesitation I said the first thing that came to mind and replied, 'Because I'm alive'. Looking at me like I was from outer space, she stormed off, angry and frustrated. I just wondered how her day, or further to that, her life, would play out due to that unfortunate choice of attitude? I couldn't help but have sympathy for her. I doubted that she actually knew how much power she had in changing her resentment towards a life she was in control of. I was curious to know whether she knew the detrimental effect her attitude was having in creating the same experiences she so often complains about. Pretty sad, I thought, but it didn't affect my day, and off I went with this great feeling. It did, however, remind me of a time when I felt similar emotions to her…

There was a period along my journey, definitely the point of no return, when I felt a sense of emptiness. I didn't have that feeling for such a long time, and I must admit a fear came over me. I was someone who was teaching people about gaining fulfilment and making real positive change, yet here I was at another point of confusion. I guess I forgot to acknowledge that I was still human; yet even more importantly, I recognised that I had left out a major part of my daily routine. I was so caught up in getting this book finished, coaching, designing verbal programs and helping others, that I forgot to stand still and really get into a **state of appreciation**. This is something that others would take as a given with me, although it totally flew over my head. I even had feelings of fear before I would go and talk to someone about this stuff, like the words weren't going to come out right. I was having thoughts that I was losing my touch in writing, and everything seemed distorted. I decided that day that another would not start unless I began with reading my gratitude list, which was the first page I had ever written. That day when I was in my room, I stopped staring at myself after twenty minutes, and pulled out a piece of paper. Still crying, I rushed down everything that I was grateful for in my life. It has never been rewritten and I still read that rough copy today. It changed my whole life, and even now is the only thing that can really get me into a state of really embracing life's greatness. It's my true inspiration.

I then realised that this experience was just another lesson learnt and a means to help me teach others about its absolute importance. I would tell them to appreciate and create a list, but this single event allowed me to discover the immense depth it has on one's life. Getting into a state of appreciation is absolutely crucial to our happiness, regardless of how far advanced we may think we are.

It doesn't matter what situation you are at in your life, consciously demanding deep gratitude will enhance the quality of it. We get so caught up with things that we want, experiences we have had, the hustle and bustle of working life, raising children, or getting our finances on track, that we neglect to be grateful for what we have. How can we ever be happy if we are not content with who we are and appreciate the only thing that is ever real, right now? I mean, even if we go and make $1,000,000, then want another million, then another, we are still back at that point of emptiness and un-fulfilment, and it goes with every area of our life. If we do not sit there and really appreciate the most important things, then we are never going to be happy. It's not wrong to keep wanting — we are human — but we can't forget the feeling that fulfils us: gratitude. The day I realised I had been leaving it out, I came up with an adage that I now repeat every morning: **A wise man never dwells on what he doesn't have. He remains in constant appreciation of what he has already, whilst being in pursuit of what he wants**.

It's the same with everything: if we don't use it, we lose it. The challenge is that most don't remind themselves how to love life, so they forget how. But what they also do as a replacement is continually practise how to hate it, so they get damn good at that instead!

Time is our most precious commodity. If you're not using it wisely, you're wasting it ignorantly.

The only thing that can ever fulfil us is to acknowledge the beauty of what we have, and who we really are. When I ask people what they think the most important things are in life, I am usually faced with the same answers. Family, friends, faith, and even being alive all make the top of the list. Would you agree? So, it's common sense to notice that **the most important things in life deserve nothing less than constant reminders.**

Then why don't we remind ourselves? There is no sensible answer, because they are the most important, right? If we do not make a daily conscious effort to recognise these things, the truth is, we will search around in the dark looking for a happiness that has been with us our whole life. Ignoring this is the major factor I see in unhappiness. I urge you to ask and answer this question with sincerity...

In your life, what means the most to you?

Now whatever makes the list, make sure you make it a priority and regularly remind yourself of it.

> 'As we express our gratitude, we must never forget that the highest appreciation is not to utter words, but to live by them.'
> *John Fitzgerald Kennedy*

Appreciation is truly the ultimate feeling, as it is the only thing that knocks down the body of ego. How many times have you wanted to tell someone that you really love, how much you appreciate everything they have ever done for you? In saying that, I bet it doesn't compare to the amount of times you haven't. The reason is our body of ego stands in the way. This one guy abused me because he said he didn't have a body of ego, and all I replied was that he just demonstrated it. We all have it — if we didn't, we wouldn't be human. We so often feel that great love and just wish we knew how to portray it without being embarrassed. When you are in a state of appreciation, it really trains you to express the qualities of life, which means you get it back just as quickly. The feeling is definitely euphoric, and something that is far away from the restrictions of our eyes. It is feeling, and feeling is power!

This simple quality of life is also crucial for success. It allows us to utilise our time efficiently and recognise every step we take. We are grateful for the time we have now, so it prevents us from just waiting around and procrastinating. We take full responsibility for our actions in the present, which allows us to really embrace our decisions as an opportunity for growth. More importantly we begin to praise ourselves for who we really are and it builds the faith and respect within us to be in pursuit of what we want. It aligns us with our friend, fear, and it promotes us to work to our peak with a broadened mind. It truly **helps us enjoy the process of success** because we go in with the attitude of 'nothing to lose, everything to gain'. Courage soon follows.

For most, there are barriers that restrict them from discovering their slumbering power. Appreciation helps break down those psychological and emotional walls. It allows you to be more vibrant, loving, and happy — all those other qualities that are crucial for a successful life. If you begin to love life, you embrace it for the beauty and mystery it is, and that's what creates empowering energy. **Appreciation is the key to letting your spirit take over your life**. If you never train yourself to recognise this other side of you, and continue to feed it, then the same feelings and experiences will continue to arise. By the addition of such a simple ritual in your daily life, you will create the world of difference. **Success without appreciation is no success at all!**

'Appreciation is a wonderful thing: It makes what is excellent in others belong to us as well.'
Voltaire

State of appreciation (SOA)

'To get up each morning with the resolve to be happy…is to set our own conditions to the events of each day. To do this is to condition circumstances instead of being conditioned by them.'
Ralph Waldo Trine

By going through a list of things that you appreciate in the morning, you could only imagine the difference it would make to your day. Most wake up in the morning complaining, feet dragging half way across the room, have two coffees and still seem to be tired. I would be sulking that much in the morning for having to wake up, that at times I came to tears.

I once had someone say to me, 'The reason I complain all the time is because crap keeps happening in my life'. I turned to him and said, 'The truth is, the reason crap keeps happening in your life, is because you don't stop complaining.' **When we complain, we become the victim. When we are the victim, we don't get what we want in life, we get more of what we don't want.**

The energy that you carry during the day from that dismal start will surely lead you to having a miserable one. In all honesty, how do you think the day is going to turn out? What hope are you giving it to improve, and what incentive is there for life to give back if you disrespect it before you have even started your day? In order to make your day fulfilled it is imperative that you begin by shifting your focus to the great things in life. If you do this for a few days, giving it up will not be an option, because the results are just too outstanding. You should also try to maintain that mood as much as you can, but even after a week or so you will see that mood starting to become your nature. If you believe that you do appreciate things, well so does everyone else at times. This is allocating time first thing in the morning to get into a 'State', because that's what conditions you.

When you appreciate something, you don't abuse it. Learn to appreciate all that's life.

I once received an email from a lady with three children, who was living overseas. She explained how she was suffering from 'depression'. I also find it amazing how people just seem to self-diagnose themselves with a tag. People just walk around saying they are depressed as soon as something doesn't go their way for that moment. It's like, 'I missed out on buying that jacket, I'm so depressed', or, 'I'm so depressed, I missed going out with my friends on the weekend'. It's just ridiculous how people tag uncertainties in life to create something to seem far worse than it actually is. How many people do you know who have taken medication for anxiety, depression, and intense nerves and still have it? Nearly all of them, I bet! They pop those pills for years to no avail, but amazingly, what I have seen from my own experience, is that as soon as they became aware of their ability to re-condition their own state, they are able to heal themselves.

Branding an emotional or mental state separates you from having full control over it. And by continuing to tell people that you have 'depression', you will never be able to take control over your life. I'm not saying that some people aren't in a very difficult emotional and mental state but I like to keep the faith that we can overcome this with the right tools, not by taking a pill every time we feel sad. See, we can continue to suppress issues with a pill, but that's exactly what it does: suppress. True healing means you must get to the source, and that is within. It's all about healing, not suppression.

Anyway, I decided to coach this particular lady through Skype. Before I was able to get a word in I was bombarded with a woman who was choked up from crying and basically having a melt down. I immediately began making the weirdest noises known to mankind. I went from high pitched to deep voiced, then back to screeching all in around ten seconds. It truly sounded like a language spoken by aliens with Tourette's syndrome. She stopped crying, began laughing and said, 'What the hell are you doing?' I replied, 'Shifting your mood. Now let's start'. It was that easy!

I worked with her on an appreciation list. Three weeks later, I received another email telling me that the last week was the best one she had in two and a half years. Speaking to her lately, she is flying high again. It's also been very effective for those who are worrying about which direction to take in life, to step up to the next level, help in relationships and really every area of life. It's very important that you follow the steps and create your list in this way. This is how I did mine, and it has been extremely effective for those that I have helped. This exercise is crucial.

Great emotions produce a great life. You have the option of generating them whenever you like. You must allocate *time to shine!*

Allocate your time to shine

If you want to have an extraordinary life, you must be addicted to life.

Your **time to shine** is going to determine how your destiny is shaped. It is to be done in the morning, and preferably for an hour. If you say you don't have the time, I have a great solution: wake up earlier! An hour ritual consists of getting into an SOA (state of appreciation) as well as creating perfect scenarios in your mind of what you want your life to be (state of certainty). You must set up an attitude that will last through the whole day. If you won't spare an hour to vastly improve the quality of your life, then at least create half that time. Even fifteen minutes if you must, but I know you can create more time if you are committed to it. Here's an example of my personal one.

SOA

Thank you for being a loving person, thank you for your great gifts and power that reign within me, thank you for being respectful, thank you for having a sense of humour, thank you for being kind hearted.

THEN: Thank you for the hands I have to write with; thank you for the legs I have to walk with; thank you for this beautiful world and the energy that flows through it; but above all, thank you for me still breathing and giving me the opportunity of life, to persist again and again, when so many others have gone before me.

We must always start with the basics, as that's what really fulfils us. If a woman came up and freely gave you, along with another million people, $10,000 each, would you make the conscious effort to say thank you? Just because she gave it to a mass of people, does it take away the magnitude of the single act she performed for you? The generous act still warrants gratitude nonetheless, correct?

Now, how do you believe your right arm weighs up against the value of $10,000? Just because most others, not all though, have a right arm as well, does it take away the importance of such a gift? If you would say thank you for receiving $10,000 and are able to clearly recognise that your arm is worth far more than that, why don't you say thank you for it? It makes no sense! We have been given so many gifts that we should value above all else but deliberately ignore them on a daily basis. As long as we do not value these and take the most important things in life for granted, we will never be fulfilled.

Next I would be thankful for things that are outside of me. Thank you for the food I have to eat; thank you for shelter; for clothes. Thank you for having a loving family and friends; thank you for the experiences I have had as they have allowed me to grow and make everlasting change.

I personally thank God for all these things, and I say each one with as much intensity as I can. I really get myself into a state. That means using my body as well. If you do not want to say thank you to God, then say thank you to something higher than yourself, because something has given you all these gifts, the qualities of whom lie within you, and that's what makes you great.

Lastly I would be appreciative of… We will add this later in the book.

State of certainty

While having a shower, eating breakfast and getting dressed I replay perfect scenarios in my mind. I imagine myself happy and having a productive day towards my goals. While listening to upbeat music on my iPod, I walk around the house in a constant state of reassurance of how I want my day to play out. At times I even dance around the kitchen while making my breakfast. Yes, in the morning! I do anything that sends my momentum through the roof.

Music has the ability to shift our state immediately, so use it to your advantage. Listen to upbeat music, or anything that gets you going. Humans have a strong emotional attachment to great tunes, so music is our ticket through most times. And, yes, I do consider myself a little crazy for doing this ritual first thing in the morning, but who isn't branded on the road of success? It's always impossible until someone does it, right?

I also think about how I am going to be the best person I know how. Not just when meeting people, but to myself. This form of conditioning can be done while performing your normal morning activities. Starting off with a state of appreciation is a must if you want a great life, so let there be no exception to that.

A close friend with over 100 retail stores under the umbrella of his franchise informed me that he would wake up in the morning doing bicycle kicks before he even got out of bed. He would then get up and sing around the house, waking his kids and wife in the process. Let's just say they weren't as enthusiastic as him when the story was being told. If you believe successful people drag their way through the morning, then dream again. While everyone else is having three coffees, two energy drinks, and sleep-walking to work, they are up and ready to go. Getting into a state of appreciation and a state of certainty at the beginning of your day is the quickest way to be inspired and create a lifetime of everlasting energy.

Task

1. **Inner:** We must write down what we appreciate about ourselves. Here's a great one to get you started — the eyes that you have to read this. Also, be thankful for all the qualities you know you have access to like love, patience, **appreciation**, respect, intelligence, trust, courage, faith and so on.

2. **Outer:** Next we are to list those things that are external but still have meaning and contribute to our life. It could be family members, a car you have to drive, or shelter. Whatever it is, it's helping you live your life so be appreciative, and take nothing for granted. Also appreciate things in nature and the world, because I don't know if you have realised, they are actually keeping you alive. You drink water, breath air, eat fruit. It's okay, this doesn't mean you are a 'greenie' or a 'hippie'; you are just opening up your eyes.

3. __?__: Stick to appreciating the first two now, and we will get to the third as we go along.

I advise that you write down at least five answers for each, and if you have any trouble look at my personal one to get ideas. It could even be the same for 'Inner' and 'Outer'. After you have written down your list in that order, you are ready to start.

 Always begin with saying **'Thank you for being alive'.** Also end with repeating **'Right now I'm alive'** with absolute conviction until you feel pumped. This task in the morning is conditioning you to change your state in an instant; a must if you want an extraordinary life. In order to be abundantly happy, you must learn to ignite your own empowering emotions. It is important that you **feel the significance** of what you are appreciating and totally embrace it. Feel those qualities within you, the house that shelters you, or the hug from your loved one. **FFF (full focus on feeling)** raises hidden and fulfilling emotions, which is the key to this exercise.

This only takes around five to ten minutes to read while stationary, so if you say you don't have the time to read it, are you really being true to yourself? The rest of your time to shine can be done while getting ready. If you don't have enough time, stop watching as much TV!

By continually practising this one exercise alone, and making it a ritual before starting your day, your life will be enhanced radically. Think of the difference when starting off your day with this, rather then nearly crying or hating the world for having to wake up. **Demanding a fulfilling state also allows you to prove to yourself that you choose your own emotions.** Allocating this time to shine will condition your nervous system to experience fulfilment on a regular basis.

You now have enough inf   on your own for **three consecutive days** an   sks. It's part of the program in this book, so if   en you should really consider passing it on. We   given the keys to life; some just refuse to open t   w you are reading this book to make real chang   so please give yourself this opportunity. Really su   le do what everyone else brands as stupid, which is why they are so different. You are to write your SOA list in the order that was given, read it for the next three mornings, and practise maintaining that mood during the day. This is it: discovering the balance between fulfilment and the drive to achieve. Remember, the change starts with you. Once that begins to happen, everything else starts to change with it. Those three days before reading on is a **must**.

And if you really want a powerful start to your day, write this on a big piece of paper, or somewhere that is highly visible in the morning…

Whatever I do today, I will commit to doing it with love and in happiness. As challenging as it may be, I will not allow anything to overpower my great emotions, and I will get through it.

Only those few who take action get the results that everyone one else dreams about.

Stop, go back. You are not to read on until this task is completed. These tasks are designed to properly train your mind and ease you into the process, as everyone else who gained abundance in their life has done. Not reading on just yet is also a great test of patience — a quality that is a must to achieve what you set out for. Take action on this or else you learn nothing. Appreciate on a daily basis, and create that **time to shine.**

4

WHAT YOU BELIEVE, YOU CREATE

*The blueprint of our greatness and true calling in life is hidden under
the collage of social beliefs that become SELF-beliefs. They include fear,
doubt, hate, and all other limitations that restrict us from discovering
our true passion. Unwrap the paper, and you will find a gift!*

What are beliefs?

I came across a story a while back about two brothers who were
both raised by the same abusive, alcoholic father. Years down the
track, one brother had a loving family, was extremely wealthy and
enjoyed his life. The other brother turned out to be an alcoholic
and was serving time in jail.

A university researcher became aware of the situation and decided
to interview the two brothers. They were in different rooms, but he
asked them both the same question: 'With an abusive and alcoholic
father, why did you turn out the way you did?' Surprisingly, they
both replied with the exact same answer: 'With a father like that,
how else did you expect me to turn out?' Both men had the same
biography, but created different beliefs around their experience.
One brother saw it as an opportunity to inspire him into action;
the other played the victim and paid the price.

Regardless of what events take place, it is always our choice on
what significance they have on our life, or what we choose to
take from them. The current beliefs we choose to live by create

or contribute to all of the experiences we have. Regardless of what area of life it is, they can be the basis for change, or the reason we seem motionless. What exactly are beliefs? They are nothing more than opinions that have been fed by other people, a chosen perception through experience, and thoughts that have been repeated.

We hear things on radio, see them on TV, through friends and family, and so forth. Do we ever sit back and think about the source from which this information stems? They are just an individual's opinion, and we know there are a lot of those flying around. It is crucial that we probe such beliefs to get to the truth. One guy I know is a great example of how other people's beliefs and opinions can affect you to the point where it becomes a self-belief. He is a great private poet, and doesn't usually share his work. I've had the opportunity to read some, and I was impressed. On this one day, he shared it with a peer at work only to have his poems and possible future life path ridiculed. He told me he didn't write anything else for one whole year, as that opinion dwelled so deeply within him; he went blank every time he tried to write. He began to believe that his work wasn't good and that he would never be able to turn it into a career.

I spoke to him for a while and we dug deep until he finally realised that he could. He had proven it in the past, so there was no reasonable explanation as to why he couldn't again. All we had to do was really criticise why he couldn't do it and direct all his energy to 'How he could'.

He started again by writing one paragraph to prove it to himself. If everyone solely based their success on critics, there would be no such thing as success!

*There are two kinds of critics. One is a coward who gains his glory
by attacking things he never had the courage to do. The other is
courageous enough to tell you that cowards never make it. Learn to
utilise both of them.*

How often do we let limiting beliefs prevent us from taking action
in our life? Funnily enough, we even let other people's limiting
beliefs prevent us. We associate feelings of pleasure or pain to
every belief we have, and that's what ultimately shapes our destiny.
The actions we take towards life every day are also the result of our
beliefs. Here are some common life restrictive beliefs that I have
also been guilty of in the past:

I can't be as great as those achievers.

I can't change.

Every girl/guy is the same.

Life is a misery.

All people are rude.

I've got serious bad luck.

No one would want me.

It's too late.

I'm too young/old.

I'm useless.

And the list goes on.

I'm sure we are all aware that there are times when we have
believed something that turned out to be very far from the truth.
Have you ever listened to verbal abuse about another individual?

We might have a friend or work colleague who slanders another person because of an experience that they have had with them. We seem to get sucked in at times and begin a belief that this person is 'bad'. We join the party of verbal abuse, and create scenarios in our mind that aren't even real. We say things like, 'Just wait and see if she does that to me, I'll fix her right up'. The whole situation is quite hilarious. But now how many times have you met that same individual and they are one of the nicest people you have met? All of a sudden they are fantastic. You may even go to the extent of defending them against things you once believed. The truth is we have the power to make ourselves believe anything we want. And we don't just do this metaphorically speaking, but scientifically as well. Those beliefs then become what we know as our 'reality'.

Building beliefs

We have found out that a belief is nothing more than an idea or chosen perception that is often repeated. An experience will take place in our lives causing us to create a specific idea of what we think that situation means. We then mentally, verbally and physically act accordingly. We stick to one perception, repeat it that many times, until we build our own beliefs around it. Our vocabulary and body language even align with the belief systems we have built. It's like someone who was in a relationship where their partner habitually disrespected them. While telling others about the situation, they use negative language, frown, and shake their head in disgust. By now it's tainted their trust in relationships altogether. The next time they see a happy couple smooching in the park, they follow exactly the same pattern. Realistically, it's just a loving couple, but to this person it represents heartache.

If you have ever heard that we cannot deliberately or consciously build beliefs then that is a lie. I know there have been things in your life that you once thought you couldn't do. Once you shifted all your focus and resources to doing it, you discovered you were more than capable. You may never have believed you could run that distance, leave that person, build a relationship, make that much money, get past that fear or break that habit. Eventually you built up that much emotional momentum with it, that it enforced a set of whole new beliefs around what you thought you couldn't do, and now what you could do. When you made yourself believe that you could, you did it with conviction.

All the beliefs that are currently shaping your life have been built by you. That means you have the power to create and build new beliefs that will change your life forever. The mysterious thing is that it actually doesn't take long at all. In order to speed up the process, you must become forceful and intense with your new way. For example when you say, 'I can't do that' or 'that's impossible', you must immediately command a physical and verbal alternative. Build up your state of mind and demand with all your power that you are taking control. Go throughout your day repeating, 'I can do it, I can do it, I can do it', 'nothing is impossible, nothing is impossible'.

When I was doing taekwondo, we had to scream during a high intensity punch or kick to get the most out of it. Raising your voice when enforcing new beliefs puts your whole being into a different state. I have forcefully built every new belief I now have about my life and success. They were not the result of one experience, nor did they magically just appear strong and certain. I knew that I had to purposely build them if I wanted to take charge of my life.

I would repeat the new things I wanted to believe with so much emotional power, that I gave my old self no real choice but to surrender. **The more you repeat it, the more you believe it!**

It is very important to understand that we create whatever we want to believe. It is also essential that we align our mental, verbal and physical actions to build a new belief. The strongest way to build these beliefs is to **acknowledge what you're doing, when you're doing it.** If it is patience you are demonstrating when waiting in traffic, don't just sit there and take it as a given. Acknowledge that you are being 'patient right now' and be proud of it. This goes with every area of our life and is an extremely strong tool in determining who we are becoming.

Re-enforcement is the number one key to building and strengthening beliefs. All successful people know that **beliefs are the foreground of creating anything in their life.**

Task

Answer the following question and come up with as many empowering beliefs as you can think of.

What would I have to believe in order to get what I want?

Example: I want to be healthy and fit.

New belief: I would have to believe that I will never get what I want in life unless I commit to living a healthy lifestyle. I would have to believe that I would never get that person I dream of. I would have to believe that my health is the most important thing in my life. Without respecting my body, I will never respect my life.

Be creative, as you are the one who picks your beliefs. These beliefs are writing your experience.

Once you write down all the beliefs that you desire, use re-enforcement as much as you can. Repeat throughout your day and in the face of experience. Over power the old limiting beliefs and you will see after a while they will diminish, and the new ones get stronger. **What you think, you believe. What you believe, you create.**

Absolute belief system (ABS)

We must also build what I call an **ABS (absolute belief system)** in order to succeed at a level that most of the world would see as unrealistic. Is there anything in the world that man has created, that someone else wouldn't have called unrealistic before its existence? If you take a good look around, you will notice that most people would have perceived every creation as impossible before it was created. Who would have ever thought that we would be able to talk to someone half way across the world with a gadget the size of our hand? Self-taught engineer Dr Percy Spencer came up with the microwave, and you could just imagine trying to tell people 300 years ago that we were going to cook food with no fire. We have flown to the moon and back, can see other people as if they are right in front of us even though they are thousands of miles away, or check the local movie times through wireless internet. I was amazed with wired internet, and then they had to just bamboozle me and create wireless!

Take a look at anything around you right now and you will see that it had to have started as a mental picture in someone's mind. Do you realise how fascinating, amazing and mysterious it is to see something in your mind, then create it to be right in front of you and tangible? So how is this possible? A simple explanation would be that it began as a vision followed by a belief system around it. Those beliefs then resulted in the vision to seem like a reality in the mind, which then caused it to come into existence through appropriate action. Trying to ultimately explain this phenomenon is impossible. It is one of the mysteries of life. And just because we don't fully understand it, it doesn't mean that it's not our gift to put it into practice everyday.

Here is a strategy and simple experiment that might help you out…

1. Concept: Close your eyes and visualise holding a piece of paper in front of your face with your name written on it. Do this for ten seconds. See the letters and feel the paper, but only in your mind. This is only a mental vision, so make sure you do nothing physically.

2. Action: Did you see that paper with your name on it? Now, get out a piece of paper, a pen, and physically write your name on it.

3. Creation: Hold it in front of your face. It's real; touch it. Do you now see that you actually just created that to be real? Where was it before you were able to touch it (Step 1)? It was just a figment of your imagination, right? You just brought something that was only in your mind, into reality. You foresaw the future, took action and created it!

For a moment, comprehend the magnitude this acknowledgement to create can have on your life.

I want you to even think back to a time when you have really felt something, visualised over it and it has come about. It may have been a new car, an outfit, or a holiday. I was coaching this young girl who wasn't grasping just how powerful visualisation in her life actually was. I went over to her house one day to see a black BMW convertible parked in the driveway. As soon as she answered the door, she didn't hesitate to show it off. When we sat down, I asked how long she had wanted that car. After finding out it was about a year, I asked how many times she drifted off dreaming about driving it, hair in the wind, friends by her side, and music playing. I then asked how many times she searched that car on the internet, and experienced emotions as if she already had it.

She burst out laughing and said, 'Yes, yes, it almost became obsession.' She explained that she made herself want that car so much, and dreamt about it, that even when the thought of not getting it came to mind, she would block it out and reassure herself that she would. I then made her realise the absolute power she had in bringing something that was only ever in her mind, into reality. It took the BMW example for this young girl to finally understand. I explained that she is able to do that with every part of her life, and she has since.

Practise this strategy with anything that you want, and you will realise that you have been creating your whole life. People ask me, 'How do I create things in my life like others?' I clearly explain they always have, the difference is that they are not aware of what they are creating. If it's something large you want to create, you might have to take more action. Going back to the paper experiment, if there wasn't a piece of paper right next to you, you would have had to get one. Everything comes with its challenges, but if you are committed to making it real, you will find a way through or around the obstacles. **This world is a plane of endless possibilities,** and it's not until you acknowledge that you have always had the power to create, that you finally realise anything is possible when you believe it is. You can actually create anything you desire; the only one ever stopping you is you.

If you think of something in your mind, see the end result, and believe it will work, then it can. See, most of the time people will talk themselves out of it or convince themselves why it won't work. This is usually due to other people's opinions or letting the idea slip before it can be reinforced. Successful people actually talk themselves into it, and will give many reasons as to why it will work. They focus on how they can do it, and repeat it many times with so much conviction that it becomes a belief that consumes their life. They don't rely on others to build their belief; they know that when they believe it enough, others will follow.

Even when we buy a car, it's highly recommended that it's equipped with ABS brakes. Having an anti-lock braking system in a car is to prevent the wheels from locking up or ceasing to rotate while braking. It also allows you to steer the car in the direction that you want in an emergency braking situation. When we have an ABS (absolute belief system) in life, we don't just sit there and wonder all day, but get those wheels rotating and acting. We view everything as a realistic possibility and that's what causes us to steer our life in the direction we want. In saying that, there are also particular beliefs that prevent us from creating such a system.

Conflicting beliefs

Why is it that sometimes we know exactly what we want, have a plan, but for some reason don't take the appropriate action? I couldn't count how many times I have heard 'I just don't know what's holding me back'. It seems that when we think of an empowering direction or something that will satisfy our wants, we automatically shift our focus to what we must 'sacrifice' to get it. Rarely do we remain focused on what we are actually gaining, hence many fall back into the trap of procrastination.

When in pursuit of what you want, if you think of 'sacrifice', it takes away the specialness of the journey.

When you think of the sacrifices, everything seems too hard. Do yourself a favour; focus on what you are gaining.

This topic also asks the question, 'Are we really losing when in quest of what we want?' If you remain focused on the benefits, it becomes apparent that you actually sacrifice nothing. But on so many occasions we neglect this fact of success, and will submit to the weaker approach. We do this because it seems easier at the time to do what we have always done. We all know that produces the same results. So, is it really easier when ten years go past and you realise you haven't achieved what you wanted to five years ago? Now is a better time than ever, so let's go through some common conflicting beliefs:

I want a partner, but if I get one I will lose my freedom.

I want to be successful, but I still want to sleep until 1p.m. and drag through my day.

I want to get fit and healthy, but if I do, it may make my friends feel insignificant.

I want to follow my passion, but if I charge people for it, they may think I am all about the money.

I want to do what I love, but if I do my parents will think I'm worthless.

If I become wealthy, the people around me will feel worthless and not trust me.

I want to sell my services, but I don't want to give off the impression that I am just doing it for the money.

I want a relationship, but I don't really want commitments.

I want to be healthy but I want to continue to eat junk food on a regular basis.

I want to get fit, but that equals pain.

I want to make massive changes in my life, but I want my friends to still like me.

I want to make a lot of money, but if I do it may mean I am not spiritual or religious anymore.

I want to be healthy but I still want to smoke and paralyse myself with alcohol.

I want to own my own business, but I don't want to be embarrassed if it doesn't do well.

I want to stop smoking, but I want to release stress.

I want to leave my job, start my own business, or do what I love. If I do, people will think I'm stupid or it may be more difficult.

I really want to go and have a chat with that homeless person, but there are people around and it may be embarrassing.

I want to start a new business, but if I do people will think I'm a failure in my first venture.

I want to apply for a better position, but I fear rejection.

These are a few common conflicts I have come across in my time. It's like one thing is pulling us one way, while something else is tugging on the other side. With all this confusion, how can we ever get what we want? Here is an extremely effective strategy when you find yourself in one of these situations.

1. Identify: First, you must discover and get to the bottom of the conflict. Have a clear indication of what you want, and be aware of what other beliefs are stopping you. An example of identifying would be the list we just went through.

2. Question: Next you need to question what you have identified. Which one is more important to you? Which one is going to have more meaning in your life? Which one can enhance the quality of your life? Which one helps you to create more energy and take action towards the bigger picture? What is going to help you grow and progress in life? Which out of the two do you value more? Will you ever ultimately be happy if you don't choose the fulfilling option? Which one can add more value to your life? How will your life look in the future if you do not face your fear? How will this decision make you ultimately feel about yourself once it's made? Could choosing the disempowering option affect future decisions you have to make? Think of more...

3. Align: From the questions, give enough great answers for the belief that is obviously going to fulfil you. Align yourself with these beliefs and reinforce them. Once you align yourself with the empowering beliefs associated with your 'real' wants, you will hit your target. There is nothing pulling you on the either side any more, because you have overpowered it with enough emotion.

Seeing that we just covered how beliefs influence every area of our life, it is vastly important to acknowledge the scientific evidence in such discussions.

Without enjoying the process, there is no success in what you do.

5

NEUROPLASTICITY

Rewiring your brain

As you continue on your journey you will soon be amazed to see that you are attracting things that help make sense of the great changes you are making. I told people about the changes I had been through and helped them with theirs. I would tell them that it was as if I was able to hypothetically 'rewire my mind'.

I remember one day in particular when this concept played on my mind. I was extremely busy that day so I let it slip, until the evening hit. Just as I walked in the door, my brother called me to watch a documentary movie on TV that was playing. He said it looked like something that I might be interested in, and it most certainly was. A program called *The Brain That Changes Itself* by Dr Norman Doidge. This remarkable show was based on Dr Doidge's travels to hunt down leading neuroscientists about a most recent finding called **Neuroplasticity**. So, to my surprise, we are not just hypothetically rewiring our mind, but scientifically and physically rewiring our brain.

For centuries the human brain has been thought of as incapable of fundamental change. People suffering from neurological defects, brain damage or strokes were usually written off as hopeless cases. Recent and continuing research into the human brain is radically changing how we look at the potential for neurological recovery.

The human brain, as we are quickly learning, has a remarkable ability to change itself — in fact, even to rewire itself. This has caused the old dogma to be thrown out. **In other words, you are physically changing your brain with every thought you have.**

Neuroscience experiment — connection between mind and body

Neuroscientist Alvaro Pascual-Leone's experiment at the Harvard Medical School was quite remarkable on this topic. All the participants had to do was to learn and practise a five-finger piano exercise.

He instructed the **first group** to play the piano, and try to keep the same beat as best they could. They practised for two hours a day over five consecutive days. When they were finished, the participants were seated under a coil of wire that sent a sudden magnetic pulse into the motor cortex of the brain. There is a strip that runs from the top of the head to each ear that makes this possible. Such a procedure is called Transcranial-Magnetic Stimulation (TMS), and gives information on the function of neurons. (There are billions of neurons in the human brain. Each one is specialised to transmit information throughout the body.) They found that after just one week of this piano practise, the volunteer's brain had physically transformed. The TMS mapped how much of the motor cortex was needed in the finger movement for the piano exercise. Pascual-Leone then found it spread and grew over surrounding areas like the growth of ivy on a fence. It was then in line with other discoveries that the constant use of one area of the brain caused it to use up more functionality of that area and physically recruit more neurons. That area is then strengthened accordingly.

The **second group** of participants were made to close their eyes and **only visually think of playing the piano**. Their hands **did not** move in the process, but they were told to totally focus on playing that same five-finger sequence in their minds. After the same amount of practise, they were taken through the TMS procedure. The findings were quite astonishing. The same area of the brain had grown, even though they had only visualised doing it in their minds. Neurons were still recruited and were wiring together to enhance the ability of such a task. Even the area of the brain that was used to physically touch the piano for group one also grew in the brains of group two, even though they had not physically touched anything.

Pascual-Leone later stated: 'Mental practice resulted in a similar reorganization'. Please keep in mind, this was only done over a space of one week and the results were remarkable.

I did this to change my whole life around, and surprisingly enough I had no idea I was physically transforming my brain to succeed and enhance the quality of my life.

Keep in mind those results of the experiment were found just after one week of *repetition*. It was definitely a 'light bulb' moment when I saw that, because I had told people that a lot of their life would change drastically after one week if they did the same tasks that are in this book. It also proves that full focus on visualisation enriches the creativity of one's being and empowers one's passion. If these findings also hold ground for other physical movements (and there's no reason they shouldn't), then it means swinging a golf club, dancing, painting, or a quick block in boxing could lead to mastery. The power of the mind is all, and any successful person will tell you that. Even if you think about it logically, everything you ever do or create is a result of your thoughts.

If you are someone who doesn't believe that mind and body are one, you have obviously never had a sexual fantasy before! Further to that, you would have never had a churning in the stomach when worried about something, never jolted when confronted with a fear, or experienced that overwhelming feeling in your chest when you see the person that you love.

Our amazing brain

In a visit to Melbourne, Australia, Dr Norman Doidge stated, 'Since all human activities emerge from the brain, any change in an understanding of the brain, ultimately has a major impact on anything we do. I define Neuroplasticity as that property of the brain that allows it to change its structure and its function. And that's in response to the actions that we commit ourselves to, in response to sensing and perceiving the world, and quite fantastically thinking and imagining'.

He later went on to explain how these new findings are the grounds for shaping every area of life, and adversely affect what we are becoming. It's an amazing breakthrough to say the least, as many philosophers have told us about how the mind is 'all' when shaping our destiny. There has also been analysis by Plato, Sigmund Freud, and a few others in history that implied restructuring the physical brain through thoughts alone.

Dr Joe Dispeza also explains Neuroplasticity in the hit film, *What The Bleep do we Know!? Down the Rabbit Hole*:

The brain does not know the difference between what it sees in its environment, and what it remembers, because the same specific neural nets are firing. The brain is made up of tiny nerve cells called neurons.

These neurons have tiny branches that reach out and connect to other neurons to form a **neural net**. *Each place where they connect is integrated into a thought, or a memory. Now, the brain builds up all its concepts by the law of associative memory. For example, ideas, thoughts and feelings are all constructed then interconnected in this neural net, and all have a possible relationship with one another. The concept in the feeling of love, for instance, is stored in the vast neural net, but we build the concept of love from many other different ideas.*

Some people have love connected to disappointment. When they think about love they experience the memory of pain, sorrow, anger and even rage. Rage maybe linked to hurt, which maybe linked to a specific person, which then is connected back to love. Who is in the driver's seat when we control our emotions or response to emotion?

We know physiologically the **nerve cells that fire together, wire together.** *If you practise something over and over, those nerve cells have a long-term relationship. If you get angry on a daily basis, be it frustrated on a daily basis, if you suffer and give reason for the victimization in your life, you're rewiring and re-integrating that neural net on a daily basis. That net then has a long-term relationship with all those other nerve cells* *called an identity. We also know that when **nerve cells don't fire together, they no longer wire together.** They lose their long-term relationship, because every time we interrupt the thought process that produces a chemical response, every time we interrupt it, those nerve cells that are connected to each other start breaking their long-term relationship.*

When we start interrupting and observing, not by stimulus and response to the automatic reaction, but by observing the effects it takes, then we are no longer the body, mind, conscious, emotional person that is responding to its environment as if it is automatic.

'A life of reaction is a life of slavery, intellectually and spiritually. One must fight for a life of action, not reaction.'
Rita Mae Brown

If all these leading doctors and scientists are discovering such breakthroughs with thought and the physical brain, then it means we are applying these findings every day. We are making those neural nets stronger as we consistently repeat those thoughts. Just think of it as someone tying a piece of rope together in your mind. When you repeat a thought, a word or a physical action, another piece of rope (neuron) is attached, only to make it larger and have more effect in your life.

The associations we have of the outside world, success, relationships, our finances and so on, only appear that way because we create them to be. So how about if we broke the pattern and replaced it with an empowering alternative? If we fed those thoughts, which become beliefs, which turn into emotion, which then cause us to act, would they force us to make different decisions that ultimately shape our life? Of course they would, and that's exactly what we are going to do. I wanted to highlight this fact so you don't think that the tasks we are going to do are just wishful thinking. They are creating new neural nets (NNN), so limiting beliefs diminish and your true power is finally displayed.

While giving a speech in the summer of 2010, I had a gentleman who wasn't grasping the idea of how the law of associative memory works. Trying not to hold up the rest of the attendees, I attempted to move on a number of times. There was a question and answer time allocated near the end of the seminar, but this guy kept putting up his hand. I had to pay his persistence, so I invited him up the front. I gave him the microphone and he said, 'Dan, I'm really not grasping this'. I started asking him simple questions such as, 'What's your name? Where do you live? How would you describe the temperature? What colour are Zebras? **What do cows drink?**'

He immediately answered the last question with confidence and certainty, and said, 'Milk'. I stopped and replied, 'Are you sure about that, Sir?' He paused and said, 'Oh my God, they drink water, don't they?' Having the room erupt in laughter, I asked whether they truthfully thought it was milk. Most stood up and admitted they weren't laughing at him, but at themselves.

The reason his brain came up with that answer is due to the law of associative memory. If I had asked him to name any drink out loud, what would have been the chances of him saying milk? You could probably agree it would have been extremely slim considering the number of drinks available. When I added cows to the question, his brain narrowed down to the one that he has been associated with his whole life. Milk and cows go together, right? Even though the answer was wrong, he made sense of it at that moment. Our life is filled with so many undesirable associations that we have repeated. It may be in relationships, work, our finances, or excuses we come up with. The only way to break them is to be aware that they are only associations, not always the truth.

6

NEURO-SENSORY ASSOCIATION — BREAKING PATTERNS

Throughout your life you have used the notion of *pleasure* and *pain* around every decision you have made. As humans, we are fundamentally entranced by the whole idea, and it is the basis of change or, on the other hand, the reason we continue to have the same experiences. The way we associate pleasure and pain is due to our perception and the belief systems we have put in place for everything in our life. As I've mentioned, **the reasons we make drastic decisions that change our life forever, are due to massive shifts of emotion.** Just think back about life changing decisions you have made that altered the direction you were going: it's quite evident they were the basis of an emotional explosion. It's similar to shaking a can of soda and then opening it. The **pressure** causes it to explode and forces the liquid in a completely different direction. You have always created that pressure within yourself, and who's to say you can't build it again with things you deliberately want to change? The truth is you can, sometimes you just need a good shake!

The truth is we can adapt pleasure or pain to anything we desire; it all depends on how we choose to look at it. People habitually do the same thing over and over again until they have created a neural net that is similar in strength to a post stuck firmly in the ground. In order to make immediate change in your life, regardless of whether it's a habit, fear, phobia or changing your perception, you must look at the effect it's having on your life and the associations of pleasure and pain you have adapted.

Neuro-sensory association (NSA) is the practice that interrupts this old association and creates a new, empowering one. This technique can be used to practically break and interrupt anything you consider a habit. Looking down when people talk to you, smoking cigarettes, overeating, or thinking negatively about a particular person are just a few of many examples. I used this to break habits such as smoking, not believing in myself, and, most importantly, my drug abuse. It got me through fears that I had and other habits that were restricting me.

NSA derives from a well-practised technique called neuro-linguistic programming (NLP). The difference in steps is what separates NSA from NLP. I found that creating steps that increase more emotional charge work far more effectively.

I invite you to take these steps and change something in your life right now. Considering that this book is about change it's only fair, don't you think? You must…

1. Know what you want

Smoking cigarettes example: To be healthy and fit; to be able to play at the park with my children or grandchildren one day; discover my power; want to know that I can achieve; attend my child's wedding; to be really successful; take control over my life. After you have written down what you ultimately want, you must pick something that is going to take the place of the old habit immediately: What do I want to do instead of smoking? What do

I want to do instead of overeating? What do I want to do instead of stressing? Whatever your habit is, make sure you choose one alternative to put in its place: 'Instead of smoking I want to eat more greens'.

2. Know what's stopping you

Normalise: To exclude yourself from a situation, for example, 'I have a poor relationship'. That is only detachment so you may feel better in the short term. It is like you are a separate entity to your experience and have no control over it: 'If the relationship is poor, it is out of my control and outside of my responsibility'.

Instead you must:

Denormalise: 'I am relating poorly.' Take ownership: 'If it's something that I'm doing, I can do it differently'.

For the smoking example, the reply for 'Know what's stopping you' would be 'My choice to kill myself by smoking cigarettes', rather than just 'Cigarettes'. We must take ownership so that we are able to make lasting change. If I told you to sit there and hear that voice telling you that 'you need a cigarette right now', really feel the sensation of picking it up, and inhaling a puff, it would most probably bring on the feeling of wanting a cigarette. But the cigarette is nowhere in sight, so was it your mind that gave you the feeling, or the cigarette itself? It could not have been the physical cigarette. It's **how you think about the cigarette that gives you the sensation, not the cigarette itself**. Someone else might see the same cigarette and want to vomit, because they think differently about it, right? This applies to anything. All sensation and desire emerge from the mind.

Once you take responsibility and acknowledge that it's actually all in your mind, you can make lasting change. It would be the same if I told you to close your eyes and imagine something really hurtful that someone has said to you in the past. Take some time now and think hard about it… How did you feel in that moment? Did the same emotions of frustration, sadness or anger churn within you? But that person isn't actually here saying it to you, are they? But you experience the same feelings through the vast neural net you have created in your brain. This is only due to your thoughts. This realisation also allows you to acknowledge that **you now have options** rather than thinking you are stuck to one. **Our thoughts are our choice.**

Tapping into your mind

Once you are aware of what you want and what's stopping you, then it's time for a small but powerful task. Nothing is going to change unless you tap into your subconscious mind. A great way of doing this is to start building the new neural net by rehearsing the reaction that you really want when faced with the old habit.

Constant repetition is what makes something a habit, so we should start breaking it right now. Close your eyes and envision the reaction as realistically as you possibly can when faced with the old habit. Feel the emotions of being faced with the old habit, and obviously create a perfect scenario of breaking it immediately with the new habit. This will bring forth new powerful emotions. Going back to the smoking example, you would visualise feeling like a cigarette, and then saying 'No'. You would imagine exactly how you would feel by doing that, and make it as real in your mind as you possibly can. Would you feel proud, strong or in control?

How would your facial reaction be? Would you be smiling after you have said no? Do this around twenty-five times, which only takes around five to ten minutes. This is a great start, because it allows you to see and create the new option that is just as real as your previous automated response of giving in. **In order to reach any desired level in our life, we must mimic how we would act if we were already there.** If you want to be mentally strong, you must practise being mentally strong!

3. Standard and value association

What do you stand for? What do you teach others? What do you pride yourself on? As you have probably already noticed throughout the book, I am extremely big on being truthful to yourself and enforcing it any way you can. We all have certain standards and values that we attempt to live by on a daily basis. We so often contradict our core beliefs due to the habits that we have put in place. Every time we do it, we seem to get weaker because we break down our emotional state. The cause of this is sometimes only due to the fact that we avoid merely reasoning with ourselves. We will refuse to look at the truth, because it seems too painful to bear. Facing those core values and standards is our ticket to an empowering life. This is the initial step in getting leverage…

Go back to your wants list and analyse it properly. It seems that the reason you wrote down all those wonderful things is because that reflects who you really are as a person, rather than what you have purposely conditioned yourself to be. Questioning is the greatest tool one can use to shift a certain mindset and begin breaking the old pattern immediately. If you have written down in your wants list that you would like to walk your daughter down the aisle on her wedding day, but you find more pleasure in smoking, then you need to re-evaluate your standards. The reason you mentioned that on your wants list is because you love her, right? But when you really love someone, are you selfish in the process? Are you demonstrating your love for her, or are you in fact stating the complete opposite with your daily decisions? If you really loved her, then you wouldn't do what you are doing. If you have written down that you want to be healthy and fit, that is because you ultimately see that you have respect for yourself. If you didn't, you wouldn't have even picked up this book.

Does someone who respects themself, and preaches to their loved ones to do the same, disrespect their life by overeating? You get my drift — these are questions that we must **enforce** to begin the leverage process. Questioning against your core beliefs, and weighing up what you want from your life against the current decisions you are making, creates a massive shift of emotion. If you think your standards are currently low in your life, raise the bar. Only by raising our standards can we ever find the power to reach new peaks.

4. Break the pattern — turn up the heat then cool down

How is this habit affecting me mentally, physically, emotionally, spiritually and financially? This is the task where you are required to get massive leverage on yourself. It's said, 'If you can't handle the heat, get of the kitchen', so that's exactly what we are going to do.

When you were a child and touched something that was extremely hot for the first time, it created a pain so strong that you knew you never wanted to touch it again. We need to hit the **maximum pain threshold of** not stopping now. This step requires you to get into some real deep thought process, and ask yourself probing questions. Basically, we are going to adapt extreme emotional pain to not stopping the habit, phobia or fear. For a brief moment, I want you to imagine the feeling you get when you see an electric appliance next to water? How have you conditioned yourself to react? In order to break the current habit, you need to condition a similar response. Go back to all those things that you want out of life, and think of never getting them. Referring back to the smoking example, this is how it would go: You would envision walking around with a tube stuck down your throat. You would imagine being terminally ill when your children or grandchildren are born and not being able to make it through. You would feel the extreme pain and torment you would put your family through. You would imagine inhaling a cigarette, follow the smoke into your body and watch it physically destroy your insides. Close your eyes, make it so real that it makes you nearly physically sick; it might in fact even just do that, and put a disgusted look on your face.

I'm sure you have heard the voice of someone who has had throat cancer and sounds almost like a robot. In your mind you would imagine saying, 'I am choosing to destroy my life as well as the people I love the most' in the sick robotic voice. Feel the emotional and physical pain you would endure, and then transmute that inner energy to good aggression. This exercise is all about emotion, so really feel and get a great mental image of exactly what it is that you are giving up in your life and what effect it's already had. It's important to really focus on the fact that **you are choosing** to give all those things up. This requires you to close your eyes and visualise.

Max leverage

Humans will always move towards something that we believe is far more pleasurable then the pain enduring option. As long as we think the old habit has more pleasure we will continue to choose it. If you want to break the pattern, you may have to attach something that causes extreme emotional pain every time you repeat the old habit. This will ensure you condition the new habit without much fight.

Now

Once you have hit that absolute pain threshold where you think you're going to get out of the chair and scream, reverse it. Begin to think of the pleasure if you stopped it **now.** The joy on your family's face, the feeling of achievement you would attain, the strength you would display. Imagine playing with your children at the park or feeling healthy and fit. Really absorb yourself in that pleasure of being free from that choice of mental state.

Also, for phobias, fears, or a situation that reminds you of pain, the **random scenario** is available. Creating a complete random scenario in your mind that seems ridiculously stupid is also effective in the face of habits. In order for this to be successful, you must look at the scenario as if you were watching it from an outside perspective. Almost like sitting at a comedy show. When you feel the sensation, or begin to think of the habit, reverse the whole scenario in your mind. Have the mental image play backwards, and then add some circus music into it. Replay it over and over again, and add whatever ridiculous things you want to it. This is similar to smashing a plate on the ground. Even if you try to fix it, there will still be cracks that make sure the plate is never the same. That's what we want to do with those patterns in your mind, smash them. For example, if you are scared of flying in an airplane, you would use this technique to change your state immediately. You will notice that fear disappears very quickly and may even turn into laughter. This practice is very powerful and is used by professionals around the world. **If you face it you can break it, if you run you're done!**

5. Build on the NNN

We live in accordance with *stimulus* and *response*. **A stimulus is something that stimulates our senses.** For the example of smoking, the stimulus would be the mere thought of a cigarette, seeing one, speaking about it, or smelling it. The automated response would be to associate pleasure with it, and go and get one. **A response is how we react to the stimulus.** We must break the pattern immediately in the face of the stimulus, which will reinforce the new response. In other words, the stimulus remains the same, but our response is going to be different.

If you hack at a tree (old neural net) enough times, it will eventually have to come down. By doing the last section, you have just created a NNN (new neural net). This is now an option and another route that your mind will always find to feed. We have created more *pain* to the old habit and more *pleasure* to the new one, instead of the other way around. The more you think of that new switch in pleasure and pain, especially in the face of the habit, more neurons are recruited to respond the way you desire. You are taking rope from your previous net and making your new one stronger every time you do it. Soon enough, once you build it enough, the other one will disappear. You will definitely notice it weakening as your repetition and intensity gets higher.

Reconditioning your nervous system (smoking example): During the process of committing an undesired habit, most people think about things away from the action they are habitually doing at that time. So if they are smoking, they will think about what they are going to do that night. It's the same when people have an overeating disorder. They think of feeding their victimisation at that time which may seem pleasurable. This then creates an automatic reaction to think that the current habit provides benefits. The reason is you are not reminding yourself of the pain as much as you are of the pleasure, right? With the smoking example, **every time you inhale, you must think of the effects that it's having on your life and what you are potentially giving up for doing it.** By replacing your wandering thoughts with the effects, it reconditions your nervous system to associate pain to the habit. It may take one, two or even three weeks, but it will amaze you how quickly you begin to change your reaction, thought, and feeling when faced with the old habit. This is truly the conditioning part to your achievement, and must be done continuously. This works in any part of your life, and is truly the gem to changing anything you desire.

6. Spread the word and reinforce the new habit

The language we use is very important to our accomplishment. It needs to be forceful and convincing. When you are faced with the old habit, pick up strength in your voice. Going back to the example of smoking, this is how it would work. If someone offered you a cigarette, you would immediately answer with, 'That's disgusting' or 'Yuck'. Say it with meaning, confidence and without too much deliberation. Be adamant about your speech in the face of the old habit. Get physical, verbal and mental with your new direction. Go and tell people around you that you are over your phobia or your habit. The more you do this, the more real it becomes, but more importantly, it becomes far more believable to you.

The final step is to put something empowering in its place and to create a ritual. If you have given up cigarettes then go for a walk every day or eat a healthier breakfast to begin with. When we put something in the place of an old habit, it sets us up for **lasting change.** We must also be extremely proud of every step we take. Even if you have stopped smoking or overeating for four hours, feel the pleasurable emotion of winning. Tell yourself how great you feel and amplify the pleasure as much as you can. **Reward will always condition what we do in life, so use it to your advantage, and learn to reward yourself.**

Keep the paper from step one where you have written down what you want. Fold it up and make it like an extra limb. Keep it in your pocket or somewhere where it will be visible for the next three to four weeks! This will remind you of why you are doing all of this and reinforce the new pattern.

2ND STEP

ENERGY — THAT FUNDAMENTAL FORCE

7

THE FORCE OF LIFE

'A strong, successful man is not the victim of his environment. He creates favorable conditions. His own inherent force and energy compel things to turn out as he desires'.
Orison Swett Marden

Boomerang effect

It seems we have become a society that thrives off the things we know are destroying us. The news is a great example, as it's something that is displayed around the world and has enormous power in getting a message across. How often do we see positive, inspirational topics, compared to those that are filled with fear and destruction? All we are bombarded with is death, betrayal, rape, theft and other damaging stories.

A vast array of energy is being emitted to the public, who in turn go out, talk about it and live their life around fear. I'm sure we are already quite aware of all those things that are happening in the world. We give them far too much attention and focus. No wonder people seem to get new ideas for crime, and why so many youth are turning to violence. Look what we are exposed to on a daily basis.

In some weird way, it seems we find satisfaction in discussing those things we complain about. Are we that distant from our truth that if we didn't have all those life sucking topics to talk about, it would be difficult to hold a conversation? Are we contributing to this destruction by discussing it and giving it our attention? You bet we are.

The main thing that most of us are so blinded to is how much this is actually affecting our own lives. Just like the indigenous people of Australia used the boomerang, it seems that energy has the same effect. When we throw it out there, it seems to come straight back at us. Think about how many times you discuss things that you dislike in one day. Do you think in order to reverse that dislike it would be intelligent not to surround your whole day with it?

I could just picture the different conscious level we would be forced to comply with if loving and inspiring stories were displayed as much as the current ones. Imagine every time we turned on the TV or opened a newspaper, we were surrounded with love and things that go towards uniting this world.

What benefits am I gaining from complaining about this particular event in my life?

We complain about our work, relationships, the world, our finances, and people around us. There are also those who do nothing but talk about other people's lives. I know because I used to be one of them. They do that to try and place some comfort in their own lives. The things they usually fault in others are the same challenges they face. The things they complain about are usually the things they are guilty of themselves. Why? It's easier to fault others than ourselves. We are scared to admit the truth, and come up with ways of dealing with it. It all starts with the person looking straight back at you in the mirror. We must identify and deal with our own challenges, and only then will we realise our ability to create…

Everlasting energy

'Passion is energy. Feel the power that comes from focusing on what excites you.'
Oprah Winfrey

Why do some people always seem tired and drag their way though life, yet others seem to be full of energy? The amount of sleep they get is definitely not the major challenge, as I discovered with myself. I have also spoken to and modelled some of the most successful people I know of, and it seems nearly all of them have less sleep than the recommended time. Before I really started embracing life, I was getting ten hours sleep with at least a minimum of eight, and I would still be tired. Now I only manage to get about six, but my energy levels are through the roof. I have realised that when energy is being used for a cause that is meaningful, beneficial, or to fulfil a self-vision, it seems to be everlasting. The greatest energy is created when we set up things to look forward to. That same energy creates more of that energy. The point being, **it is not physical tiredness that needs as much rest as we think, but our mental state that needs more stimulation.**

One of the first things to understand when it comes to energy is that you are the boss of the production line that is within you. As long as we are complaining about things, focusing on why our life is so bad, why we are the victim, or repeatedly reminding ourselves of things we do not want, our opportunity to produce empowering energy is nonexistent. It is in fact quite the contrary, as it does nothing but drain energy straight out of our system.

We all know that when we complain about something, our energy level is down and that's why it feels like crap.

One day I decided that I would refuse to complain about anything. Even when people would tell me about their 'problems', I would never feed them. I would try to help them to see another side, but if they didn't want to hear it, then I would simply start to discuss a completely different topic. I would even go to the extent of telling them that if they ever wanted to complain about anything, and were looking for someone to join the party, then don't bother calling. If they were really going over the edge, I would tell them to stop feeling sorry for themselves or physically grab them by the shoulders and shake it out of them. It's great to show compassion, and I highly promote it as being one of life's greatest qualities, but you also need to do what is in the best interest of the one you care about, and yourself.

If you submit and consume yourself with everyone else's petty complaints, you leave yourself vulnerable to producing those same feelings they have. I'm quite aware that we all know someone, or a lot of people, who do nothing but whine their way through life. They are always feeling sorry for themselves yet never seem to do anything about it. They try to place all their issues on you. They are subconsciously leaking their own energy and trying to fill themselves up with yours. So there are a few outcomes; they just drain their own energy, or you consume yourself with theirs and go straight to their level. Speak with a powerful tone in those situations; be compassionate, but don't go along for the ride. You will notice even after one day of fending off negative vibes from others that it will be far more productive towards the life you desire. When we focus on the great things in life our energy levels are high.

Have you ever had three parties in one weekend that you want to attend? On that weekend you will live off four hours sleep a night, but still be energetic enough to attend them all, and have a great time. Your energy levels even cause you to stay up until 5a.m. when you're usually tucked in and sound asleep by 11p.m. Uplifting energy always creates more great energy. You are able to identify this great energy, because it makes you feel good, while all others have the opposite effect. To be able to **command your own emotions,** a must if you want an extraordinary life, you need to imagine a group of security guards waiting at the front of your production factory. Every time you feel someone or something is trying to break in to the great energy you are now deliberately creating, take it down. It may seem a bit challenging at the start for two main reasons: Firstly we are surrounded with so much negativity, and secondly, we become like addicts to complaining.

Don't let people infect you with their negativity; you control the situation by displaying how much you love life.

Do not let newspapers, TV, family members, friends, work colleagues or anyone else shift your empowering direction. If you do, you bow down to a life that is less than what you're worth, and do nothing but manifest poor results in your life. You will have friends and family asking what has gotten into you; just be honest and feel your truth. Some may not be able to handle it, because they don't want to feel insignificant or may feel as if they are 'losing' you. Keep at it though; you are being much more of a friend acting this way than feeding emotions that are destroying their life. As well as that, you are stopping yourself from destroying your own life in the process. The funny thing is that it will eventually rub off on everyone around you, and you become infectious. People will cling to you and start asking how you do it.

I couldn't count how many people bagged me out for loving life more. They would say I'm being a fake for being so positive, that life can't be that great, and all the rest of it. Their comments proved that they were vastly unaware of their own lives. Funnily enough, they were always the people who were lost and never believed they could do anything great. Knowing the effect they were having on their own lives forced me to be compassionate. Months would pass, and those same individuals would ask for guidance. Did I help them? Of course I did, or else I'd stoop to their level. Now we all know that we cannot feel great all the time, but by practising it, at least you will know the feeling you want to get back to. That will help you come up with ways of regaining it.

It's crucial that you always remain you, and express that great person you know you are deep down. By the way, this is a journey, so you are going make mistakes. The most important thing to remember is that you are always in control of how you feel. Use the great gifts you have been given; **think and feel for yourself**.

Produce that great energy by focusing on the great things in life like that appreciation list, things you want to achieve, and the beauty that surrounds you. Put down your phone or your laptop and go and breathe the fresh air. For a brief moment, just look at the birds, or up in the sky. Truly take in and focus on the beauty of this magnificent world we live in. We get so entranced by what we want, we forget about what we have. What most don't realise is it's what we have that gets us what we want, in happiness.

'Life is full of beauty. Notice it. Notice the bumble bee, the small
child, and the smiling faces. Smell the rain, and feel the wind. Live
your life to the fullest potential, and fight for your dreams.'
Ashley Smith

Also acknowledge that practice makes perfect. Just like anything in
life, we have to practise loving life in order to get better at it. When
faced with a disempowering experience, you must look for an
alternative route immediately. That curiosity and determination
will always help you find a way through.

8

FOCUS AND FIND

'Ask and you shall receive; seek and you will find; knock and the door will be opened for you'
Jesus Christ

Have you ever thought that someone was deliberately ignoring you or deceiving you behind your back? How did you feel in that moment? Were you frustrated, hurt, angry or upset? How about when you found out that they had not done it to begin with? How did you feel then? Did you feel embarrassed, upset with yourself, or even stupid? So how were you able to feel those emotions initially, even though the deceit never happened? Before I tell you the answer, let's do one more. Think of someone you really love for a moment. Really feel them next to you. Take a minute, close your eyes and imagine their presence. Before you read on, do this. Did you just feel full of love, as if that person was actually there with you? The reason this happens is because your mind doesn't know the difference between something you are actually experiencing, and something that is only in your mind. **What we focus on we will surely feel.** So by knowing you have this power, how quickly can you change the way you feel?

In order for us to fully enhance the quality of our life, and achieve at our peak, we must choose wisely in the way our attention is being focused. Life is defined on the notion that **our mind is definitely going to find what we focus on.** Now whether that is a blessing or a curse is entirely up to you, as you're in total control of directing that energy. It becomes so frustrating when the experiences that we don't want to keep showing up, do. The reason they show themselves so often is because we are putting so much energy towards them. When we focus on the things we don't want, we get more of them! That uneasiness then begins to consume our reality. This may create a feeling of hopelessness, anger and disappointment until other areas of our life suffer because of our inner turmoil. It's quite obvious in everyday life experience. When you are feeling angry, everything outside will seem distorted and get under your skin. When you are irritated about something, everything will seem to irritate you. When you are happy, then everything seems great. It's a law of life — there is no escaping it. We must learn to enhance our emotional fitness, and that comes from what we choose to focus on. **When you continue to focus on what you want, your whole demeanour adapts to your desire. Body language, vocabulary, tone of voice, and even subconscious movements all shift to mould you into the person you need to be.**

Don't make things you don't want a priority in your life. If you do, they will consume your reality.

Even in an advanced driving course, the instructor will stress that directing your focus is a crucial part of survival. It is said that if we look at the pole or a tree whilst losing control, we automatically get drawn to the object. The same principle goes in every area of our life. The more we look and focus on not having enough money, always seeming to find the wrong partner, someone not letting you live your dream, not having enough resources, not having the time or always being sick, to name a few, they become stronger. Your mind is going to find every way to attract the things you focus on.

The Bible says: 'Seek and you shall find,' which I think is a pretty good concept that we need to grasp. What you find depends on what you're choosing to seek. You have always got what you have asked for, however you might not be exactly aware of what it is you are asking. Are you really taking notice of what doors you are knocking on, because they are opening? **When your mind wanders, so does what you create.** If you have ever walked a dog on a leash, you would know that sometimes it seems as if the dog is walking you. When it begins to wander off, you direct it back to position with the leash. That's exactly what you have to do with your thoughts, keep them on a leash! If you don't, you lose control.

Think, feel, act, create.

When you think about what you don't want, how does it make you feel? It personally makes me feel disempowered, unmotivated, sad, and even frustrated. All these human emotions cause us to act in the same way that created and attracted those things we didn't want in the first place. As soon as we shift our focus towards things we want, our attitude changes instantly, and we begin to feel inspired. And when we feel great, we get great results. By redirecting our focus towards what we want, **our mind is also more inclined to finding it.**

Have you ever bought a new car and all of a sudden you begin to notice that same make and model everywhere? When you hear someone call out the same name as yours it grabs your attention immediately. It might be a parent calling out to their child, but you will look around.

This power of 'focus and find' truly displayed itself while my brother and I were shopping for his wedding. All we needed was a navy blue tie, so we made a pact that our focus for the day was strictly a 'navy blue tie'. The amazing thing was that blue began appearing everywhere. It was like we had our own personal scanner, and as soon as blue was in sight, everything else seemed to fade away. If you have ever seen the movie *Terminator*, you know the closer he is to locking onto a target, the quicker his scanner beeps. That's exactly what it was like. I was noticing blue everywhere, even baby blue. I began relating irrelevant colours to my initial focus. It even reached a point where I was looking at black ties, and concentrating my hardest to see if they were navy. Even after the store clerk reminded me a number of times that they were black, I was still convinced that some were blue. Blue shoes, blue socks, blue hats and blue suits all began to catch my attention. By the end of the day, I told my brother that I didn't want to see blue for another year. The reason all these things caught my concentration, is because I had made it a priority in my life. **The things you prioritise, you find everywhere.**

Your emotions derive from where your focus is being directed.

As much as being able to focus and find what we are seeking among so many possibilities is another phenomenon of our amazing existence, there is also a part of the brain that allows such experiences to take place. With every thought of the mind, there is a physical action in the brain. The reticular activating system (RAS) is composed of several neuronal circuits connecting the brainstem to the cortex. This part of the brain acts like a filter between your conscious and subconscious mind. It's responsible for taking notice of, or relating outside information that was always in existence, to enhance the picture you have mentally created. There are billions of bits of information going on in one single moment, and if we were able to notice them all, we would definitely go crazy. The RAS helps narrow it down to the information that is important to you. In Dr Maxwell Maltz's 1960 self-help book, *Psychocybernetics*, he describes it as being our own 'servo-mechanism'.

With doing a bit of what I love — research — I discovered that auto-focus cameras contain a servomechanism. I'm not sure if you have ever used one of these, but it automatically creates sharper focus and a clearer picture once the lens is moved to the desired location. **When we make something important in our life, be it a benefit or not, it becomes a priority. The RAS in your brain is going to seek it everywhere and make the picture a whole lot clearer.** Guess who's in charge of moving that lens? You are.

Shifting focus — move your lens

'Most people have no idea of the giant capacity we can immediately command when we focus all of our resources on mastering a single area of our lives.'
Anthony Robbins

Why do some people have such a great outlook on life, while others seem to be surrounded by so much misery? Why are there some who succeed at a much greater level than others, and are fulfilled? Why do those few find inspiration everywhere and are always motivated, yet others find it difficult to come up with any ideas? The answer to these questions lies in the understanding of how life actually works. I hear people say to me, 'I know how life works;

you wake up, go to work, and come home. It's the same thing every day'. My reply is, 'No, that's how *your* life works'. The truth is, the more we think about the same thing, it repeats the same feelings and hence we repeat the same actions. See, most people believe that things must change on the outside to affect their inner self. They believe that they must have a sense of achievement in order to feel great about themselves. If you have met anyone who is really successful, rich in all areas of life, you will notice they don't attempt to live life backwards. They live it the way it was intended, which is to **feel great first**, then that causes them to **act great**, which results in **achieving great**. The only way to make yourself feel great first is to be intelligent in the way you command your focus.

'Concentrate all your thoughts upon the work at hand. The sun's rays do not burn until brought to a focus.'
Alexander Graham Bell

All of our emotions arise from where our focus is being directed. Once we shift our lens over to something else, it's going to pick up detail that once went unnoticed. It's like getting a spotlight and moving it from one area to another. Once that is successfully completed, the other areas of our life, which once contributed to its destruction, will be left in the dark. On the other hand, if we do not shift that light, these experiences and situations must keep happening so you think the world as you know it is still in check. We revolve many situations around it, relate irrelevant things to it, and create scenarios that seem worse than what they are; all to satisfy the stories we play over in our mind.

Let's take someone who is paranoid. They repeatedly focus their energy on someone doing wrong by them, being unfaithful, or trying to rip them off. They have focused on that idea so hard, they believe that everyone they meet is the same. Did it ever occur to them that the reason they feel that way is because they have trained their mind to believe that is the case. Could our intention cause a situation to actually turn out that way, or is that we are expecting it, so we will relate anything back to that scenario? Is everyone really trying to take advantage of them, or is it just a reflection of how they are feeling internally, which causes them to perceive it that way?

I vividly remember how excited I was when I bought my first car. The last thing I thought about was that this car might have any faults. I was rapt; I'd just bought my first car, and I placed the bar high on it. In my eyes it was perfect — until it started breaking down and overheating. All of a sudden my perception totally changed from this car being 'perfect' to me being 'doomed' with cars. When I bought my second car, I had tarnished my thought of having a reliable car due to my choice of perception from my past experience. Even though the problem might have been something as simple as the window not working, I would refer back to being 'doomed' with cars and would just wait for the next thing to go wrong. I would freak out at any unfamiliar noise, forgetting that it was a metal box and they make noises. I would tell people about how I was cursed with cars and stress about it every time I jumped in. As I would start the engine, it was as if I expected something to just blow up. It was driving me mad and took up far too much of my energy.

This paranoia of my car breaking down continued, until I got in my friend's car one day and his window stopped working. I smirked, shook my head and said, 'We must be doomed with cars'.

I expected him to go along with the victimisation, but he turned around and said, 'Relax, it's just a window'. So in fact was it me that was 'doomed' with cars, or was it just the uncertainty in life that everyone experiences that I personalised to play the victim and feel worse?

Thinking about it, there are people dying of starvation in the world, and yet here I am complaining about a window not going up. Further to that, it seemed okay to spend $400 on alcohol every week, but I would whine over having to spend $100 on fixing a window that would allow me to breathe. I guess it's easier to put the blame on things externally, than to take accountability ourselves. My belief of being 'doomed' with cars diminished and I realised it was 'just a car'.

This might sound like a simple scenario but, when I tell people the story, I realise I'm not alone. How often do you focus on something so hard that it begins to consume your life? How many times does something then happen, and you realise you actually had nothing to worry about in the first place? Or you eventually get over it and it has no power in your life? That surely creates different emotions.

We create our own reality, and when it has its hiccups, we think it's not living up to the high standards we have set, and start to doubt. We then shift our focus and believe that is the best life has to offer. Very far from the truth, but we must put something beneficial in its place in these times.

Successfully directing energy

The beauty of life is just as real as the ugliness of life. It all depends on which one you choose to see.

A few years ago while working at a call centre, I noticed one of my colleagues had his head down and looked quite upset. He was never really the type to say much, so I decided to approach him. He told me that he didn't want to talk about it, so I knew I had to take action in order to help. The next day I walked past, and again his head was in his hands. I decided to clap as loudly as I could next to his ear. He jumped up, startled, and I said, 'You see how quickly your mood can change'. After that, we got into a conversation and his perception of his girlfriend leaving him changed drastically.

Rather than beating himself up over everything he apparently did 'wrong', he acknowledged through reasoning with himself that it was what he had wanted for a while. He told me that he had a gut feeling it was never going to work. He also wanted to travel and experience things that he knew he couldn't do while with her. I explained that by shifting his focus towards reasons that would serve him, he would be able to pave a new direction for his life; that unless he stopped lying to himself with playing the victim, and took charge of the benefits he was already aware of, he would never be able to move on. In an instant he was able to come up with a list of visions he could work towards, and that would allow him to be free of the emotional attachment of his past love. Challenging times would still face him, yet he created empowering routes that his mind would now always find to feed, rather than the pain enduring option. As long he continued to reinforce the new idea of his deep truth, the other one would diminish.

When you stop focusing on things you don't want, you break the pattern of letting them consume most of your life. It also prevents you from associating irrelevant things to a situation that just 'is'.

It's like watching a guy run across the street towards an old woman. We might perceive him to be heading in that direction to rob the lady, which causes us to become distressed. Someone else might perceive the situation as a good gesture, where the guy is going to give back the change she left at the store. All of a sudden the guy runs straight past and makes no contact with her at all. Both scenarios were just as real for that moment, but only because we created them to be. This is the case for every thing that happens or has happened in your life. That external stimulus was, or is open for whatever you wish to attach to it. Analyse it properly, put things into perspective, think of something that you should be really grateful for in that time, or focus on what you want, and you will experience pleasure.

Focus on how the situation could benefit your visions in life, rather than distance you from them. What knowledge can you gain to take action and better your life? As long as you look hard enough, benefits can be drawn from any experience. So in fact, **every situation is open for an alternative view, and never just set to one.** Things once thought of as 'bad' will become your greatest opportunities for self-growth, and allow you to take another step towards a quality life. By practising this strategy, even just a few times, you will soon discover that the only reason anything ever seems a certain way is due to the thoughts and hence emotions you **choose** to attach to it. You will relate this exercise to past and new experiences, and that's when you really take massive steps to positively shape your destiny.

When feeling down about something, you know it is actually just due to your perception. These times call for full focus, and not letting your mind wander. We must not just settle for how things

might seem in an instant, but search deeper, looking for ways to turn it around. Once you have discovered a better way of looking at an experience, even if it's only slightly better, hold onto that new thought, and feed it like mad. Once that is accomplished, you have learnt how to successfully direct your energy.

3RD STEP

THE SYSTEM OF ACHIEVEMENT

9

TAKE INSTANT CHARGE

'It had long come to my attention that people of accomplishment rarely sat back and let things happen to them. They went out and happened to things.'
Leonardo da Vinci

We have all achieved something in our life, regardless of how small we might think it is. There are times where things seem hard, almost unbearable, until we finally overcome them. Achievement is when we accomplish something in our life, whether it is having the courage to overcome a situation, the attainment of personal goals, a heroic act, or putting extra effort into a task. All achievements, from the greatest to the smallest, will play a major role in what you set out to achieve next. Raising a child, providing the essentials for your family, getting a relationship back on track, or overcoming one that wasn't working are all types of achievements. Whatever we achieve in our life, the process is quite systematic. We get a vision of what we want, passion then builds up, we align ourselves with fear, consistently think of how it can be achieved, work our action plan, and follow it. Regardless of whether you have taken notice of this or not, it's usually the way it happens.

Achievement never dropped out of the sky and knocked on your front door with a bunch of roses — you had to go and get it. And just because you may have achieved something, it doesn't mean you are ultimately fulfilled. I couldn't count how many times I have

heard of someone achieving something great, yet a month down the track they are empty because they don't know what to do next. I've met multimillionaires that are some of the unhappiest people I know. They exclusively went for the money, only to find that is not a passion, but rather an attempt to find lasting happiness in a material way. That sent them to another dead end. I'm sure we have all heard of stories where very wealthy people end up as drug addicts or commit suicide, while others with very little material wealth are the happiest people alive. They are all great achievers, as that word achievement is personalised to individuals wants. However, it is only achievement and fulfilment together that brands someone truly successful. We must learn how to gain them both, and that's what I have dedicated my life to finding. I have worked tenaciously to unravel the powers that allow us to shape our destiny on our conditions. The following knowledge and strategies steered me towards a true success in no time.

The reality of compelling visions

'Dreaming is not enough. You have to go a step further and use your imagination to visualize, with intent! Forget everything you've been taught, and believe it will happen, just as you imagined it. That is the secret. That is the mystery of life.'
Christine Anderson

On 1 October 1971, just four years after the passing of Walt Disney, thousands of people swarmed near Orlando, Florida to see the grand opening of Walt Disney World. One of Mr Disney's closest companions said to Walt's wife, Lillian, 'I wish Walt was here to see this'. She turned to him and said, 'If Walt didn't see this, it wouldn't be here now'. She was referring to his vision. The

Walt Disney Company is worth approximately $35 billion, and it all started with Mickey Mouse, who Walt said '…popped out of my mind onto a drawing pad on a train ride from Manhattan to Hollywood at a time when business fortunes of my brother Roy and myself were at lowest ebb and disaster seemed right around the corner.' I guess that's why Walt is also known for his famous quote, 'If you can dream it, you can do it'.

In order for us to live to our full potential, we must embrace the dream visions that flash before us. Most people I know will use this powerful tool to feel worse in their daily lives. They envision that dream body, that nice car, or big house, and immediately begin to get angry or beat themselves up for not having it now. I think the reason is due to their disbelief that they are actually able to attain them all. It is absolutely crucial to focus in on the great emotions of such visions, because that's what inspires us to action. Going on a holiday is a perfect example. We visualise being on the holiday way before most of our preparations are even organised; we build the emotion around it, and that is what inspires us to action.

The reality is that if we don't create absolutely compelling visions as to what we want out of life they will never come into existence. We must understand that a dream and a vision are two different things. The word 'dream' gets thrown around like a fairy tale. It's regarded as something that is not real, cannot be worked towards, or has no ground for creation. Everything that has come into existence was the result of someone's vision.

In Corey Turner's book, *Vision — The key to your future*, he states, 'Living life without any clear direction for your future is like trying to drive a car blindfolded. It may be really exciting for a few seconds but incredibly dangerous because of the very real danger

of crashing and hurting others.' I think it's also clear that we will be hurting ourselves in the process, and I know that one is real from personal experience.

If we don't have visions as to what we want to achieve in our life, then how are we ever going to bring it about? We won't know where to start, resort to things that never fulfil us, and live our life in the desperate rage of just hoping something will change. Now you might be sitting there thinking that you don't know exactly what you want in life. I've had this discussion with many people, especially youths, but we must think deeper. Is it that we really don't know, or is that we don't believe we can achieve the things we dream about? The people that never achieve much are those who wait for things to happen on the outside, to help make their visions become clearer. What they are unaware of is that they must create a vision first, of anything at all, and that makes everything on the outside align and assist to its accomplishment. You rarely get it straight away, but it will come if you hold it close to your heart and firmly in your mind. Then there is the balance of action you must take, but all successful people know that it starts with a compelling vision.

'Good business leaders create a vision, articulate the vision, passionately own the vision, and relentlessly drive it to completion.'
Jack Welch

That vision of a special person in your life, that Ferrari, that house by the water, that increased pay check at the end of the month, that good relationship with your family, being free from drugs or an addiction, are but a few goals. Visions don't necessarily just revolve around money, but abundance in our whole life. **The more clarity you have about what you want, the more you're**

willing to work for it. Most people seem to use broad terms such as 'I want more money', 'I want someone in my life', 'I want to own my own business', or 'I want to be more successful', unaware that they might get them, but only in the broad terms in which they ask. For example, saying you want to share your life with someone, and then falling in love with someone who isn't right for you. It's because you didn't have a clear indication and vision of what that person would be like. Their traits, their qualities, and things you must have or really want out of a partner weren't clear to you in the beginning. We just end up settling for the same old things. The same goes when we make an extra $20 for the fortnight and then we complain. You asked for more money didn't you? In order for you to get exactly what you want you need to be absolutely clear about it.

'Your past is important, but it is not nearly as important to your present as the way you see your future is.'
Tony Campolo

Creating visions also calls for common sense, as we know things might not result in exactly the way they first appeared in our mental image. Accept the imperfections in life, because things are unstable, impermanent, and naturally subject to change. This may also be caused by our mere inability to ever see perfection. I mean, if we meet that person and they don't have the size eight foot that we imagined, I would probably suggest putting down the judgment sword and see it for what it really is. It's like when you plan a trip away and you are visualising lying on the beach. You envision how the hotel room might look, and the beauty that surrounds the place. When you get there, it's not exactly the same, although you still appreciate it for what it is, sometimes even more. Look at the true essence of the creation, and the right passion from which it stemmed. Paintings are not looked at as perfect, but those who understand them are able to see the passion of the painter within them. Appreciation is then stemmed accordingly. **Allow room for error, but never allow room for giving up on those things that you know you must have.**

Knowing what I want — or do I?

'Don't ask what the world needs. Ask what makes you come alive, and go do it. Because what the world needs are people who have come alive.'
Howard Thurman

Sitting down in a café one evening with a close friend, I overheard two young guys discussing how they didn't know what they wanted in their lives. I know it's not very polite to eavesdrop, but in a place where tables were almost connected, I felt as if I was meant to be there. I politely asked if I could interrupt. My friend was kicking me under the table because she was embarrassed, but I couldn't leave after hearing these guys' distress, and knowing I could help. I asked them, 'If I said to you that you could have the woman of your dreams right now, would you take her?' They laughed and said, 'Yeah, for sure'. I then asked if I were to offer them a mansion with a Lamborghini parked out the front, would they take it. Again the answer was yes. I then asked if they could wake up every morning feeling great with an inspiring outlook on life, contribute to the world, have a fit body, and be in a position where they were in charge of their emotions, would they embrace such a life? One guy turned around to me and said, 'Did you just win the lottery and feel generous?' I laughed and replied, 'No, I'm proving that you know exactly what you want, you just don't think you can get it!' This is one of the major challenges I see in society today. **Most people know what they want; they just believe it's out of their reach.** It's then easier to say they don't know as an excuse to escape with some dignity.

How many times have you wondered what you really want out of life? Further to that, how many times do you change the mere thought of what you want? With all this confusion, it is almost impossible to manifest a single idea, because your focus and energy is too widespread to make one real. Besides the fact that you are changing your mind, it is imperative that the choices you do decide on don't conflict with who you are.

Now you might know exactly what you want, and that's great. For some, like me, that wasn't the case. To know what you really want, you have to know yourself first. I mean, how can we ever really know what we want if we don't fully know who we are? How will we know our powers? How will we ever be able to build a relationship with ourselves to the point of trust, in order to get what we set out for? It seems most cloud and hide who they are every day, until they are confused and doubt their true ability. If you know who you are, then you will know what you want. You are able to identify your passion, and live a life that reminds you to be conscious of every action you take.

Exploring yourself, nurturing your everyday life, and feeding who you really are is the basis of finding out exactly what you want. The more you stress and worry about not knowing, the more it clouds your true identity. You must have the faith that through making changes in everyday life as it is now, regardless of how small the changes might seem, your truth is going to display itself.

As I mentioned, I didn't have a clear indication of what my passion in life was, I just knew I loved to help people. The last thing I thought I would become was an author. To be honest, in the beginning of my change, all I wanted to do was alter what I was doing in the present. It worked quite well, because instead of fogging my mind with what I thought I wanted, I decided to change what I was doing, which built the belief that I could achieve anything. I needed to rectify the concept of **feeling, acting** and **creating** of my own accord. That allowed me to recognise that it could be done in any area of my life.

We must also be aware of *conflicting beliefs*, and the influence they have on our decision-making. If your appreciation list states that you are very grateful for your family, then I'm guessing they are important in your life. If you wanted to open up a brothel, that could be a conflicting belief. Realistically, the choices you make are up to you, but it calls for some deep thought processes. Go back to that part of 'Absolute power of questioning' where I invited you to notice those great qualities within you. You will realise that your choices should be in line with who you really are, and how they could be of benefit to the things most important to you. This may also be the cause of why you have changed your mind so many times, as you will always adapt pleasure and pain to a 'want'. We are emotional creatures, so the feeling that you get from something you want is compelling. **Always go for the feeling, because that's the pinnacle of what you want.**

Create massive purpose with everything you do

'It doesn't matter what you do if you don't do what matters. If you do what matters it doesn't matter what you do.'
Unknown

There are so many people that use the excuse of 'having to' or 'needing to' do something in their life. I would like to point out that you never 'have to'. And 'needing' also gets thrown out most times as well. We complain about our cars, our jobs, and the people in our life. If you are continually complaining about how crap the car is, then why don't you get a baseball bat and smash it to pieces? No one is stopping you. You don't *have to* keep it, and you definitely don't *need* it. I'm sure the bus or other transport can take you about. If you don't like that person in your life, then it's your choice to stick around. If you find yourself always complaining about your job, get up now, and go and tell your boss how much the company stinks. Also let him or her know that you are picking up your things and leaving. Come on, you only live once so go and do them. You don't want them, remember. If you are wondering whether I'm serious, you bet I am. But are you? If you are saying to yourself, 'I'm not going to smash my car or say that to my boss,' why not? When you answer the 'why not' you will realise it's because you actually want to be there more than you don't want to be there, or else you would have already done something about it.

Your complaining is creating your own disaster.

What about doing chores around the house? Doing the dishes or mopping the floor is something that people believe they *have* to do, or *need* to do. The answer again is, 'No, you don't.' You can quite easily walk around with grime seeping through the floor or eat off a plate that has crusties left over from last week. If you get my point, all these things are **wants**. You want to keep the car because you don't want to walk everywhere you go. The reason you won't say that to your boss is because you want money. You want to wash the dishes because you don't want get infected with bacteria. Even if someone held a gun to your head and asked you to do something, it's still a choice to obey or not, right? The solution to your complaints: Stop whining and take massive action.

A while back, I had a friend ring me up complaining about helping her sister and nephew move into a new place. She had no sleep, was drained, and was acting like she was giving something up by helping. I asked her, 'Do you have to do it?' She answered, 'Yes, because who else is going to?' I quickly reminded her that she didn't have to do anything, and could have slept all day knowing that her sister would do it on her own. Then she replied, 'No, I wouldn't let her do it on her own'. Laughing to myself, I said, 'Well, that means you actually want to do it, because you recognise it's a great thing to do. The fact that you're doing it means that you want to more than you don't want to. Stop complaining and be proud of yourself'. She called me back an hour later and said, 'You know what? I feel really good about what I just did for my sister'.

When you create meaning with everything you do, it gives you the drive to go that extra mile that no one else is willing to go. **Successful people do not just do something, they acknowledge why they are doing it.**

People ask me, 'What is the purpose of life?' But I think the question should be, 'What isn't the purpose of life?' Everything in life has its purpose.

When you start acknowledging that you **want** to do things, it increases purpose.

Creating purpose in your life is by far the number one way to create self-motivation. Just remember, you are far more willing to do things that you want to do, rather than those things you feel that you have to do. **Turn your 'have to' into 'want to' by giving enough great reasons as to why you are doing it in the first place. This also increases your appreciation. If you find that it's not actually something that you want to do, then also acknowledge that you never have to. Once you grasp that everything you do in life is a choice, there is no room to play the victim.** If you choose to do it, do yourself a favour and stop dwelling on what's 'wrong' in the experience. Shift your focus to why you want to, or the compelling visions that you're about to write down.

How to unleash a smothered passion and allow it to drive your life

'Reduce your plan to writing. The moment you complete this, you will have definitely given concrete form to the intangible desire.'
Napoleon Hill

Task

This is the third section of your appreciation list that I said we would get to. You must add this to your list to complete it.

3. Wants: This is the part where you are to put all limitations aside and write continuously. Write down everything you have dreamed of having, and be creative. Give thanks for the things you want in life, and do not hold back at all. I don't care how big or how small, you must write it. Be as specific as you can, because clarity brings forth courage. If you want more money, then how much do you want? Do you want $10,000, $100,000 or $10,000,000? When your visions become too vague, you will never hit your target. **When**

you're not clear about the result you want, you result in getting anything.

Most people aren't specific with what they want because they fear the feeling of failure if they never get it. But why worry in advance? I have discovered that in order to create an extraordinary life we must raise the bar so high that it scares us. Only by raising our standards do we give ourselves the opportunity to step up to such a level. Besides the fear aspect, most find it easier to wishfully think that what they want will just appear. What these people must realise is that the reason they will never get what they want is actually caused by their reluctance to create more clarity in the first place.

I had a client who was going overseas at her dad's expense. Attempting to create more independence in her life, I asked her to set an amount of money she would like to have extra for her trip, which she had to earn. Scared to write down a large number, she came up with $2000. I knew that she would always cut her ability in at least half because of her dad's involvement, so I raised it to $4000. She eventually reached $3800. What a great achievement! If she never set $4000 as a target, she would never have reached $3800 and may have even saved less than her original $2000. Not to mention the massive growth and self-respect she gained in the process. If you shoot an arrow with no target set up, where do you think it's going to go? How can you hit a target if you don't have one to begin with?

'Clarity: The ability to think clearly or understand things clearly.'
MacMillan Dictionary

When in pursuit of what you want in life, there are two things you must have in order to get it: clarity and enough emotional charge. Without either or both, you don't stand a chance. Clarity helps create that emotional charge. I hear so many people tell me that if they meet that 'special' person, they will make changes, or if they had more money, they would then decide what they wanted to buy. I am quick to remind them if they aren't clear on what that person is like, so they can make the changes **now**, then that special person will never be attracted to them. And as far as the money theory goes, it's actually the complete opposite. By having a clear indication of what you want initially, it forces you to produce more emotional charge, which will ensure you create the money needed. You must be specific with what you want first. Creating clarity is not wishful thinking; it makes what you want more real. And when something is more real, you believe it more. When you believe it more, you take action!

The only way we can accomplish beyond our known limits is by frequently raising our standards.

There is one point you should take note of. That is, make sure you don't drive yourself crazy filling in all the minor details, like your business having electric doors instead of a manual one. Just write down the bigger picture, and you will end up filling in the details as you progress. By staying conscious of the bigger picture, it reminds you of why you are taking all the small steps now. All exceptional achievers reached a point in their life where they stopped dwelling on not having their wants, and forcefully brought forth emotions as if they already did. **You must celebrate your success now.** Imagine and create the same feelings you would have if you had all those things you want. If you do this it allows you to experience the powerful emotions which master your willingness to act and your goals will draw closer. Unless you build the belief by consuming yourself with what you want, you will never get it. **You can't get to a place that you don't believe exists!**

Go for it right now. Again, you must not read on until you have completed this task. Get out your appreciation list and start writing. Stay away from writing down what you don't want. Focus on what you want. An example in the 'Financial' section would be, 'I want to own a condo in Miami with a swimming pool on the balcony, and **not**, 'I don't want to live in the one bedroom apartment that I am currently living in'. To make it easier, create sections or a table such as:

Financial	Physical	Mental	Emotional/ spiritual

Note: This list is subject to change. It will evolve over time, but you must have an indication initially. Think hard and dream big. **Make sure you always begin with 'I want…'**

At the end of reading my list I would really get into a state and use my body. Sometimes I would walk around with my eyes closed and beating on my chest if I had to. I would do anything that would put me into an overwhelming state and repeat:

'Thank-you for giving me everything I ever wanted; financially, physically, mentally and emotionally. For everything I ever desired and have. Thank you, God, for being one with the qualities that reign within me and giving me the gifts to obtain and attain anything I desire.'

Focus on your 'wants' first thing in the morning. Carry that energy throughout your day and you will see the path begin to light up for you. Write down any progress or ideas that flow.

Do not read on until you have completed this crucial task for your personal growth.

Creating purpose and enough emotional charge

In order to be successful, you must have purpose. In Napoleon Hill's masterpiece *Think and Grow Rich*, he presented the idea of a 'Definite Major Purpose' as a challenge to his readers to ask themselves, 'In what do I truly believe?' According to Hill, ninety-eight per cent of people had few or no firm beliefs; this alone put true success firmly out of their reach. His journey also consisted of researching and interviewing 500 of the most successful people in the world at the time. Thomas Edison, Alexander Graham Bell, Henry Ford, F W Woolworth, John D Rockefeller, William Wrigley Jr and Franklin Delano Roosevelt were only a few.

These highly successful people displayed definite patterns in their attitudes, but at that time, which was not so different to our era, most people had serious misconceptions of the qualities they thought brought them success. It was evident that negative emotions such as fear, selfishness and resentment were the sources of failure. This came as a big shock to most. The opposites of these attributes were found to be some of the secrets to success, but it was said that everyone must discover this on their own and thus gain the knowledge to really influence their lives.

In my experience, achievers who think that winning means they have to be arrogant and heartlesss in the process, actually lose more than they gain. They may have gained money, but they lost everything else, including themselves. There is a way of gaining what you want and staying true to yourself in the meantime, and that's what real success consists of.

'Your worth consists in what you are and not what you have.'
Thomas Edison

Task

Why do I want what I want?

Look at your wants list, and note down as many reasons *why* you want what you want. Also **write down why you must have them and why you will not settle for less**. If you do not have a clear indication about *why you want what you want*, then you will not enhance the emotions that create the certainty to obtain them. Passion builds up; it is not something that you just find at its peak. This exercise is crucial for assigning passion to your wants. Stay away from writing what you don't want. For example, '**I want… because I don't want to be poor**'. *Instead you would write*, '**I want… because I want to feel like I have accomplished what I'm worth** or **because I want to give my family great opportunities**'. Go and write a list now.

These next sets of questions also create an enormous amount of *emotional charge*. Focus on each one individually for a few minutes and write down the answers.

- How would it make me feel if I **didn't** get what I wanted in my life?

- What would I think about myself?

- How would my body language be?

- What are the emotions I would experience on a daily basis?

- Are some of the answers to these questions things I am doing now?

If you are acting in the same way as you would if you never got what you wanted, how on earth do you expect to get anything!

Now

- How would it make me feel if I **did** get what I wanted?

- How would I hold my body? What would my body language be like? What would my shoulders, facial expressions, or attitude be like?

- Throughout my day, how can I produce those same emotions I would get when I attain what I want? How would I have to think, talk and walk?

- Must I allocate time to really think about their accomplishment and continually embrace the emotions?

- How can I create rapid change from the answers I have obtained from these questions? What can I do differently? What are the different emotions I need to start commanding?

Only by answering these crucial questions can you bring forth the **emotional charge** needed to achieve. Take the same feelings that you imagine you would get if you gained what you wanted with you all day. Let those feelings drive your decisions. Remind yourself of why you really want what you have written down.

10

THE PERSISTENCE PUNCH

'Nothing in the world can take the place of persistence. Talent will
not; nothing is more common than unsuccessful people with talent.
Genius will not; unrewarded genius is almost a proverb. Education
will not; the world is full of educated derelicts. Persistence and
determination alone are omnipotent. The slogan "press on" has
solved and always will solve the problems of the human race.'
Calvin Coolidge

Have you ever thought of an idea or something that you believe
people would want, and a year or two years down track you see
it on the shelves? It could be on TV, a new product out in the
supermarkets, or an invention that you once thought of. You then
say things like 'that was my idea' and you go and tell others that
you had once thought of it. Well, the difference is, the person to
whom the idea flowed after you, decided to persist that belief. We
let so many dreams, visions and ideas slip because we think others
might find them stupid, that it will be too hard, or we give up
due to the hurdles we come across. An Olympic hurdler doesn't
run off the track if he misses the first jump; he gets back up and
finishes the race. **Falling down doesn't mean failing.**

The concept of 'failing' was only created by those who were too
scared to succeed, and only exists in the same world as 'giving
up' does. If we never stop persevering, then failure will not be an
option. There is in fact no such thing as 'failure', but everything

is knowledge we can put into practice. The reason there are great achievers is due to their reluctance to see something as a failure. They stick to the belief that there is no failure, only feedback. You don't fail — you only get results. These achievers are like a bulldog with a bone clenched firmly in its mouth. The more you try to take away the bone, the harder it grips.

If you read biographies of high achievers you will notice most of their first businesses or trials weren't the ones that took them to greatness. Some did, but the others used every experience as an opportunity for learning and growth.

It is easy to give up, but only in the short term. I couldn't think of anything worse than just settling, and to me that's a lot harder to live with. It's normal not to feel 100 per cent motivated all the time and to have moments where you feel like you are being defeated. What you need to master is moving forward even an inch in those times, because that's how you win. Every time you win, you become stronger. Relentlessly holding onto your visions is winning in essence.

One of the most inspirational stories of persistence I have ever seen was of an Australian man stuck in a South East Asian jungle for eleven days. The documentary is called *Miracle in the Jungle*, and it was based on Hayden Adcock's amazing story of survival. On a trek that was only meant to last a few hours, he got lost in some of the roughest terrain known to mankind. With no food and faced with every challenge that seems possible during a national storm alert, he thought his time was over. His wounds were so deep and became so moist that his body became a feeding ground for disease. Parasites entered and hallucination started to kick in. Half way through his ordeal, Hayden found himself at a waterfall, where he considered jumping off. He said that just as he was about to jump and end his own life, he thought about his parents and all his loved ones. He thought if he if he were to give up now he would be leaving absolutely no hope, so he didn't jump because of his strong love for his family. Hayden survived another six days in the jungle after that before being rescued, and faced challenges that most would consider insurmountable. It just goes to show one man's persistence can defy all the odds against him. It is a documentary I highly recommend.

'Permanence, perseverance and persistence in spite of all obstacles, discouragement, and impossibilities: it is this that in all things distinguishes the strong soul from the weak.'
Thomas Carlyle

In order to stay persistent, you must truly cut every avenue of retreat. Succeeding needs to be the only way in your mind, because that's when you will go that extra mile and push past the limit that was once thought impassable. There needs to be no other way than that to which your passion directs you. If you believe something can work, then it can, because you have been there in your mind. Every creation began from a vision and belief, even when most people called that same idea nuts. When you really believe in yourself, it will eventually rub off on everyone around you, and you will notice your persistence is desirable. **Don't forget that we build our own beliefs**. It is said that Colonel Sanders went to 900 chicken shops with his recipe, and had the door closed in his face. They said his recipe would never work and that his idea was crazy. Yes, 900 times! Ask yourself how many people would have given up after five refusals? He believed in his idea, and finally got his first break. His sheer persistence and determination transformed his recipe into the franchise we all know as KFC.

Tommy Hilfiger started by selling his jeans out of the trunk of his car. Not many would have the guts to do that. If he hadn't persisted do you think he would have one of the greatest clothing companies of all time? Even those who have won a medal, passed a test, owned a local business, or dedicated their life to contribution have remained persistent to see it through. **There are certain breaks that successful people hit, but in order for them to arise, they know they must persist**. The problem with most people is that they give up, unaware that their big break might have been just around the corner. That's why it is imperative to continue pushing on, because these breaks do happen, and when they hit, they hit big. If you are finding it hard to believe in yourself, then prove it to yourself.

I'm sure there has been a time in your life when you had to do a new task. Let's take getting a new job as an example. The first day you walked in, how nervous and excited were you? That job may have been really difficult to comprehend and do. It may have even got to a point where you thought you would never get the hang of it. A few weeks go by, and you wonder why you ever stressed because it now seems so easy. If you look for it hard enough, your ability in life will astound you. But most people don't take the time to notice it. The truth is, we have the ability to do anything in our life. People throughout history, with all different biographies have proven that time and time again.

There will be times when you feel as if your head is under water, and you will question what you are doing, doubt your ability, and have others call you stupid. What will bring you to greatness is acting the way the great do. **Everyone on the road of achievement has experienced self-doubt. Those who win, though, always overpower that doubt with self-assurance**. If you have ever bought a new car, you will be familiar with that uncomfortable feeling when you sat behind the wheel for the first few times. Then we sort of miss our old car because of its comfort, but there is no way we will go back, because we know the new one is better. We will persist in driving until it becomes second nature.

> 'By perseverance the snail reached the ark.'
> *Charles H Spurgeon*

I have had some people get confused with the notion of 'letting go' compared to that of 'giving up'. Letting go of something you don't want anymore is not the same as giving up on something that you truly do want. For example, if you are in a relationship that is not working, and you don't want to be in it anymore, then following a new path is imperative to your happiness. Letting go of something you do not want any more displays strength, and that's why it is not called 'giving up'. In truth, you would still have to persist in your letting go to achieve it. Your truth never lies, and letting go isn't giving up, because if you know deep down it's not what you really want any more, then what are you giving up? Common sense says nothing. Your mind tries to play tricks on you sometimes and tells you that you may want something when you know deep down you don't. So your truth will always ask, *'Is this something I really want, or am I just scared to let go and push past my known limits?'*

It's just like when we want to grow a particular muscle in our body. We work out, and we have to strain and stretch to the point of discomfort, and then as time goes on the muscle grows. If we only ever stop at our limit, we see no improvement. This goes for any part of our life. You will know in your heart whether it's a sign of weakness for hanging around in a situation that you know you don't want to be in anymore.

In saying that, you will also know when you are using excuses to not go and get what you know you deserve. We all face challenges when we go after what we want, but not many persist in the face of them. **Challenges are also there to help you eliminate what you don't want, so what you do want becomes clearer.**

Sheer determination is crucial for manifesting our visions into reality. Your idea or vision is probably just as good as the last great achiever's — you just need to let your passion drive you. Stay strong, keep the faith, believe in yourself, and never give up or accept less than what you know you must have. Most importantly, make sure you enjoy the process. **As soon as you stop adding pleasure to what you are doing, you are certain to experience pain.** Living the dream isn't just when you get what you want; it's actually the process of getting it. Things may seem hard at times, but remember, they are never so hard that you can't get through them!

People we know — in the face of obstacles

'Adversity has the effect of eliciting talents, which in prosperous circumstances would have lain dormant'.

Horace

The vice president of Columbia Pictures told Harrison Ford that he was never going to make it in the business.

John Grisham's first book was rejected by twelve publishing houses and sixteen agents.

A recording company said about the Beatles: 'We don't like their sound and guitar music is on the way out'.

Charles Darwin's father told him that he would amount to nothing and be a disgrace to himself and his family.

A music teacher said about Beethoven: 'As a composer he is hopeless'.

Enrico Caruso was told that he couldn't sing at all.

Walt Disney was fired from a newspaper because he 'lacked imagination and had no original ideas'.

The author of *Chicken Soup for the Soul* was told by publishers that 'anthologies didn't sell' and the book was 'too positive'. It was rejected a total of 140 times. It now has sixty-five different titles and has sold over 80 million copies all over the world.

Thomas Edison was told by a teacher he was 'too stupid to learn anything'.

Winston Churchill failed the sixth grade.

Albert Einstein wasn't able to speak until he was almost four years old and his teachers said he would 'never amount to much'.

Isaac Newton did poorly in school and failed at running the family farm.

F W Woolworth was not allowed to wait on customers in the store he worked in because 'he didn't have enough sense'.

Michael Jordan was cut from the high school basketball team, went home, locked himself in his room and cried.

A producer told Marilyn Monroe she was 'unattractive' and could not act.

Jonathan Livingston Seagull by Richard Bach was rejected eighteen times before it was published. It then sold over one million copies the first year.

Julia Roberts auditioned for *All My Children* and got rejected.

Abraham Lincoln's fiancée died, he failed in business twice, had a nervous breakdown, and was defeated in eight elections.

We all fall down, but not everyone picks themselves up. NEVER GIVE UP!

'All the adversity I've had in my life, all my troubles and obstacles, have strengthened me…You may not realize it when it happens, but a good kick in the teeth may be the best thing in the world for you'.
Walt Disney

Achievement adversities — be swift and bold on your road

'Adversity exasperates fools, rejects cowards, draws out the faculties of the wise and industrious, puts the modest to the necessity of trying their skill, awes the opulent and makes the idle industrious'.
Unknown

A very good friend of mine who began importing stock from China hit a massive rut after his launch. He had seen a 'success mentor' who told him that if he put it out there to the universe, it will come back at him. This 'expert' forgot to mention the massive action taken by people who actually achieve. So is it that easy that you can just think wishfully? Throw it out there to the universe and it will bounce back at you? I'm not even going to tell you the answer to that because you already know it. We all know that we can't sit there and think *'my car is going to be in the driveway, my car is going to be in the driveway'* then open our eyes and our car is in the driveway. If you think that sounds ridiculous it's because it is. Unless we get up and move the car, it's going to remain on the street. But people still buy the concept. There will be a lot of people, many books, documentaries and seminars that try to sugar coat achievement. I even heard this one speaker and author say that we can 'manifest effortlessly' when it comes to what we want. If you ever hear anything like this and believe it, realise you are setting yourself up for a big disappointment. There never has been, and never will be an easy way of achieving something great.

The positive side, however, is that even though sometimes in life there is no way out, **there is always a way through**. You will always hear from others that someone out there is worse off, although that's not really inspiring, is it? Inspiration comes from acknowledging that there was someone worse off that actually got through it! There is always a way. You must accept and make peace with a challenging situation, and look for every way to push forward or move swiftly around it. Don't resist, instead embrace how your experience can change your life for the better. We so often focus all our energy on the obstacles and not on the desired outcome. It's just like when there is a car in front of us that is indicating, we automatically look for a way around, right? The last thing we want to do is stop the flow of where we are heading. **We must focus on the outcome not the obstacles**.

I think we are all very aware that if we want something in life, we must go and get it. If you wait around and just bliss out all day, it will never come about. There is never an easy road to success, so put down the books and skip the seminars that portray that. Most of the population also want the easier option because we like to believe we can do less and gain more. Definitely not the truth, and that's why most of the population never get what they want. Great selling tool for liars though, because they're not telling the real story. Notice that only a few tell you about their adversities. Wonder why? It's a shame for those that ten years down the track are still sitting in their bedroom waiting for the Ferrari or dream partner to drop out of the sky. Life is about learning, and the only way to grow is through challenges, so they will be around for ever.

'Adversity is a fact of life. It can't be controlled. What we can control is how we react to it.'
English proverb

This particular friend of mine did so much in the lead-up to his launch and expected such a great outcome, that he neglected the 'after' plan. When the phone wasn't ringing like mad and stock flying out the door, he assessed his whole success on this outcome. What he wasn't aware of is that most business launches don't actually go to plan.

It is absolutely crucial that your road of success is not based on one particular event. If it is, you leave yourself open for great disappointment. I believe it's far worse preparing, building up momentum and taking massive action, then being disheartened. To me, that's worse than never going for it in the first place. This usually happens to people who have one set way to achievement, which could have detrimental effects. Don't ever change your ultimate want if you truly believe in it, but be able to move around. You must be diverse on your road.

Bruce Lee summed it up beautifully when he said, 'When you put water in a teacup, it becomes the teacup, when you put water in a bowl, it becomes the bowl. It can also crash or flow. Be water, my friends.' What he was referring to is how water is able to mould its shape into anything it is put into. We must be able to mould ourselves into any situation we find ourselves, as there is never one set way to be. There are many different avenues to be taken at all times. When you do find yourself at points of challenge, be aware that they are actually for your benefit. Any successful person will tell you that it was times of challenge that made them push harder and think broader. Adversities and challenges are actually **learning points**. I may just add that twelve months later, a businessman walked into that same guy's showroom and bought $60,000 worth of stock in one day. The ball rolled from there. He was quick to remind me that he had nights when he felt like his head was underwater and would run to his toilet to throw up, but he refused to put a time limit on what he believed in. He kept the faith, persisted, and finally got his break.

Life is a gift, my friends. You may only be one step away from unwrapping the paper.

So if happiness is looking forward to something, and great emotions inspire us to act, then we must continue to set up new challenges, yes? Never lose sight of your passion and set up new visions and challenges far before the completion of the imminent one. The most important thing to recognise when out to achieve is that every step you take is one step closer. You must have your eye fixed on this notion so it builds *massive* incentive, and never lose sight of your goals. Continue to take action and walk those steps that light up in front of you every day. Keep the faith if you believe in what you are doing, and there you have the ingredient to great achievement. Here's a strategy to ensure the strength of your success…

'Adversity precedes growth.'
Rosemarie Rossetti

Step 1: Create many plans

If you have a plan, that's absolutely great. Create another one! Even create five more if you can. Always have many options for improvement. If you don't have a plan, then create one. If you're thinking you don't know where to start then my advice is to keep your eye fixed on the prize. Feel it, be it, breathe it, meditate over it, talk about it, pray for it — I don't care what it is, just consume yourself with it. This will allow for inspiration to appear everywhere, and then write stuff down. Even if it seems extremely small at the time, make sure you catch it on paper, and things will flow from there. Create the after, after, after plan. **If there are roadblocks, this will allow you to change direction.**

Step 2: Take appropriate action

You must take action every single day. Do two, three, five, or ten things a day; just make sure you are doing something. This will create momentum. Small steps equal massive progress. If you beat at a piñata enough times, the sweets will eventually fall out. Use that concept with your visions.

Step 3: Acknowledge challenges/adversities correctly

Don't just accept how things seem in an instant; that's narrow-minded. You must have an open mind on the road of achievement. Every time a challenge or adversity appears in your life, it doesn't matter how small, see it as a **learning point** instead. If you commit to making this simple adjustment, you will be inundated with great options for growth.

Step 4: Never lose sight

Never ever take your eye off the prize. Always remain focused on what you believe in. If it makes your heart sing, then never stop. Holding your ultimate visions close to your heart and mind will continue to light up the path for you. It's our true inspiration.

> 'Boldness be my friend.'
> *William Shakespeare*

Getting down to business

> 'Take up one idea. Make that one idea your life — think of it, dream of it, live on that idea. Let the brain, muscles, nerves, every part your body, be full on that idea, and just leave every other idea alone. This is the way to success, that is the way great spiritual giants are produced.'
> *Swami Vivekananda*

Seeing we just covered that wishful thinking doesn't work without action, now it's time to see how action might not always work without some sort of plan. They say hard work always pays off. Well, I know people who have worked hard for thirty years and still don't have the things they wanted twenty years ago. I'm the first one to admit that achievement doesn't come easy, but when you enjoy the process it doesn't seem that hard either. This is because you have created so much emotional attachment to its accomplishment that you wouldn't live any other way. If you did, then it would be much harder living a life away from what you know you're worth.

We must learn to work smart and have strategy. In the beginning of my change, I made a promise to myself that I would only model the elite of whatever industry I wanted to learn about. What would be the point of finding patterns from those who weren't as successful as others? Why not just go straight to the top and find their patterns? When I wanted to learn how to play tennis, I researched Roger Federer's style. The way he held the racquet, his motion and his game mindset became the new foreground to my practice. When I wanted to learn about business, I looked at the Chinese and Japanese. I was always fascinated with the way they did business. It always seemed secretive and mysterious to me. It was as if they knew things that the west had not yet grasped. The way they went about their business had me wondering. Through my quest to find answers, I stumbled across a book called *The Art of War*, written by an ancient Chinese military general, strategist and philosopher, Sun Tzu. I discovered that the Chinese and Japanese use this book, and similar war books, as a basis for their business ventures. They view business like going into battle, and I guess in most cases it is. Courage, honour, strategy, preparation, when to attack or defend, or when to retreat are all important aspects for these people's success.

In order to make money from your passion, or even increase your wealth, you must think business. Does that mean your work isn't coming from your heart? If you are selfish and have no intention of sharing your success, then I guess it's not. If you are going to, then of course it's still from your heart. It depends on the belief system you choose to build around monetising your passion. When looking to build beliefs about money, think of the use of a knife. If a knife was given to a humble man on an island, he could use it to cut fruit, which would make his life a little easier. If you gave the knife to a serial killer, you could probably bet what he would use it for. The knife can be two different tools; it all depends on how you look at it.

Most of the people I have heard say 'money is evil' or slander those who have a lot are usually the same ones I hear complaining about not having enough. A contradiction if you ask me, but that's because the majority don't think they have the capability to increase their wealth. It's then much easier to attack people that do, in order to gain some quick satisfaction. How many of those people do you think would refuse a $10 million cheque? How many of them would refuse a double income bonus for the year? So is it money that is evil, or is what some people do with money that seems evil? Society will attempt to blame a piece of paper, or other outside resource to escape accountability for human action. There is a broader challenge, and that is the conscious level of some people.

While I was in Thailand learning about the power of the mind, I had the pleasure of staying with some monks over three days. Even they were reliant on money donations from the lay people. In order for them to survive and keep the temples running in Bangkok, they needed money. Love it or lump it, it's a major part of our society. You might not want millions of dollars and that's fine. I know people who have money that will last them a lifetime and are unhappy, and those who are just comfortable and are the happiest people alive. I also know people with no money that are the biggest haters alive, and those who have a lot and are doing great things for the world. How you deal with your financial situation is your choice. If you want to turn your passion into a lifelong career or create massive amounts of wealth, the reality is you must be prepared. Business is not for the faint hearted, so it means we must set ourselves up and build strength. If history has taught us anything, it's that everyone is capable of achieving. You could be buying a business, starting your own, or you alone may be your business. Whatever it is, here are some questions to get your mind racing…

- How can I make my idea feasible and profitable?
- Do I have a marketing plan? How can I market? What can I do to reach a mass amount of people without taking the edge from the image I want to portray?
- Do I have some sort of business plan?
- Do I want investors? If so, when do they break even? At what point do they see profit?
- Are my visions still too vague? Do I need to create more clarity on what I want?
- Are their operational skills in the business I must learn? Do I need six to twelve months' practice in that type of business first?
- Are there people in the industry I can talk to and gain ideas from?
- Do I want a loan? If so, how much capital versus loan do I want?

- Am I likely to make profits instantly? If not, do I need another job to survive and continue to invest?

- What are the **principles** and **culture** I want to promote in my business? (Examples: honour, integrity, loyalty, fun, trust, etc. All successful businesses have these two areas cemented. They pass through to customers, staff, advertising and marketing. It's also crucial that the owner practises what he preaches.)

- Do I need to lengthen my days to get more done? Is it beneficial to condition myself to six hours sleep rather than eight or ten?

Why do you want to achieve in business? Are you going to treat it like your own mission? Is it because you want to be your own boss or like being in charge of your life? Are you passionate about what you do? If you are only doing it for the money, not the feeling, you will never be happy. **The cause must always override the materials. If it doesn't, you're in trouble.** It's fine to want the big toys, but never let them be the basis of crucial decision-making. Instead, let your passion be the sole decider. People do things that destroy their life when driven by materials. So make sure you keep on top of it.

'A business that makes nothing but money is a poor kind of business.'
Henry Ford

Don't be scared off by those listed questions. Sometimes we ignore these things, but I guess that's why so many businesses crumble or people give up. I never went to university to learn how to answer them, and most successful business people I know didn't either. All you have to do is get the ball rolling. Even taking notice of some of these questions will help you fill in the gaps as you go along. For example, my marketing plan began on a notepad with a pencil. I just began by listing down a few ideas of how I could market the book. After about a month, it turned into about ten pages. I would even pull over when driving so I could write a new idea in my phone. Then I began structuring it into sections and time frames. If you are yet to browse the internet for things you think will improve your business, do so immediately. You can find practically anything on the internet, and it's a free source. I'm not saying you will base your success on it, but it's a great reference to use. I typed in, 'Ways to market a book,' and was instantly bombarded with thousands of ideas.

Only build on progress

'Correction does much, but encouragement does more'.
Johann Wolfgang Von Goethe

When we are working towards our visions, it is crucial that we acknowledge every step we take. It seems we go around reminding ourselves about when we make 'mistakes', but how often do we pat ourselves on the back for doing something great? Even if it's having the courage to tell someone how much you love them, sending one email towards your vision, or finding growth from self-criticism. They are all things to be really proud of.

Any great achiever has used this critical tool in reaching their peak. If you take a minute, you will actually realise that it's impossible to gain growth from something that you see as a negative. We have to shift our mindsets to reward ourselves with every step. The way we train police dogs is a great example. These dogs are the elite of the elite, and are very disciplined and trustworthy. The officers know that when it's time to deliver, these canines step up to the plate with accuracy and certainty. They are not beaten or screamed at to teach them. It doesn't matter how small the step they take towards their outcome is, they are conditioned by being rewarded every time they make progress. When this is repeated, it gives them incentive to do it again and again, until they are like machines. The only way to really enjoy our life and achieve our goals is to condition ourselves to the great feeling we attain when we are rewarded.

When you were a child and your parents screamed at you to do something, even though you might have done it, you didn't want to do it again. On the other hand, when you did something and they mentioned how proud they were and how well you did, you felt happy enough to repeat it. We even live in a society where punishment for doing the 'wrong' thing is seen as the solution. It seems that misbehaving gets far more recognition, so it becomes quite appealing to those in search of attention. But how often do we praise people for doing great things for the world? How often are they recognised? Is it any wonder why there are so many people that are lost and confused? The only way the world, and our own life, can change is if we build on the positive progress we are making.

Our true motivation lies in repeatedly being self-proud. If you ever wonder how some people seem to stay so motivated in life, this is why. They don't wait for other people to come and praise them for their efforts, they do it themselves. This creates others to do it, because they feel your passion. Even if it's something that you think you might have done poorly, always look for the growth in it.

I was coaching an aspiring singer who would really beat herself up over not hitting the correct notes. All she focused on was how poorly she had done, and forgot to recognise the great parts. Instead of looking at it and saying, 'How can I improve these areas and work on them?' she would view them as a failure. We are our own biggest critics, but once you recognise that your own criticism is the best life coach you will ever have, you will excel. You need to get physically excited with every step you take, regardless of how small it might seem at the time. This allows you to realise that accomplishment feels great on all levels. Get physical, vocal, jump up and down, dance around your house, look like a mad person, it doesn't matter; just build incentive. **Your feelings of today shape tomorrow.**

'Most of us, swimming against the tides of trouble the world knows nothing about, need only a bit of praise or encouragement — and we will make the goal.'
Robert Collier

11

TIMES OF CRISIS — LET'S BE HONEST

'Every crisis offers you extra desired power.'
William Moulton Marston

Nothing in the world stands still — it either depletes or grows. We are no exception to that law, so if you're not appreciating, you're sadly depreciating. At times, it even seems as though we are proud of being worse off than others, and will brag about it saying, 'Oh, I've got bigger problems to worry about'. Attempting to prove you are worse off than others is like competing for the most miserable life and I don't see that as something to boast or brag about. If you don't like your job, then leave, if you didn't have enough sleep, then go to bed earlier.

And, going back to the common social complaint about work, is it really the actual job one doesn't like, or is it the belief systems one has around 'work' itself? I used to be someone who would complain about the job I had, yet every different one seemed just as bad as the other. We will find every excuse not to like our new job, continually saying the same things. I have discovered that it's usually the attitude one takes towards the word 'work'. If we have no vision for ourself we will never be happy with feeling as if we are making someone else wealthy, while we are missing out in the process.

A great friend who is like a brother to me said, 'The system I was brought up to believe would grant me success was a lie'. He completed a university degree, and then worked for multiple companies over ten years. Even the thought that his approach to life would be the 'safe' one failed him. Two separate companies, who had no mercy at the time of the cull, made him redundant. The last company he worked for gave him a role where his target revenue was $17 million for the year. He made the target, but only made a salary of $80,000 himself. Besides that, he contacted the owner of the company to ask for a raise, only to have a return email saying his boss was 'too busy' to discuss it because he was on holidays on his yacht.

He made a conscious decision to take his knowledge and start his own marketing business. So even if you are an employee of a company, make sure you are doing it for your own cause. Build the belief that work is the stepping-stones and foundation for your own endeavours. I think having a solid known income is a great thing, but if you are looking to expand yourself, then use it for your own benefit. Look at it as working for yourself, rather than working for somebody else. It may even be something you have on the side, like investing in property or shares. At one stage I had two jobs, and partnership of my own business. I would finish work at 6p.m., go deliver pizza until 10p.m., then go and work on my business. You will always find the time if you are committed, and excuses won't get in the way.

You may call it work; I call it building a dream.

People become addicted to their victimisation and start believing that it's an escape for feeling better, but we all know that is not true, as not long after we are likely to break down and give up. People make things worse than they are so they don't have to do anything about them. In whatever area of life, it seems like a pretty good escape, but we are in fact cornering ourselves into self-torment. Then those same people don't want to be disappointed, feel rejection or failure, so they say things like 'I'm sceptical' or 'I'm pessimistic' when faced with an empowering alternative. I believe it's just being too weak to face the truth and admit they see a better way. It doesn't take courage to be a pessimist. What's 'wrong' is always accessible, but leaders and those who take control over their own lives decide to look at what's right in that same situation.

The answer in any time of crisis or victimisation is not 'positive thinking'. Too many take positive thinking as the bubbly, vibrant attitude it is portrayed to be. Yes, it is great to be like that, but we are not going to be like that all the time, period. We can never just be one way in life, because different situations call for different reactions. If your house is on fire, I'm sure you are not going to be skipping down the street singing nursery rhymes. At that time you are not going to be even conscious of thinking positive, but you can be **intelligent**. And by thinking intelligently, you would quickly get yourself together and say, 'Okay, what am I going to do here? How can I make this better? I better start by calling the fire fighters'. Intelligent thinking helps you to assess a situation properly and create a strategy. That's how positive thinking should be portrayed, especially with any crossroad you find yourself at. The challenge is that most people I come across attempt to think positively but very few ever get to the core of what they are actually feeling or experiencing. It's always about intelligent thinking. **When you decide to see things for what they really are, not**

worse than they are, you will always find another avenue for growth.

I once had an overweight client who told me that he had a slow metabolism and was big boned. He victimised it every way possible and made it sound worse than what it was, so he didn't have to face the short-term pain of hearing the bald truth. I looked at him dead in the eye and said, 'No, you are obese, and need get off your arse and run like you have never run before'. Call me the bully, or call me someone who cares. A few months later I received an email from that same guy in China where he was then working. It was a picture of him by a hotel pool, and I must say even I was shocked at the achievement. He thanked me dearly because all he needed to hear was someone blatantly spit the truth out, and that was enough to shoot him off into an empowering direction. For his whole life his family members and friends had covered the truth because they didn't want to feel 'bad' by telling him. That was obviously selfish and contributed to his health problem. I've trained many clients with the apparent 'slow metabolisms' or those who are 'big boned' and they get fit just like anyone else.

They say the truth hurts, but don't they also say the truth sets you free?
The things that usually hurt us the most are the same things that set us free.

I came from a family that didn't have a lot of money and I always had to think of my own way to make it. My parents didn't buy me my first car, pay for my holidays or invest in my business. I never actually asked them for it, because I knew if they had it, they would have given it to me. For a long time I told myself I was the victim of an unloved destiny, while seeing people around me

getting all those things handed to them. I had decided to look at it in the worst possible way rather than to look at it how it actually was. Here I was in a country where I was surrounded by so many resources and opportunities. My parents provided me with food, education, shelter and love, when so many others never have those experiences. I finally realised I had a compelling future, if only I decided to look at it that way, and then all of a sudden the situation seemed like a pretty good one. **Most times we complain about things that we have full control over**. We need to stop lying to ourselves and be completely honest, or else we will never make change. Others will say they are being realistic when looking at a situation in the worst possible way, but is that the truth, or are they just exaggerating? We will also blow it up until we say things like 'it's impossible', again thinking that's an easy escape until we are forced to wake up once again. Being real requires you to be honest with yourself.

Take ownership. Observe the situation as it really is, not worse than it is.

Now that we have stopped looking at our situation as worse than it is, and see it as it really is, brings us to the next step. If it's true that we can look at things as worse than they are and that can be just as real, who's to say we can't look at things as better than they are? It would have just as much impact in the way we react to it, but for the better. It would actually change everything about the situation, and, more importantly, change the outcome of our total approach. It's very important to now look at the situation as being **better** than it is. Even if something seems to be a massive challenge now, if we have something great to look forward to, we will find a way to get there. Set up a compelling vision, put things into perspective, and draw out what you can learn from this. Make the vision as real as possible, and you have automatically set up another path to go on.

Vision. See it better than it is.

Now that we have created something beneficial to work towards, it's time to make it the way we see it. This calls for an action plan, or a strategy that is aligned with your new outcome. Take action in order to bring that very vision into reality. Focus your decision making around it, remind yourself of the desired outcome, and become it. What would you have to believe? How would you have to stand? What would you have to remain focused on? Who could you talk to? What other action can you take to create it to be that way?

New strategy. Action the way you now see it.

12

THE ACTION TRILOGY

Through speaking to so many individuals about life, it's clear that they see their physical actions as having more effect than the mental and verbal actions they commit to. I'm here to smash that belief and tell you that every thought you have and word you speak has just as much power in shaping your destiny. Most do not acknowledge that everything is initially outsourced from their thoughts, which cause the words to come out of their mouths, and are the basis of all decision making. The balance is symmetrical, but our greatest downfall is not being aware of this major fact. We are continually shaping our destiny through these three types of action, and creating it to be our nature and beliefs. If you got offered the mind of Bill Gates, would you take it? How about the dancing ability of Michael Jackson? Or the golf swing of Tiger Woods? If the answer is yes, then why don't people set out to learn the traits and skills they desire? These professionals must have learned to become that great, right? Surely it wasn't easy.

The reason that most people refuse to believe they can be great is because they condition themselves to believe that they are stuck with the actions they have always chosen. Further to that, they create an illusion that their previous choices and experiences sum up who they are, and what they are becoming.

'It doesn't matter where you came from, it matters only where you're going.'
Condoleezza Rice

Take a look at those individuals who seem to have had everything given to them on a silver platter and end up in rehab, while others who have been through the most horrific experiences set out to make the biggest impact in the world. **We are not stuck with our experience, and it does not sum up who we are**. What's happened doesn't determine what's going to happen. A wise man once said, 'tomorrow doesn't equal yesterday'. In saying that, we are the sum of our thoughts, and what we choose to do right now. We have an addiction to those things that are away from common sense, and that's why common sense doesn't seem all that common. Surprisingly, those people who use common sense are actually branded as uncommon these days. They are usually seen as crazy until they prove they are a cut above the rest. Are they special? No, they just used common sense. There are patterns that we think we must continue to be slaves to, because we always have. That's a lie, as the choices we make right now ultimately shape who we are becoming.

It seems that most of us have a clear indication of what we should do, but the statistics are alarming on those who don't actually do it. This is why obtaining knowledge in life is not the same as learning. If you gain knowledge, but don't put it into practice, it leads to nothing being learnt. I've had so many people say to me, 'I know this stuff'; my response is that knowing doesn't seem to be making a difference, you **must do it**. They continue to act the same way, have the same experiences, the same emotions, and are never fulfilled.

A man twice my age once abused me and said, 'What have you learnt about life, you're half my age?' The reason this friend of a friend was so angry was because he just found out his girlfriend cheated on him for the third time. I explained to him that it only took one similar experience for me to make my decision. It seems he knows a lot about what he should do, but what has he learnt by going back to a relationship that causes him so much pain? He has learnt nothing. It doesn't matter whether you have had ten experiences or one, the only time you can learn is by taking action.

We must shift our thinking that change is painful to thinking that change is pleasurable. Basic methods of discipline might not seem to last long, but what does work is when you become addicted to something positively new. You must exchange one disempowering addiction for an empowering alternative. Really embracing this concept allows for a conscious shift, and enforces real growth. It's not until we action our knowledge that we achieve growth in our life. Only by this formula, can you experience the never-ending cycle of self-growth.

Personal growth formula:
L = K + A
Learning Knowledge Action

The battle

The battle has only ever been you against you!

Theoretically, being able to condition our state sounds simple, yet that's what scares some people off. They find it hard to believe that our greatness in life is found through its utmost simplicity. **Most great things in life do lie in its simplicity, although we have made things so complicated, that being simple again is the challenge in itself.** We race around trying to figure out all these complex ways to gain fulfilment and success, but we have always had the qualities within us. The challenge is definitely putting your knowledge into practice. As long there is life, there will be challenges. Our character is not based on not having challenges, but how well we handle ourself in the face of them.

I once had a conversation about life and change with a lady who definitely inspired me to add 'The Battle' section to this book. I would say it's an essential part to take note of. As we were discussing all this stuff, I was full of energy and she said, 'You make it sound so easy, just like other motivational speakers'. I had to remind her that I was not a motivational speaker. It's one thing to be pumped for an hour by hearing some inspiring words, but it's another thing being pumped for life, and that takes strategy. I educate, not just motivate, and there's a major difference. I educate people on how to motivate themselves, because I won't be with them night and day. I thought about what she said for a second, and it reminded me how hard it was at times and how strong I had to remain. It was a battle in its truest form, but by being equipped with the appropriate strategies and solutions, I wasn't setting myself up to be defeated anymore.

Change is a challenge. It's not a mere walk in the park. The great thing is that it's a simple equation. **If you want change, you have to make change, or else nothing is going to change**. We seem to be oblivious to it, or on the other hand, we do realise this point, but are scared to embrace it. We are scared that it might have the power to actually change our life forever. It's a positive way, of course, but we still seem to fear the unknown.

In order to win any battle, you must be equipped with the most powerful arsenal. The battle of the mind is no exception.

Life is about learning and growing, and it's not that easy at times. Who you were is more than ready to battle who you're trying to become. That self is not just going to give way without a fight. You have trained that self to fall into guilt or depression, along with the fear that you can't achieve, and so on. I'm sure you can help me out with the list. You have the power to rewire yourself. The way you physically, mentally, and verbally act must change if you want change; there is no other way through. I can only show you ways to get there, and make your walk as comfortable as I possibly can. You have to go on the journey and walk your own path. I just want you to know that it's not all a bed of roses, so you can be prepared. When a mental, verbal, or physical battle does come up, don't think you're alone and submit to being the victim.

Everyone that has been on this journey, achieved great things, or made massive change in their life has acknowledged that it's not as easy as giving up is. Anyone who says that it was must be supermen or women. If they make you believe that all of a sudden their whole life turned around completely, and everything they knew or thought changed instantly, they're taking you for a long ride. You may never get to your destination, and even crash pretty hard along the way. I've seen too many people left in the dark by misguided 'motivational speakers' or authors out on their own selfish agenda. We must use our intelligence on this journey. **Nothing in life that is great is easy. If it were easy then it wouldn't be great.** We wouldn't be able to tell the difference between living an ordinary life and an amazing life. Now knowing that it's not going to be a breeze, it's also important to acknowledge that it's not that hard either. I've come to realise that human beings do not like problems, but we thrive for a challenge, and that's what re-conditioning yourself to find your truth is.

> 'The gate to life is narrow and the way that leads to it is hard, and there are few people who find it.'
> *Matthew 7:14*

In order to overcome these challenges, especially the mental ones, we need to have an army always waiting at the entrance of our mind, not so much anticipating a challenge but always ready. Every time you take down thoughts or emotions that are preventing you from excelling in that moment, more recruits jump on board. Before you know it, the army within is far more powerful than anything else. **Experiencing something vastly different to what you are experiencing in that moment of inner conflict is the key to winning back control.**

> 'Your worst enemy cannot harm you as much as your own unguarded thoughts.'
> *The Buddha*

Think of this reconditioning process like that of a right handed boxer who is preparing to lead with his left. The trainer's instructions are that he has to learn to lead with his left hand to win the fight. The boxer will get confused during sparring and will swap to his right numerous times, but **now** he knows what he has to do to win the fight. He stays conscious of it and quickly corrects himself, until it becomes a part of his nature.

Whenever your limiting side seems to be winning a mental battle, here is a quick strategy to gain control again:

- **Stop resisting.** When you feel you are resisting your mind too much, just stop! Make peace with the situation and tell your limiting side, 'Okay, you're here and I know what you're trying to do, but you will never win'. Say it in a relaxed tone and nod your head as if you are certain about your comment. Just think of a time when someone has tried to upset you, but you have assured them that their efforts are pointless. It's the same when you try to upset yourself. Your limiting thoughts will eventually pass over by doing this.

- **Write.** You must write down how you feel. When you feel great, write it down. When you feel down, write down how you can turn it around. You can always go back to when you felt great and read that again. As you are probably aware, the times that we have resistance building up within ourselves are the same times that everything seems to irritate us. It could be an issue we have with a friend, a partner, or a job. It's not until we get it off our chest that we feel free again. The same goes with resisting our thoughts. Get them out and write them down.

Mental action — all in the mind

'Men get rich by doing things in a Certain Way; and in order to do so, men must become able to think in a Certain Way. A man's way of doing things is the direct result of the way he thinks about things.'
Wallace D Wattles

Once you become aware that every thought you have is shaping your destiny and recreating your reality, you have won half the battle. The best way to come to terms with this is to take a good look at the thoughts you are having. Notice the pattern with experiences you have had, and continue to have. Check whether your thoughts are making you act in a certain way and attracting experiences. Once this is done, you will almost always see a pattern that can be broken. We are usually just reacting to our environment, which causes us to believe we are on automatic. We feel as if we have no real control over our experiences or how to think when a challenge arises. The truth is, we have always been in control of which direction we take, and until we take full accountability for where we are in our life, we cannot make change. Obviously there are experiences and people we cannot control, but we can always decide what significance they have on our life, our perception, or how we react to them. **Most people believe our thoughts are at the mercy of our eyes. I disagree. Our eyes are at the mercy of our thoughts, and hence our feelings.** As long as we just let our mind wander all day we get set up for having many unexpected experiences. In this instance we are not in control of what we are creating. The only time your life is really affected is when you lose control of your mind.

When we monitor our thoughts, we are able to shift their direction to where we want to go. In order to live an outstanding life, we must capture the great thoughts and let the other ones pass. Everyone has the same thoughts flowing through them; certain people just choose to capture certain ones. It is your choice to hold onto a thought that is disempowering, and it will also be up to you whether you let it flow out of you the same way it came in. You don't need to hold onto them.

Relate every experience you have, to benefit the bigger picture you have set for your life.

Human beings have approximately 60,000 thoughts a day. How many of those are you using to create the life you want? As you would probably agree, it seems difficult to change those thoughts that you normally have subconsciously. We have repeated these thoughts so many times that we have them with no real thought process. The only way to truly rewire your subconscious mind, which is crucial for success, is to **look at the effect that every one of your thoughts is having on your life,** rather than just thinking them.

The reason why humans like analogies and stories so much is because we love looking at things from an outside perspective, then relating that to our own experiences. When you look at your thoughts from an outside perspective, you find a clearer way to relate to them. In order to have an extraordinary life, you must stay conscious of everything you do. Breaking the unconscious pattern of disempowering thoughts and getting off that wheel that brings you unhappiness requires you to look at the cause and effect of every thought you have. If you need a refresher as to how every thought physically changes your state as well, go back to where we discussed the power of neuroplasticity in our 1st Step. Also, use this question against your thoughts:

Is what I am choosing to think about now being productive towards what I want?

I've explained this throughout the book, but I'll give you another detailed example. Let's say someone cuts you off in the car and you react with anger, as most normally would without too much thought process. It is going to affect what you create next in your life, as the energy of that anger will flow on to whatever activity is to follow. More importantly, it builds the belief that when a challenge comes up, the option is to get angry and not be productive towards your growth. On the other hand, you could react, but instantly correct yourself, because you now see the detrimental effect your thoughts are having on your life. I'm not saying you won't react at all, but by being aware of your thoughts, you are ready to turn them around if a challenging situation arises. This allows you to take a different approach and build on something that is important for success. Monitor your thoughts throughout your day, and correct yourself or counter-think. Sometimes it's a battle because you have been used to looking at something in a particular way, but you must look for another avenue that will benefit you. It's not hard to see every day that your thoughts create your life.

> 'A man is but the product of his thoughts; what he thinks, he becomes.'
> *Mahatma Gandhi*

The commitment to do this is one that is taken on board by every successful person. If their thoughts are not monitored and continually corrected towards what they want, they know they will never get it. It comes naturally to some, so a lot of the time they might not even realise they are doing it until questioned deeply on the topic. For others, like me, it is something we learn to do. I just knew I was sick of feeling the way I was and never being happy, so I decided to take mental action. It wasn't until I discovered my emotion was due to my thought patterns that I was able to take control of my life. I did this to turn my whole life around and surprisingly it didn't take long at all. It's actually quite amazing how much you learn and grow by monitoring your thoughts for one week.

You should also challenge yourself to think big during your day. To reach our peak we must think about the bigger picture. If all you think about is achieving small, then that's all you will ever get. When you stay open to thinking big, the rest in between doesn't seem overwhelming because you are keeping your eye on that prize. I remember sitting down in my bedroom only a year and a half before my book was finished; I had written one page and I had no clients at the time but knew what I wanted. I asked myself, 'Daniel, how on earth are you going to write a whole book?' Every time I would begin to stress over the number of pages, or begin to think about not being able to put my ideas on paper, I would fight it. I mean, I had never written anything in my life besides a few literature projects at school that I had completely forgotten about. I would block out the negative thoughts with as much power as I had. I continued to reassure myself that it was going to happen. I would envision myself opening up the finished product, and only a few months later I created it. The ideas and words of the book just flowed. I would meet people who were in search of coaching and I began attracting all the things I had remained focused on.

Realistically, there is only one way to change your life: Change the way you think.

Thinking about the end result also has this funny way of cutting time. Even the smaller steps are achieved at a much faster pace. After a week or two of staying focused on the bigger picture, you will notice the massive growth spurt that was available to you your whole life. **When you think on a large scale, ideas will flow to and from that direction**. Even if you learn something that you think is small about the new direction you are heading, write down that progress. Turn the imaginary thought into concrete form by making it as real as you can. Any growth or idea, big or small, don't miss it or let it slip, and soon enough they will be flowing on a regular basis.

To strengthen and expand our mind we must invest in it. You must read books, listen to audiotapes or CDs, go to seminars, but most importantly guide your thoughts successfully. Individuals that have had an influence in my growth and to whom I pay homage to are Ralph Waldo Emerson, Napoleon Hill, Kahlil Gibran, Wallace D Wattles, Maya Angelou, Deepak Chopra, and Mahatma Gandhi. These people are just some of the giants who have played a hand in the positive turning of this world in the last century. Learning from extraordinary people is a great way to invest in your development. **Investing in yourself is like investing in the greatest shares — the more you invest the greater the dividends.** By feeding your mind the right information, you strengthen it towards that great life.

'I am no longer cursed by poverty because I took possession of my own mind, and that mind has yielded me every material thing I want, and much more than I need. But this power of mind is a universal one, available to the humblest person as it is to the greatest.'

Andrew Carnegie

Verbal action — what you say is what you are

'Great people talk about ideas. Average people talk about things. Small people talk about other people.'

Tobias S Gibson

Kids say the darndest things, don't they? When I was a child there was a particular retort we would fling to other kids after they sent off a judgmental slur: 'What you say is what you are.' I didn't realise how much truth that one saying held until recently. People have no idea of the giant impact their choice of vocabulary has on their lives. **The words we commit to shape and condition who we are, just as much as our thoughts and physical actions.** It does not matter in what context or subject, as long as you use words that have limitations, you are limiting your state and hence your success. A quick example is when we use the word 'can't' in every day conversation. Take a second to ponder on this and you will realise that nearly every time you say the word 'can't' it is untrue because you do have a choice. It's not so much that you 'can't' do something; it's that you don't want to. The more you say you can't do things, the more your mind conditions that notion, and it will appear every time a challenge comes up.

By replacing our current vocabulary with new empowering substitutions, we will influence the emotions we experience throughout our day. That emotional experience then determines how we act, and then the results we get. We are linguistically programming our subconscious mind with every word, which then turns into ritual and becomes our nature. We say things unaware of the massive effect they have on our lives. I cannot overstate the importance of this; it will be the 'be-all' or 'end-all' of your success. Here are some example words and sayings that we must stay away from in everyday speech and some **great ones to put in their place**:

- I could never do that – **I can do that**
- I'm not smart enough – **I am infinitely intelligent, have the resources, and will learn**
- I'll never be wealthy – **I must be wealthy**
- I'm always sick – **I feel great**
- I'm too fat – **I must get fit for the feeling**
- I'm unattractive – **I'm beautiful**
- If I start my own business I'll fail – **I'll do whatever it takes to succeed**
- I can't earn more than my parents – **I can earn more than my parents**
- I'm a loser – **I will win**
- I can't be bothered – **My existence is energy**
- I'm too tired – **I must demand an energetic state, now**
- That's really bad – **What's great about this?**
- That's impossible – **Anything is possible**
- I feel drained – **I'm a powerhouse**
- I can't – **I can**
- What a coincidence or What luck – **Cause and effect**
- Maybe one day – **I'll make the day**

- Hopefully – **I'm certain**
- That's too hard – **I love a challenge**
- I'll do it later – **I must do it now**
- I'm over it – **I'm just getting started**
- What if… – **It's not, so don't worry in advance**
- I should have – **I didn't, but I'm always in control of myself now, which means I can**
- I'll try – **Do or don't do**
- I hate my life – **Love is life**
- I wish I was happy – **I choose to be happy or not**
- He's lucky – **He's successful**
- I hate him/her – **I love myself enough not to hate**
- I wish something bad happens to them – **I wish the best for them, which means I will be blessed**
- I hope I get there – **I know I will get there**
- I won't find that person – **I have faith and I'll make sure**
- I need that/it too – **I want that/it too**
- I'm okay/not bad – **I'm great**
- I don't know – **I'll find out**
- There is nothing I can do about it – **Is there really nothing I can do about it?**

All these first sets of words are limiting. By habitually repeating them, they are causing you to never get past those views. The second words in bold are empowering and will benefit your life. It doesn't matter how hard it may seem at times, you must replace words that have no benefit to your life with empowering substitutes. When a sportsman is playing poorly for his team, does the coach leave him on the whole game? If he is a good coach, he will take him off and put someone on that will enhance the team's success. You must coach the words you commit to strategically.

Another myth I would like to clear up is the concept of being jinxed. We are taught to believe that if we say things that will benefit our life, we will jinx ourselves. I'm sure you have heard this outright lie throughout your life. The power of it really occurred to me when I heard my friend repeating how well he was going to do on a written test that was going to ultimately determine the grades he received for his last year at university. His father overheard and said, 'I wouldn't be talking like that, son, you don't want to jinx yourself'. That sounds absurd, doesn't it? But just think how many times you have heard that, and more importantly submitted to that belief. Some people see it as a way of being less disappointed *if* the worst happens. Exactly: **if**! Why on earth would you predict the worst possible outcome? Why would you worry in advance over something that isn't even real? Where is the intelligence in that? And realistically, does it lessen the disappointment? The reason that some people never achieve what they want is due to their lack of self-belief. What hope do you give yourself if you are too scared to have faith and believe in your own ability to begin with?

It doesn't matter if you are using restrictive words in a joking manner, or in a serious or destructive manner, they all have equal effect. Only use words that have power in helping you grow: I can, I will, I am, and I must. These words make you feel great about yourself. For a brief moment, think about how many conversations a day you are involved in? Now count how many contribute to creating what you want in life, compared to how many contribute to things you don't want? How many of the conversations make you feel empowered and inspired, compared to the number that make you feel the opposite? How many are you complaining in? **Stay away from negative notations and words.**

You might feel a bit funny walking around and only spitting out words that you think are positive, but the notion of 'positive' isn't the only factor here. It's all about using the common sense we are built with. **Is there any sense in using vocabulary that restricts us from excelling in life?** What you decide to say on a daily basis becomes your reality, so is just as real in conditioning you. If you say it's too hard, then it always will be. If you say it's impossible or you can't, then your reality will be perceived accordingly. Whatever you decide to say is in fact real, because it will force you to act that way. I ask people how they are and they say 'not bad' or 'okay' as an answer. If you want to be great, then say it, and you will start believing it. I would be focusing on why I said 'not bad' in the first place and immediately do something to turn it around. We must train ourselves to speak with powerful, inspiring and productive language.

By being aware of how powerful language is in shaping our destiny, you can now watch the pattern with those who use limiting words. Look at their whole demeanour. Notice how miserable their day is and usually how unproductive they are towards any real visions. Next time you hear people talking at work or at a café, listen and notice how much their conversation contributes to the very feeling and situation they are complaining about. Observe how much energy they are giving it. Most importantly, use it as an eye opener to observe and correct yourself. You will condition and reprogram your state in no time.

'Death and life are in the power of the tongue, and those who love its use will eat its fruit'.

Proverbs 18:21

Do you think the most successful people or those who add value to the world waste their day discussing irrelevant things? You bet they don't. If you want to add value, talk like it; if you want to achieve at your peak then speak like it; and if you want real success then surround your conversations with it. Hype it up so much to yourself and those around you that you know you have to deliver. They say 'talk is cheap', but what I think they mean is 'talk is cheap on its own'. Talking big is actually quite valuable when you know you are going to follow through. **If you don't speak it, you won't get it; if you don't talk like it, you will never be it.**

Physical action — small steps are massive progress

'A journey of a thousand miles begins with one small step.'
Lao Tzu

I truly believe that most people know exactly what they must do to get what they want, but their biggest downfall is never taking action. They will listen to other people's opinions on the 'secrets of success', but they never put them into action. What they don't realise is that the 'secret' is in doing! Only then will they truly understand how the concepts they have learnt actually work. The strategies in this book create extraordinary lives, but even they are useless if they are not practised. It's those who act that get the rewards instantly.

Even if you just get a little inkling that something will be slightly beneficial in the shaping of your life, you must act. Those inklings usually turn into great satisfaction. Even if you commit to doing five different activities that are only ten per cent a week better than what you normally do, that increase in performance will vastly improve your life.

> 'You don't have to be great to get started, but you have to get started to be great.'
> *Les Brown*

It's obviously one thing telling yourself to get up and take action towards your growth, but as we all know, it's another thing actually doing it. Do you ever have those times where you really want to do something, but your mind gets so bogged with ideas and things to do, that you just seem to stand still? It was happening to me while I was writing this book, and I just knew other people would have gone through it. All these ideas seem to flow, but it's a lot easier just to think about them rather than actually do them. We have all these great ideas for our business, sorting out our finances, schooling, and our relationships, but we never seem to act. Why is that? It's because most of the time we are collecting so much information that it almost feels unrealistic to see them all through. The amount that we have piled up scares us, so it's much easier to run, rather than to face them. We say things like, 'I'll do it later' or, 'It can wait until tomorrow'. Do you really get it done later, or tomorrow? By the time you have piled up all these things to do later or tomorrow, you're going to need a day to transform into a year. Then, on the other hand, you will find absolutely anything and everything to do except for the task that you must do. If there were rankings for that, I would have been a champion in the game. **Stop weighing up too many options. You are most likely weighing yourself down in the process. Just do it!**

> 'A life which does not go into action, is a failure.'

Arnold Toynbee

The great solution is that small steps equal massive progress. Nothing in the world starts itself, so it means we have to get the ball rolling. Think of it as a snowball going down a mountain and picking up mass and speed as it takes each new turn. We still have to begin by pushing it down the mountain, right? In David J Schwartz's self-help book *The Magic Of Thinking Big*, he states: 'Action must precede action. That's a law of nature. Nothing starts itself, not even the dozens of mechanical gadgets we use daily.' He then goes onto explain that even an automatic heater that regulates temperature in our house requires us to set the temperature. I don't care how small or insignificant it may seem to the bigger picture at the time, I promise you that every step counts. Without those small steps first, you will never gain the strength and momentum to get to those bigger steps.

We don't enter this world running. Life requires us to grow, just like anything else that exists in the world. All successful people know it's about getting into gear and kick starting without too much deliberation. The others who don't achieve are those who focus on why they can't do it, why it's too hard, and why they shouldn't, instead of actually just doing what they know they must do. Instead, successful people convince themselves of the complete opposite of those limiting questions. They give reasons as to **why they must do it, how it can be done, and reaffirm that it's the only way**. Most decisions we make are due to a strong level of self-convincing, and that requires a build-up. We must use our convincing tool to direct it towards what we know will ultimately benefit us. People can become overwhelmed because they see all the small steps as an alliance with pain. They will evaluate a million different things to do, instead of focusing on the massive value of the end result. Imagine a lazy person thinking about washing his own car. He will think of all the 'undesirable' activities he has do to get the job done before he even gets there. He thinks about getting off the couch, getting a bucket of water, grabbing the soap, sponge, and changing his clothes. Then he must wash the car, dry it, undress, have a shower, and so on. All this overwhelming thought helps him to talk himself out of it. He then wiggles his backside further into the deep grooves of his favourite couch and dozes off for his sixth nap for the day. His partner then walks in the door and tells him there is a car wash up the road that has a special discount of $10 just for today. He gets up and shoots out the door. Now $10 is still more than he would have paid for washing it himself, yet he puts more value on the end result and adapted more pain to the other scenario. He neglected that he would now **still have to** get up off the chair, change his clothes, get in the car, drive there, and so on. He left out all the small steps because it was easier to think of the pleasurable outcome. In order to get things done in life, we are required to remain focused on the pleasure of the end result. If we do, most of the steps in between switch from pain to pleasure.

When you don't set up something to look forward to, the little things frequently get to you.

All great achievers know that their accomplishments begin with taking the initial step. Once you get started by doing the small steps first, your interest in doing more skyrockets. The results and how much you grow in such a short amount of time are actually quite amazing. After persisting in doing a few small tasks, you will notice that you willingly take more time out to do more. Those ten minutes will turn into thirty, which will turn into an hour. It becomes exciting working towards something that you actually want, and soon enough it will consume your whole life. It doesn't feel like a boring process because you have that vision.

Throughout history, we have heard that if we believe in ourselves then we can achieve anything. There is no greater truth, but how do we do that? Once you spark yourself into action, it builds faith in your ability to create the life you desire. You acknowledge the mass of energy you have within you that can be accessed in an instant, which helps build your self-belief. A sense of pride soon follows every step forward, and that's when you become a very powerful being. I urge you to spark your life **right now** and take action towards something on your wants list. When I say do anything, I actually mean it. Send an email, make a phone call, go and get a brochure, speak to someone, inquire on the 'net, go and get the materials, book a dance lesson, write down an idea that you thought of — absolutely anything.

'A superior man is modest in his speech, but exceeds in his actions.'
Confucius

The main message I am trying to get across is that if you think something as small as making a phone call is insignificant towards the bigger picture, then you have automatically gone back into the majority. Seriously, how do you think these great achievers did it? Where do you think they started? You must take action every single day towards what you want, no matter how small it may seem at the time. Do **at least one thing each day, make sure you recognise the progress, and be proud of yourself for doing it.** Each day's progress means you are one step closer than you were the day before, and then a after a week, that's a great improvement. The small steps you take now determine exactly what your outcome will be. Sometimes you're only a little bit off, and directing those steps intelligently in everyday life will make the world of difference.

There was a day when I was faced with a mental battle. I was considering whether I should continue fighting for my dreams. To reassure myself, I kept repeating, 'It's all going to happen,' referring to the bigger pictures I had set for my life. But then I stopped! It was as if someone said to me in a loud voice, 'It's not all going to happen — it's already happening'. I'm in the process of creating my visions with every step I take. There is no real end or destination. The growth is consistent and never ending. Where do we stop? Our visions don't just come one day; we contribute to creating them every day with the actions we commit to. Success is the journey.

Everyone is too concerned with what they are going to do, instead of what they are doing.

Task

Go and take action right now, anything at all, just get it started and push that ball down the mountain. Do not read on until you have completed at least one thing, it doesn't matter how small, then come back and write it down below.

....

It's also great to set short-term goals, but keep your eye on the bigger prize. The small steps will light up for you as you keep your eyes fixed. You will be far more empowered to take them when the emotions around the bigger picture are produced.

Have you ever been driving on the highway when all of a sudden the speed limit reduces to almost half because of roadworks? It goes from 100kph (60mph) to 60kph (37mph). How slow does it feel? It almost feels like you are crawling, doesn't it? On a suburban road, however, that reduced speed is the normal speed, and hence feels quite normal. You then wait in anticipation for the end of the roadworks so you can zoom off again. So why does it feel so slow on the highway? Once you have been driving at 100kph, there is no way you want to go back to feeling like a snail! Once you speed up your life, you will never want to go back to the way you were. Every time your action starts to slow down towards things you want, your awareness will immediately remind you to speed it back up.

And don't be disheartened if you don't hit a target in the time you set — it's happened to the greatest. In saying that, it will come if you continue to persist. Funnily enough, it usually comes when you are ready for it. Whoever warrants these gifts to us is very intelligent, and most times I have been thankful for them coming after I would have initially liked them to. I noticed that if certain things had come my way when I really wanted them, I might not have been mentally or emotionally ready. Does that mean I didn't do everything I could to bring it about? No, of course not, I took action every day. You have to build and stick to the belief that, **'No matter how long it takes, or what it takes, I am going to get there.'**

'You don't have to see the whole staircase, just take the first step.'
Martin Luther King Jr

State of peak physiology — body language

Are you aware of the enormous impact your body language has on your life? In order to build confidence and get into a state of certainty, your body must align with your new thoughts and vocabulary. When you complain about something, you will be able to notice the shift in your face or your shoulders. You may even be someone who has a permanent frown on your face. Some people I have met would actually strain muscles in their face if the thought of smiling even came to mind. It's as if there is a single grey cloud hovering over their head, raining, while the sun is shining all around. Okay, a little exercise. Right now, I want you to push your shoulders back and sit upright. Come on, straighten that back. Now put on the biggest smile you can possibly do. Don't read on until you do… I'm guessing you did that. How did you feel when you just did that? Ridiculously stupid? Did you feel more in control? Increase in confidence? More enthusiastic? A state of happiness? Or are you laughing because you can't believe how quickly your mood and physiology can change from a sudden shift in the way you hold your body? **Your body language assists in creating your emotions.** By acknowledging this, how quickly are you able to change your state from lazy to energetic, sad to happy, or nervous to confident?

Changing state formula: body + focus = control

Our body must be used when getting into a state of certainty. Even when going to do a deal or in any form of negotiation, it is the one who is more certain that usually gets the best part of the deal. While the other person is trying to build a state of certainty when you walk in the door, you have already hit your peak far before your entry. Most people attempt to build certainty by succeeding more. They still subconsciously think that succeeding more guarantees more certainty in their life. But the fact they neglect is that it's certainty that actually brings success in the first place. All successful people live by this and unfortunately for others who don't, their dreams will go untouched. Our body language is also crucial in the way we communicate with others.

It is estimated that **it takes the average person three to seven seconds to unconsciously judge someone they meet for the first time.** That could be someone we are interested in, someone we are making a business deal with, or someone we meet casually. That initial response decides how comfortable we are with that person. We either get a perception of pain/danger from that person or a sense of comfort. Once we have that initial perception we adapt our feelings, language, posture and tone. The most crucial signal in this initial response is — you got it — the **smile!** The mouth area is the first impression we get, and a smile signifies a happy, friendly demeanour. There are two types of smile: the genuine smile and the fake smile. I know you know what I'm talking about when I say the fake one because you notice when others are doing it. Well, guess what, they see you too. A genuine smile consists of using the upper muscles of your face as well as your mouth area. A fake one usually consists of just using the mouth area and excluding the eyes and upper face. The fake one usually restricts the person from seeing your teeth as well. Do not fake a smile when meeting someone. Research shows that a large majority of people unconsciously recognise the sincerity of your smile by simply looking at the top half of your face. So that means using your whole face when smiling could be the great difference in the initial contact.

The physiology of a smile is also remarkable. When you smile, your body releases endorphins, which send a message to your brain. That message is to feel good, confident and satisfied. If you 'genuinely' smile right now and try to bring forth sad emotions at the same time, you will notice it's extremely difficult. As babies we learnt to smile when someone else smiles at us, so that is programmed with nearly everyone you come in contact with. This means when you smile at someone, they smile back, which then releases endorphins in their body. Voilà! The unconscious message they receive is 'this person makes me feel great'. That also means when we smile to ourselves, it makes us say 'hey, this person makes me feel great,' and you will notice the power you have in creating and controlling your own emotions, even in times that could also be distressing. This is what abundant people do to shift their outlook immediately, and create a clearer mind to find a more benefiting avenue to focus on.

I spoke to a guy one day who I hadn't seen in a while. I asked him how work was, and before I knew it, I was bombarded with complaints. It was like he was waiting for years for someone to ask that question. His tone dropped, he sounded drained, his shoulders slouched, he frowned and he was in a mega state of hating life. I knew he had planned a holiday with a few of my friends so I decided to shift the subject and ask him about that. It was as if the sky had just opened up and the sun shone right on him. His whole mood shifted within a second. He sat upright, his tone was stronger and more confident, he began to smile and his whole demeanour changed. It was as if I was talking to a completely different person. I decided to point out to him what I had just done, and he was pretty surprised. It's so simple yet it usually flies right under our radar. I told him to take that same body language to work or when someone asked him about it, and it would enforce a different mood. He called me two days later and said he had the best day at work in six months. He finally realised it was the attitude he was taking out to life every day that was affecting how his day was panning out. He was always in control of how he perceived his day, he just needed someone to make him aware of it.

I'm sure you have met someone who is successful in life, so I want you to think back for a second. I don't mean successful in just achieving, I mean in all areas of life. I bet they didn't talk in a voice that sounded depressing, have their shoulders forward, their head down or feet dragging. They were energetic, confident, shoulders back, head up, strong tone of voice and certain. Don't be a fool and think you should only hold yourself like that when you are successful; holding yourself like that initially is what creates success. That's what makes a leader in life, and the way you carry yourself everyday is crucial to success. **The petty thinkers mope around and only live because they were born. True winners acknowledge they were born to LIVE!**

The balance

As with anything in the world, life requires balance. Without balance things seem out of their nature and don't seem to function properly. Doing too much of one thing without doing other things to balance it out usually results in us burning out. If you have ever really got stuck into gym training, you would notice that it doesn't seem to last too long unless you have a balanced life. If all your focus is on your body, then other areas start to lack. You may have a great body for the next two years, but then the other areas of life seem to weigh it down, and you can find yourself back where you started. That is the same for every area of our life. It is also crucial to have balance when it comes to your actions.

I know we all cross paths with individuals who go around talking themselves up and say they are going to do these great things in their life, yet five years down the track we see no progression. We must attain a balance between how we think, the words we say, and the physical actions we take. If we say it but we think otherwise we will never be able to create the way we say it. If we physically act like it, but we do not speak like it, then we cannot create it. If we think like it, but we don't act or speak like it, then again we cannot create. We must think success, speak success, act success, and then your gift to create will absolutely astound you. Once this balance is accomplished, your growth amplifies immediately.

If it's just positive thinking that you believe will change your life, think again. If you don't act accordingly, you're never going to get what you want, are you? We get a concept in our mind first, but we create with the balance. The 'Mega-state challenge' further in the book is crucial to gaining this balance. It also helps in mastering our emotions, which are the basis of all decisions we make. **When we align our mental, verbal and physical actions towards what we want, we create the way we intend.**

13

FEAR — FRIEND OR FOE?

Too many people are thinking of security instead of opportunity.
They seem to be more afraid of life than death.
James F Byrnes

As a child, if you ever woke up facing the other side of the bed, you would know how scary it was for that moment. Nothing looks the same. A place that you sleep in every night begins to be out of the ordinary, everything seems out of place, and panic begins to set in. But the more you start to focus and take a closer look, the more your surroundings begin to make sense. Relief takes over your emotional state, and you realise you had nothing to panic about in the first place. In order to make peace with fear, we need to take a closer look.

Throughout our life we have been bombarded with the notion that fear is a foe that should be avoided at all costs. I'm here to tell you that fear is actually the best friend some never had. Fear has this tendency to send us unconscious messages that will benefit our life. Just like any best friend, it is telling you to step up and pick up your game. It might be an area of your life that you are lacking in, and all fear is there to do is remind you that you shouldn't forget about it and walk off. Think of it as your own success alarm clock that says, 'If you don't listen to me carefully in this instance you can't get the most out of life'. If we never get scared, it means we aren't taking any chances. Being scared also tells us that something important is up, right? We must search deeper into the feeling and listen carefully to what it's telling us. Once that is achieved, we will be able to see a new way in which to take action against it.

The more we attempt to eliminate fear, instead of using it to our benefit, the more it becomes like trying to put out fire with petrol. This creates more fire and more fear. As I was writing this book I was scared that my writing wasn't up to scratch. There was a period when I thought I was losing my touch and it began to worry me. Knowing that I had to quickly question this feeling, I began probing. I discovered that it was fear in not knowing whether this would relate to people from all different walks of life. I wanted it to be adaptable to everyone, regardless of financial, religious and social position. I knew that I had to align myself with fear and, just as any good friend does, it reminded me when it was time to raise my standards. I went to people from all walks of life and gave them the same section to read. It was the questioning chapter, and it seemed they were all fascinated. That was the power of getting to the heart of the feeling. **Fear is only looking at something with the worst possible outcome.** Is someone really scared of snakes, or are they scared of getting bitten by a snake? Do they fear the tall building, or do they fear falling off the tall building? Are they really afraid of venturing into business, or are they scared of failing? People are only scared of an outcome that is imaginary! The three initial questions I would ask are:

1. 'What am I really scared of here?' rather than, 'I'm scared'.

2. How can I view this differently, and what new beliefs would I have to implement in order for it to benefit my life? Would I have to believe that overcoming this fear is the only way to get the most out of life?

3. How can I use this to take action and help me grow?

Again, it is a process of deep questioning rather than just accepting. This is how we grow and exceed our expectations. Let's say you have made an important appointment to be somewhere at 3p.m. on Monday. The day comes, you hop out of the shower and realise its already 2:40p.m. Fear starts to kick in because you just missed the bus. All the positive thinking in the world isn't going to help you if the next bus comes at 2:55p.m., so you now use the kneejerk feeling of fear to support your action. You call the local taxi service and off you go. Your fear has taught you that next time you should plan better. This is a very basic example, but one that seems to be very common in our society. In essence, if we don't align ourselves with fear in everyday life, then we will never learn, and we all know that learning equals growth. **Don't resist fear: embrace it!**

'You gain strength, courage, and confidence by every experience in which you really stop to look fear in the face. You must do the thing which you think you cannot do.'
Eleanor Roosevelt

You must give strong reasons as to why you want to overcome the particular fear. What this will do is add massive purpose to its accomplishment. Replay these new reasons with intensity every time the thought of the fear comes to mind. If we have a fear of snakes, but common sense tells us that there are none around, does it mean we won't be scared from the thought? We definitely will because it's only ever in our mind. A particular client of mine would almost be in tears when her friends would say, 'Howssssss your day been, Jesssss?' Seems pretty funny, but hearing a similar noise that a snake would make caused her to shake in her boots. **By enforcing new reasons as to why you want to overcome the**

fear, you break the neurological pattern and get into a different state. Surprisingly it doesn't take long to condition the new one. It can happen so quickly that I've seen people's habits, phobias and fears literally disappear in one week. Sounds simple enough, but how many people do you think take the time out to do it? Not many, I can tell you. Or they will repeat 'this stuff doesn't work' because they don't believe how quickly they can turn their life around.

In the face of fear

Confidence is self-trust. The only way to build trust in your ability is to face and overcome your fears.

I've always said there are two sides to our life; the scared guy and the inspirational guy. The scared guy is the weak one, and in the face of a fear will tremble, think his life is about to end and will look for the closest exit. The inspirational guy is trying to help you and will say, 'You're not going anywhere, you're coming with me'. He will drag you if he has to and make you stare at the fear straight in the face. The question is, how do you empower and grow your inspirational side and weaken the other one? **We must counteract in the face of fear, in any way possible**.

We all know that when we are feeding a baby we don't shove two steaks down its throat to ensure nourishment. The aim is to build your strength, so act as soon as fear shows itself, but don't kill yourself in the process. Let's look at a treadmill for example: most would initially see that as being painful, too hard, embarrassing, or a waste of time. In order for us to shift our mindset we must first sort out our belief system. We would begin to see the treadmill as being very pleasurable. It would represent a healthy life, a fit looking body, confidence, strength, a must in order to be successful, and a must to achieve a lot of things on your wants list. The major tip is to feed this little by little, so you could start by walking. Now isn't that a different approach? Most would look at that equipment and automatically think 'running', which equals embarrassment and more pain, but start off by walking, and then all of a sudden it doesn't seem that hard. If you hit it really hard the first time, it could come as a big shock and cause even more pain. It will be more fun this way, and more desirable the next time that scared voice tells you to run away. You will eventually want to push yourself to the limits and be much stronger when faced with your limiting side.

'Courage is not the absence of fear, but rather the judgment that something else is more important than fear.'
Ambrose Redmoon

Fear is also a physical emotion, so it means we have to counteract with our body and get into a state of certainty. We know it's physical as much as mental and emotional because we feel fear throughout our whole body. So you must get really physical and loud with yourself when encountering it. This rule can be applied with any fear we face, as we must learn to drag out the strength that lies within us. It's never a question of whether your strength is there, but rather what you do to drag it out. As time goes on and you begin to feed your strength, you will also notice that you become fearful when you think of settling back for that life that once made you unhappy. It creates you to act even harder just with the thought of it, because there is nothing scarier than living an undesired life, once you have created a compelling vision of what you really want.

1. Ask yourself how you have overcome fears in the past. What did you do? Who did you talk to? Who else has been in a similar situation and got through it?

2. Shift beliefs around the certain experience or object — add massive value to its accomplishment, and make it pleasurable.

3. Stay focused on the desired outcome. This will **turn your fear into excitement**.

4. Counteract immediately in the face of fear. Use your body to get into a different state to overpower it.

Note down all the great things you can attain from overcoming this fear. Keep your eye fixed firmly on these benefits. Your fears will soon turn into challenges, and that will turn into excitement!

Fear of achievement

'At Microsoft, there are lots of brilliant ideas but the image is that they all come from the top — I'm afraid that's not quite right.'
Bill Gates

I have heard so many people talk about top athletes, people who are worth massive amounts of money or those who share a great relationship. They say things like, 'He was born to be a golfer,' or 'She has always been a smart businesswoman'. I know because I used to join in those conversations. We say it as if these people had no real choice in the matter. In some way we try to believe that it was planned out for them and no matter which way they went in life, that's how they would have ended up. I don't believe any view could be so ignorant after seeing the passion these people put into their success. If you are one of these people who have this thought, instead of just lying to yourself in believing they are vastly different, I urge you to look fear in the face and prove yourself otherwise.

Underachievers will always pick out the few stories where people got 'everything' on a silver platter, and use that excuse when they hear of anyone achieving. For example they will say things like, 'He has a rich dad,' 'They were lucky,' or 'She did that in an era when new ideas were available to create'. We all know that's only an attempt to shade the lack of action they are taking in their own lives. It's nothing short of garbage! There are more young, innovative self-made millionaires now than ever before. There is even a saying in the financial world that 'billionaire is the new millionaire'. It takes someone to be courageous and wise to recognise the hard work and determination taken by those who have achieved. By acknowledging that truth, it helps you respect the game a whole lot more. It even promotes the understanding that you're not the only one that has or will experience hardship on your road, and that's inspiring.

> 'That some achieve great success, is proof to all that others can achieve it as well.'
> *Abraham Lincoln*

Being guilty of undermining achievers myself in the past, I have now come to realise that my limiting thoughts were just me being afraid of achievement. I never believed I could be great, so it was much easier to escape in fear than to face the truth. What I came to acknowledge is that the major difference with these great achievers is that they conquered that restrictive view of success. Were they born programmed with that powerful mindset? Was their journey a perfect walk? Some of the greatest achievers have been through experiences we would never trade with. We live in the same world, with the same capabilities.

Look at Tiger Woods. Regardless of his off field antics, the guy is the best at what he does. Playing golf, of course! At the age of five, he went on the American show *That's Incredible* and declared that by the age of twenty he would beat the best golfers in history. Now do you ever believe he lost sight of that vision? No matter what challenges came up, that vision stayed cemented. He continued to create his reality around that concept. This is a man who worked extremely hard for his achievements. Tiger even asked his dad to give him military style coaching. His dad would be in his face or use loud and annoying noises every time he went to swing. He would do anything to distract Tiger in a moment of concentration. Towards the end of the intense program, Tiger did not budge when faced with these challenges, and his dad then told him that his training was complete. His father also mentioned that he now has the strongest golf mind on the planet. He wasn't wrong! Tiger knew the importance of mental training so much, that a mind coach was even hired. Dr Jay Bronzer would make him sit down and visualise hitting perfect shots over and over — the same technique of visualisation we are learning in this book. Tiger Woods built an **absolute belief system** around his success. And who's to say there aren't fifty or a thousand other potential better golf players than Tiger Woods? There may just be, but will they fight for their vision, or will they let their fear get in the way of achieving?

Life is not to be feared nor resisted. It is to be embraced, to be the best you can possibly be, and live the life you dare to dream.

We see the aftermath of what we think is the success of great achievers, like the money they spend and the way they live, yet we rarely take the time to find out how they did it. We ignore that these achievers are just normal men and women, yet they decided to pursue their true potential. We neglect everything that was before; their persistence, their compelling visions, their passion, or the strength they had to build. All these things needed to be conditioned. Albert Einstein once said, 'I'm not particularly intelligent or particularly talented. I'm just very, very curious'.

Oprah Winfrey is a woman who was sexually abused and who lived in poverty as a child, but her passion for life became so overwhelming that she had to live it the best way she knew how. The guys from Google are another example of defying the odds and starting off in their garage, competing against the large company 'Yahoo' at the time. It almost seems impossible to think that someone could actually achieve that much in one lifetime, let alone a few years. But they all came to a point in their life where they decided they would never just settle, but go on a quest for their dreams no matter what challenges came their way.

When you surrender to this commitment, the world smiles with you and you get those breaks you never believed possible. You don't have to want to make billions or even millions of dollars; it is entirely up to you. It's whatever makes you happy; just understand that taking a chapter out of the book of some of the greatest is the best start to obtaining what you want. I have researched and met some of the greatest succeeders I know, and there are patterns. This book is based on those very patterns. They all stopped thinking, speaking, acting and believing that they had no purpose in this world, and began learning how to add value. They learnt to use fear to grow, researched what successful people did before them, and lived by the exact strategies and values you are reading, rather than escape in their fear.

Appreciating other people's success is also vastly important when enhancing our own. Being jealous or in disbelief will distance you from ever understanding the qualities you have within you. We must look at them and find out what they did differently to everyone else. As soon as you start doubting them, or believe that it was luck or coincidence, you fall back into the mass of underachievers. When you start to question and get intrigued in others' success, that's when you enter the minority of the greatest achievers in the world.

'Every person who wins in any undertaking must be willing to cut all sources of retreat. Only by doing so can one be sure of maintaining that state of mind known as a burning desire to win — essential to success.'
Napoleon Hill

14

SHAPING YOUR DESTINY: MEGA-STATE SEVEN-DAY CHALLENGE

Mega state = mental + verbal + physical

Having the ability to quickly and intelligently change the way you feel in times of emotional challenges is critical on the road to achievement. It's time for us to raise the bar and take enormous action. The following tasks are things we are going to apply to our daily lives, so saying we don't have the time is unacceptable. Remember, you signed that contract at the start of the book and said you were ready for change. If you do not act then close the book and pack it up. You cannot be helped unless you are willing to help yourself. If you want to excel, then make it happen.

Look at yourself in the mirror, and **repeat this ten times before you start each day for the next seven days**. Make sure you get very vocal, emotional, physical and forceful until it gets you into a complete mega-state of certainty:

'I am in control of shaping my whole life through my state of mind, the emotions I choose, and the actions I take every day. No matter what challenges I am faced with in these next seven days, my spirit will display and direct my strength to my success. It will empower me to do it forever. I can do anything I want in my life.'

By doing this every morning for the next seven days, you will prove your commitment to yourself. It makes what you are doing concrete and helps condition your state immediately. All people with an extraordinary life are able to change their state in an instant. That is the advantage they have over the masses. What is worth more than your life? What are you willing to do to enhance it? Are you really committed to changing your course of direction forever? Is your truth telling that you are doing enough as it is, or lacking drive? It doesn't how much you are doing towards empowering your life, it's still not enough. **The moment you think you have done enough is the moment you stop growing**.

Task 1

Commanding focus

'Since belief is all important, it behooves you to guard your thoughts; and as your beliefs will be shaped to a very great extent by the things you observe and think about, it is important that you should command your attention.'
Wallace D Wattles

Requirement: Monitor your thoughts and redirect them intelligently

Duration: First three days

Description: You have already been implementing great changes with the previous tasks, but now we are stepping it up. When you start thinking of something that makes you feel down, worried, or stressed, you know that it's only through your choice of focus and must be corrected immediately. You must look at the *effect* that every thought is having on your success. Once you look at the effect of your thoughts, rather than just thinking them, you jump off the 'automatic wheel' and are able to enhance your life. Being aware of the power of your thoughts is absolutely crucial in attaining happiness and gaining what you set out for. Only by doing this are you able to begin forming the mindset of the most successful people in history.

Don't deliberate about the disempowering thoughts too much, just block them out with as much power as you possibly can and replace them with something that you love, something that makes you happy, or something that would put you in a state of excitement or fulfilment. **A projection of a desired vision you have put in place for yourself or something that you really appreciate is a great way to shift your focus and emotion immediately**. Even if you feel that you shouldn't, it doesn't matter, you must! If there is a secret to true fulfilment and achievement, it's being able to take control of your mind.

I don't care what you have to do to get that thought out of your head, you must do it. Scream at yourself, or forcefully let it know it is not going to take control over your life anymore and repeat the new thought over and over. One day my aunty thought I was crazy because she heard me screaming from outside my house. She said it sounded like a lion that hadn't eaten in a week. Quite a funny comparison, I thought, because that's how hungry I felt for my success. Good aggression is different to anger, so don't be mistaken. It's fine to get forceful with yourself, and is a must in some challenging situations. No matter what it is or how challenging it may seem, you have to fight. Keep repeating that it's going to be okay, it's all in your mind, and that you have full control of you at all times. There is always another way at looking at something. **You choose the way you feel through your choice**

of thoughts. Tell your mind that you are now in control and you are not going to let it wander.

The way you determine if a thought is having a detrimental effect on your life is by the feeling you get from it. You must have that army always ready at the entrance of your mind. For example, if you are thinking 'I can't make it', you will quickly repeat 'I can make it, I can make it' over and over with more force. This is training your mind, and what goes on in your mind determines the outcomes you get in life. You must maintain focus on your new direction. Even after a week you will notice that disempowering thoughts diminish just by being aware of them. **Proper attention doesn't just miraculously appear, it needs to be directed and deliberately commanded with intensity**.

Task 2

Shift vocabulary and body

'A helping word to one in trouble is often like a switch on a railroad track… an inch between wreck and smooth, rolling prosperity.'
Henry Ward Beecher

Requirement: Take control over the words you say and your body language

Duration: Next three days

Description: We previously covered the importance that your language has on your life. Now it's time to monitor and correct back to the empowering options. Go back to the list of options in the 'Verbal action' section and use that as a guide. For these three days, there are to be strictly no negative connotations or limiting words whatsoever. Speak with confidence and enthusiasm. Every time you say can't, impossible, I'm drained, or too hard, you are to change immediately. Even by staying conscious of this, you will break your old pattern and the emotions you experience throughout your day. Your day will be surprisingly better just by doing this one exercise. When people complain to you, do not join in. The results you see from this are actually going to make you laugh after the week is over. You will be wondering why you ever chose to shape your life with your previous discussions. Even avoid the news on TV, newspapers, or anything else that can implant anything negative in your mind during this exercise. This way you will not be able to talk to others about these emotional draining topics, **unless you use it to benefit yourself or others**. It will force you to come up with intelligent things to discuss; an important aspect to living a happy life.

This also goes for the way in which you are going to hold your body in the next three days. When you are humble yet confident, you become a powerhouse. Don't be egotistical, or walk around like you have stick up your backside because it may just have the opposite effect of what you want to achieve. It's not brain surgery to figure how to stand confidently. Unless you are aware of your actions, you will never achieve or be fulfilled. Take as much physical action as you can towards one of your wants on your list. Emails, phone calls, browsing the 'net for information, and speaking to people are all taking action. It will build up.

Task 3

Have fun with faith

Don't wait for experience, create your experience!

Requirement: Take the leap of faith and do something that you have never done

Duration: Last day

Description: Are you ready to explore? This is the task where you are to turn your fear into excitement and explore your ability to enrich your life experience. This exercise is so important to every part of your life that it must be completed. Do something that you have always wanted to do, or think of something new. Bungee jump, sky dive, ice skate, go kart, drive in a professional super-car for the day, go to the gym, rock climb, go horse riding, paint ball skirmish, or whatever you can think of. If you're sixty-five years old and think you're too old to go paint ball shooting then think again. I was up against one such player the last time I went. Let's just say I got my butt kicked. That senior could shoot. Not to mention the team of girls digging into to me as well. My point is that there are no excuses, only fear. Put that fear on the shelf for one day and just do something that electrifies your spirit. **No matter what it is, if it's pushing the boundaries for you, then do it**. We get so caught up in routine that we forget to live. We experience the same emotions, day in and day out. In order to create happiness in your life, you must stay excited and have something to look forward to. Set this challenge up, but most importantly, enjoy it!

15

QUALITY DRIVEN SUCCESS

'Educating the mind without educating the heart is no education at all.'
Aristotle

Too many people have become misled by the concept of achievement and the word 'success'. We have proven many times throughout history that the common view of 'success' that so many people take on board is a myth. It was February 2010 when a close friend rang me up to tell me that famous clothes designer, Alexander McQueen was found hanged in his apartment. But he had all this money, and all this fame, so why would he commit suicide? He is just one of many great achievers who have taken their life. Edwin Armstrong, US inventor of FM radio in 1954, Pierre Beregovoy, French Prime Minister in 1993 and Brian Epstein, the British manager of the Beatles in 1987 all ended their own lives. The list goes on, not to mention how many top actors, athletes and artists suffer from drug abuse and emotional torment. However, on the other hand, there are many who have it all in life: fulfilment and great achievements. What's the difference between the two? Some searched for a feeling of success only in their achievements; the others acknowledge that success is in who they are and how they live their life, not in what they have!

The truth is, we can continue to achieve in our life and still be unfulfilled.

You might want to be successful in raising a child, in fitness, your finances, in your relationships with others, one particular area of your life, or all of them. I just want you to understand that success does not exist in anything outside of you, and should never be looked at as a thing you must chase. Success does not lie in a Ferrari, a mansion, or any of the achievements mentioned above. Just like any purchase or singular desire you have ever wanted in your life, the feeling doesn't last. All people who base their success on external desires eventually ask themselves, 'Is that it… what now?' I know that's happened to you in the past with regards to something, so you should understand that it will never change. It may have been the new watch, the handbag, the holiday, or the new car. Regardless of what it was, there came a time where you were once again at a standstill. **You need depth and meaning in your life**. True success is to discover the enormous power you have within, discovering who you are, and the attitude you take out to life everyday. Once this has been grasped, everything else will flow. So success must come well before ever obtaining those external wants. Once you attain real success first, and begin to live a great life, all the rest just becomes the cherries on top of a beautifully made cake. If the cherries are taken away for whatever reason, it won't really make much difference, because the cake is already complete. It's extremely important to realise that it's success that actually gets what you want, not the other way around.

When one isn't at peace, nothing makes sense.

Many people have based the word 'success' on money, for many years. In recent times it has taken a whole new approach as more people are striving to be genuinely successful, which focuses on abundance. Surrounded by so much external pressure and demand by fast moving societies, we are now striving for quality success. This is a balance between an inner peace and the constant self-growth that leads to achievement in all areas of life. Obviously, the degree of achievement is based on an individual's particular wants.

Time doesn't stand still, so we always aspire to grow to that next level in our lives. Driving our success with important qualities will prevent going around in a circle, just waiting to achieve that fulfilment. Being stuck in that cycle always results in ending up back at those points that feel empty and isolated. I think it's also very important to note that even people with a lot of money will end up back at that point if they do not find true success. Don't be mistaken — just because someone is a great achiever doesn't mean they are successful. **In essence, success equals fulfilment**. We all seek different dreams but everyone strives for a balance. This is why I have worked to discover and find the qualities that must drive success — QDS.

QDS is the process of eliminating negativity from within and hence from your surroundings right now, so you are able to attract and create more intelligently. If we allow the term 'success' to drive the quality of our life, then we may become misled along the way and continue to go against what will really fulfil us. **Never let it be the notion of 'success' that enhances the quality of your life, rather let it be the qualities of life that enhance success.** It's like trying to build a state of the art house on a poor foundation. It will never be stable but, more importantly, it will never be that state of the art house. Building on those qualities are that great foundation. When challenges arise on your journey, your strong foundation will prove that you can resist the pressure.

I used these qualities to attract the most marvellous experiences, discover hidden knowledge, strengthen persistence and achieve at a greater level. This stuff is powerful. What's great about these qualities is that all of us have them now, accessible and ready to use. Don't be someone who blindly walks around life believing they have to get patience, love, strength, or the truth. **The sudden reality is that you have all the qualities you have been searching for; they have always been within you.** Whether you choose to use them or not is up to you.

1. Love — the ultimate quality

'A coward is incapable of exhibiting love; it is the prerogative of the brave.'
Mahatma Gandhi

They say love comes in many forms. They also say that love can drive us crazy. Is it really love that does those things, or are we tarnishing the reputation of the divine emotion? Are we undermining love and giving it unnecessary associations? I believe love comes in one form, only in the purest state. I had someone refer to love as 'coming in many different forms' when they explained how they heard a story of a man who became so obsessed with his ex-girlfriend, he stalked her for three years. Love doesn't drive these actions — jealousy, greed, hatred or vengefulness should never be mistaken for the almighty love, for true love opposes such things. Love doesn't drive us crazy; our inner demons battling it do.

Love is the pinnacle of qualities that can set us free from that feeling of emptiness. I am speaking of a love that is so pure that it is not restricted by what we see with our eyes, but is the feeling we attain from within; like the love some have for their mother, pet, child, husband, or life itself. The love is far beyond our eyes. Your dog maybe the ugliest mutt to some, but the love you have for it is not restricted by its outward appearance. True love asks nothing but to fulfil itself. **You alone are the only one who can fulfil yourself with that love that lies eagerly within you**. It will appear, but we ignore it on so many occasions. Love is the true guider in life and only that shall be served. If we do things out of pure intent, love will surely answer. Through love your dreams become real, and everyday life will show itself in the most beautiful way it knows how. It takes the cloth from your eyes and allows you to see the world in its truest essence. You align yourself with the world and everything in it, which is the basis of your dreams coming true.

One man who had much controversy surrounding him, but who I believe demonstrated much love that went unnoticed, was Michael Jackson. A particular statement of his that I thought was truth in essence was, 'Let us dream of tomorrow where we can truly love from the soul, and know love as the ultimate truth at the heart of all creation'. Regardless of perception or judgment of this man, that saying is undeniably true. The great know that greatness is Love.

Once you experience true love in your heart, you dedicate your life to showing the earth what you have discovered.

All the important aspects for achieving fulfilment stem from love. My plan is to cover some of the main ones that I see have a direct impact on obtaining that goal. Love is like the seed of a plant. The seed is already planted within us. The seed is then fed by water and sunlight, which in real terms are your experiences and time to act. The two must correlate; the seed must be ready to be fed, in order to be fed, correct? The root then shoots out to the world and is exposed. It then begins to blossom, which is all the effects of love — inner peace, patience, respect, and appreciation, to name a few. Its roots grow far and wide until they eventually intertwine with other plants. We all have that seed and it's just waiting to be fed. Love, by its very nature, creates, and we are no exception. All men in history who have accomplished great things have used love as their driving force. It's the true essence of your being that will make you go well past your previous limitations and achieve things you once thought impossible. When love takes over your life, buckle in and get ready for a ride beyond your wildest dreams. This love is so great that it reflects in everyone and everything. It is one where your intention is to be the best person you know how, and treat everyone and everything with that same respect and love. That's the secret to fulfilment.

> 'Life without love is like a tree without blossoms or fruit.'
> *Kahlil Gibran*

Greatness also stems from love. In fact, everyone is great right now, but most are unaware. Loving yourself is an essential part of success. If you don't, you can never trust yourself to gain it. Would you really trust someone with your life that you didn't love? Well, if you don't love yourself deep down and embrace it on a daily basis, how can you trust yourself to get what you want? **There is a difference between loving who you really are, compared to loving who you pretend to be.** Loving yourself is not about putting yourself above anyone else; rather, a true self-love equalises you with the world. You are able to understand yourself more, and it allows you to better understand others. We have been conditioned to believe that loving ourselves is egotistical, but not loving ourselves actually displays EGO, because we **E**dge **G**od **O**ut of our life. If you truly love yourself, you won't allow yourself to go against your claimed morals.

You would acknowledge that others' growth is your growth and vice versa. In saying this, you can't really help anyone until you help yourself first. While helping yourself, you will be helping them. Contributing of your true self is far greater than materialistic help. We must not judge people on appearance, religious status or environment; we are all human and have an equally important role to play. If you do commit to those limiting actions, you are only tarnishing a relationship with yourself and it will never be a means to gain a true success. When you treat others with respect, it grows the respect you have for yourself. It's like when we meet someone who backs the same sports team or has the same cultural background; there is an instant bond and respect. We gain a sense of belonging from that person and will immediately get into conversation, maybe have a laugh or two. There's the feeling of camaraderie that seems to arise. Imagine considering mankind as being on the same team. Picture the sense of belonging now, and the rapport you will be able to build with others. Picture the difference in attitude and your approach towards those you come into contact with.

Everything you do to others, you are equally doing to yourself. That is the law of life; no one escapes.

My way of dealing with others is quite simple. I always take notice of knowing that they have the potential to love, were created by love, and I am convinced that they are a great person deep down. I choose not to see what others see, and it greatly affects my experience with them. By doing this they will feel your genuine approach and lack of ego. This method unconsciously forces them to react in a similar way. That's truly acting out of love and that's when it reflects in everything and everyone around you.

We are in this together; it's called networking. But remember, no one wants to help those who aren't willing to help themselves, so do things out of love and great intention and there will always be people willing to lend a hand. WE is greater than ME, but the change must start with you. Look in the mirror and tell yourself how much you love that person you see, regardless of what you have been through. It might seem stupid at the start but that's only because social myth and other unfulfilled people have influenced the belief you have built. Look at what this person in the mirror has been through, yet they are still there to face the music. That's something to love and respect, because it shows strength and the determination to never give up. If you want to give love and be loved, you must love yourself first. **When you feel love on the inside, you will see love on the outside. You are love!**

Pure love is freedom

'Eventually you will come to understand that love heals everything, and love is all there is.'
Gary Zukav

Freedom begins with the power that comes from understanding that you control your life. It is the absolute knowledge that you choose the way you feel, and hence the way you live is structured by freedom of choice. We have been socially programmed to believe that our freedom is based on outside events. In other words, we must wait for things to make us happy on the outside, to complete our inner self.

In order to experience true freedom in your life, you must realise that your perception of the outside world is nothing more than a mirror reflection of the internal self that you create. **How you feel is what you see!** The inside must change first, in order for the outer to be seen in happiness. At a deeper level, when we change our perception of the outside, it really does change what happens on the outside. We choose to create our physical, mental and verbal actions every day. Without realising we make them stronger by repetition. Mostly we are oblivious to the fact that we are creating our lives under such slavery.

Our freedom is not dependant on a job, a holiday, or in any other person. We may change a job or decide to go on a holiday, but essentially it is the freedom that was discovered first that allows us to do those things. Attaining freedom by choice is the only way to discover fulfilment. If you are looking at the substantial world to free you, then you will never find it. Eternal freedom stems from pure love of oneself. A love so strong that it trusts you to feed your intuition, all the while projecting that same love out to the world. The cold and wet nights seem to be appreciated just as much as the warm ones, challenges are seen as life's growth, the faith in yourself blossoms and you finally witness the beauty that surrounds you. You choose to be free, or not, everyday.

And what is it about love that makes it so fascinating? Could it be its ability to transcend the earthly concept of time into nothingness, its power to defy all the odds, its infiniteness, its courage to conquer all things, its dwelling in all creation, or just its very existence?

2. The quality of knowing your truth

Since love and not understanding is the starting point for the journey of self-truth, all who wish to walk it can take the first step.

As I was cleaning the mirrors at a boxing gym I once worked at, something dawned on me. Looking at them from a distance I wasn't able to tell whether they were dirty or not. The closer I looked, the more unclean they became. The only way I was able to clean the mirror was by having a closer look. With my reflection staring back at me, I wondered how I could use this principle in my life. We don't truly notice our truth or the uncleanliness we surround ourselves with unless we decide to take a closer look. From a distance we can be fooled into thinking that we are following our heart and need no improvement, but dare to take a closer look, and the real answers begin to appear. **In order to be truly happy and obtain what we desire, we must be honest with ourselves**.

Why do we undermine our ability? So often we act ignorantly towards what we know will ultimately benefit our life. I truly believe that we all have a sound understanding of our truthful side when it's time to make a decision, but think it may be the easier option to lie to ourselves. Initially this might seem like the case, but the truth has an uncanny way of catching up to us, doesn't it? Someone asked me a challenging question on this topic. He said, 'If the ultimate truth is love, that inner voice, and we are all able to distinguish between it, what about a terrorist's truth? Their truth is to kill people'. This was how the conversation went on:

Me: Does a terrorist love something; it could be his mother, sister, pet or anything?

Chris: Well, I guess he would, yeah.

Me: Okay, so he knows that love feels good, right?

Chris: Yes.

Me: So what would happen if someone came up and killed that something that he loved, how would that make him feel?

Chris: Being human, I'd say it would feel like hell.

Me: Okay, so the terrorist is able to distinguish that love feels good, and having something killed feels rotten?

Chris: I see where you're going with this.

Me: Yes or no?

Chris: Yes.

Well, that's the truth right there, isn't it? When the terrorist goes and kills someone who he knows is loved by somebody else, it's for greed, ill power, and selfish satisfaction. It's not the truth; he is feeding his lies and he knows it. He will never find fulfilment during such an act because he is separating himself from his true essence. Humans have a fundamental tendency towards truth. Call it common sense, conscious ability, reasoning, it doesn't matter, we are all able to distinguish between a loving act and a hateful one. We are built with love, that ultimate truth, so it will question every decision we make. Lying to yourself doesn't hide the truth, so you can bet your life that it will always come and display itself.

We don't have a very high tolerance for psychological dissonance of any kind. Self-deception can have terrible consequences for a person's experience of their conscience, even in a person who carries a not-so-advanced conscience.

'A man may imagine things that are false, but he can only understand things that are true, for if the things be false, the apprehension of them is not understanding.'

Isaac Newton

The greatest indication of knowing our truth is by listening to that deep voice within that tells us what is correct by us, and at the expense of nobody else. It's also that same voice that tells you one way will make you ultimately happy, while the other path will only bring you short-term satisfaction. Some call it the heart, and science is proving now more than ever the connection between emotion and physiological changes in our body. Dr Deepak Chopra is a great source of how these two correlate and the vast impact they have on our lives. I never realised how crucial the saying 'follow your heart' is in shaping our destiny. The challenge is we rarely listen to it. Realistically, **we can ask as many questions as we want, to as many people as we need, until we get the answer we desire. Surprisingly enough, we always know the truth is different; we just occasionally think that feeding a lie will fulfil us. But it doesn't**.

'A lie stands on one leg, truth on two.'
Benjamin Franklin

We also judge ourselves on those decisions we choose to make. We are our own judge and decider on where we go in life — another God-given gift we all have. We are able to distinguish between a lie and the truth, but instead of taking action, we submit again to what we know is creating suffering. This continues to create a life we don't want to live. Don't we judge ourselves? We lie to ourselves and are forced to visit that inner courtroom a thousand times over, with the same faults.

Most will play both parts and not always fight for their truth, even though they are able to acknowledge it. They aren't just in their judging. They do things that they know are against their moral laws or who they really are. The more they lose in their courtroom, the harder it is to believe they can win the next trial. They live a life of losing their truth to lies, and are never happy. We must be fair and just judges.

If you have a particular belief or have heard of one from someone else that causes you to act in a certain way towards yourself, life, the environment, or others, I urge you to ask this one question: **Does this belief or decision help me ultimately demonstrate more love to myself, and everyone and everything around me?** If the answer is no, then it is not worthy to hold up in the courtroom of truth. No one escapes this law of life. It's supremely important to refer back to love in your beliefs and I'd suggest even questioning it against the teachings in this book. I don't want you to just believe this because I have said so; I want you to reason with your own truth. Just acknowledge your truth has always and will always hold love as the pinnacle of your fulfilment. If you make decisions that don't display love, especially for yourself, then life will force you to. And at times, it has no mercy in the lengths it must go to to wake you up. I'm sure we can all relate to that at one stage in our life.

All the answers you seek are within; they have never ceased to exist.

You must be willing to reason with yourself in order to bring out the truth. As the famous poet, Kahlil Gibran says so superbly in his masterpiece, *The Prophet*, '... God rests in reason... God moves in passion. And since you are a breath in God's sphere, and a leaf in God's forest, you too should rest in reason and move in passion.' **I must say, I truly find peace in not just knowing I have the ability to reason with myself, but in putting it into practice.** The only way to know a wise person, a great teacher of the truth, or an enlightened soul is if they speak of a love for all as the ultimate truth. If they don't teach you this, you are, sadly, being lied to.

Now, it's one thing being able to distinguish between your truth and your lie, yet it's vastly different when it's time to act. Mastering this next quality is the key to experiencing a joy most people only dream about having.

3. Feeding your truth is the quality to everlasting happiness

'There are only two mistakes one can make along the Way to Truth:
1.) not going all the way; and 2.) not starting.'
Gautama Buddha

When we feed something it grows. For some, fear, sadness, lack of direction and unhappiness has become daily indulgence. Every time you make a decision or commit an act that is against your truth (love, kindness, happiness, giving, patience), it sabotages the relationship you have with yourself. Is it any wonder that so many people don't know what they want or which direction to take? On the other hand, when you feed your truth it will grow to a size you never imagined possible. In your truth also lies fulfilment. When we begin to feed that truth, our happiness gets fuller, and in that is found inner peace. There is no limit to the growth; it's a never-ending supply, because you are supplying it. You are the hand that feeds you, so you can always rely on yourself! However, if your hand is always reaching out to be fed by an external supply, it can stop at any time. Those people, money, and situations may not last forever. The more you grow, the more the supply grows.

I'm so glad I trained myself to feed my truth because it's definitely the reason you are reading this. If I hadn't, I would never have been able to discover what I'm great at. I've spoken to excellent achievers, but more importantly those who are successful, and they all have the same thing to say. They began listening to and acting on that deep voice inside. Not only on major decisions that had to be made, but even to the smallest acts of everyday life. There is a distinguishable truth in every moment, opportunity or experience. If you are willing to reason with yourself, you will be able to clearly identify it, but more importantly, act on it.

We must really start listening to that intelligent and wise voice within. If brushing it off has become a way of life you must change immediately. Here is one example of how I conditioned myself to feed my truth: We all know what a rubbish bin is used for, so we are able to distinguish that the bin is there to do the correct thing and throw rubbish in. (Common sense reminded me of this my whole life but I chose to ignore it on so many occasions.) The difference now was that I began to amplify my truth (common sense), which clearly told me to throw my rubbish in the bin. Throwing something on the ground when I knew there was a better alternative was disrespectful. And I guess **if we want respect,**

we must give respect. By taking my truth into consideration and actually listening to it, I was able see the important role it played in my own life. This change in action also taught me a few other things. One of them was that I was able to commit to doing something that I actually wanted to do. I fed that deep voice, and it instantly created new emotions.

'Follow your heart, but be quiet for a while first. Ask questions, then feel the answer. Learn to trust your heart.'
Unknown

This simple change in behaviour will also train you to have patience. When something (bin) isn't accessible 'right now', you don't do something that is against what you really know you should do, just to obtain some short-term satisfaction. Can you see a similarity here with how this could benefit us in reaching our greater visions? You might see this as being very insignificant, but this is what allows you to acknowledge that you have the power to think, act, and create for yourself. It allows you to **create your own happiness**, which in turn helps you to respect more of your decisions. More importantly, it proves that the feeling of fulfilment does exist. Even when you make a decision that is extremely hard at the time, you will never regret it if it's aligned with your truth. When you believe something enough, you live by it. It seems **we always force ourselves to feel down when we know we do something that is against our truth, but how often do we recognise or acknowledge when we do something great?** To condition a great and rewarding feeling when acting on that conscious voice is the ultimate advantage in life. Remember, it starts with the small things, because that's what gets the ball rolling. If you don't have the energy to do the small tasks, how are you ever going to believe that you can actually reach your peak in performance or get the most out of life? When you do make the decision to feed your truth, don't dither about it. Make sure you create the energy if you must and do it with great intention.

A smoker is a perfect example. When I ask people about their smoking habit, they say, 'But I want to smoke'. Nearly every time I ask if they were in an ideal world and could be free from smoking, would they, I get the answer, 'Yes, of course'. The truth is the voice that tells them to give it up, and they know it.

That voice is always speaking, and you know when it does. Are you going to stuff up along the way? Of course, you're human. In life we may not make all the best decisions, but we are not meant to. If we did, we would never know growth.

'The seeker after Truth should be humbler than the dust. Only then, and not till then, will he have a glimpse of Truth... In the march towards Truth, anger, selfishness, hatred, etc. naturally give way, for otherwise Truth would be impossible to attain.'
Mahatma Ghandi

A social term for acting on our truth is **integrity**. In western ethics, integrity is regarded as the quality of having an intuitive sense of honesty and truthfulness in regard to the motivations for one's actions, and can be regarded as the opposite of hypocrisy. The word 'integrity' stems from the Latin adjective integer (whole, complete). In this context, integrity is the inner sense of 'wholeness' deriving from qualities such as honesty and consistency of character. As such, one may judge that others 'have integrity' to the extent that one judges whether they behave according to the values, beliefs and principles they claim to hold. Just really listen to yourself, then act on it. That's all it takes.

Mahatma Gandhi summed up our inner voice the best:

There comes to us moments in life when about some things we need no proof from without. A little voice within tells us, 'You are on the right track, move neither to your left nor right, but keep to the straight and narrow way.'

There are moments in your life when you must act, even though you cannot carry your best friends with you. The 'still small voice' within you must always be the final arbiter when there is a conflict of duty.

Having made a ceaseless effort to attain self-purification, I have developed some little capacity to hear correctly and clearly the 'still small voice within'.

I shall lose my usefulness the moment I stifle the still small voice within.

Penances with me are no mechanical acts. They are done in obedience to the inner voice.

Excerpt from *Mahatma: A Golden Treasury of Wisdom — Thoughts & Glimpses of Life*

4. Quality of forgiveness — don't live in regret

'You think you look strong because you can hold on, but strength lies in letting go.'
Alan Mandell

You can spend your whole life hanging on to what could or should have been, but you can't go back in time. When we read a novel we turn the pages forward, not backwards. If we did read it backwards, the story would make no sense and confuse us. Having regrets is taking away the essence of life, because at that very moment when the decision was made, it was exactly what you wanted. You didn't do it any other way, even though the thought might have slipped your mind. The decision was made for a particular reason. The great thing is that you may now see a different path of greater benefit. Using this new-found knowledge for current experiences is the advantage successes have over the masses. It is absolutely crucial to obtain knowledge from our experiences, but we should never be remorseful over past decisions that helped shape our destiny. Residing in regret is like being stuck in a dark hole, where your mind is telling you there is no hope or means to get out. If you switch on a light bulb, cover it with a thick piece of material that makes the room dark, does that mean there is no light? No, the light is still there, it's just covered.

We have the ability to take off that material at any time. Just think of that material as being your regretful mindset and the illusions that come along with it. Previous experiences that so many people let control their life are literally only a mental image. It is a story that we replay over and over again, tormenting ourselves, but it is gone in reality. Take a look around, are you physically there? Being a figure of your imagination means you have the power to change the way you think about it. It is never the situation that is making you feel like you can't move on; it's your perception of the situation. No experience has one set way of looking at it.

'When you change the way you look at things, the things you look at change.'
Max Planck

I can't think of anything worse than living in regret. It's true that we shaped our life around those decisions but in the same sense we have the ability to shape our life around our current decisions. **As long as you regret the decisions you have already made, the ones you must make will be sabotaged**.

In the process of eliminating regret, forgiveness must be used to conquer it. Forgiveness is one of the greatest gifts we have. It grants us permission to break free of burdens that restrict us from being at peace with ourselves. Resentment and remorse leave no room for growth. If we do not forgive ourselves we will remain stagnant and hateful, and that will definitely affect what we create next in our lives. We must be at peace with our past in order to gain a full view of opportunities, to stop being restricted by a narrow mind, and to allow for different decisions to be made in the future. There is no future in the past.

'Accept the pain, cherish the joys, resolve the regrets; then can come the best of benedictions: "If I had my life to live over again, I'd do it all the same."'
Unknown

It is essential that we accept our previous actions and those of others as an opportunity for growth. You may even say sorry to someone, but don't expect their acceptance. Such an expectation could lead to constant disappointment. You must accept that you did your part. Apologising to someone is not admitting that you did something wrong, it's allowing the other person, but more importantly yourself, to acknowledge that you now see a better way. The most important thing you can do is forgive yourself. This will allow you to move on and make progress towards visions that you never trusted yourself to obtain. And if you think about a time when you have forgiven someone, wasn't it the case that you truly only came to forgive them once you forgave yourself for being in that situation? What someone does to you cannot change, but how you see it can. So in order to forgive yourself, and others, you must accept inwardly that it was your choice to be in that situation, feel the way you did about it, observe it the way you did, or what you decided to learn from it.

I once spoke to a woman who was raped as a young teen. The hatred she felt towards her attacker stopped her from excelling in life, especially in her relationships with other males. It wasn't until she found peace within herself, that she was able to forgive him. She explained to me that through such an evil act, she found liberation within herself, and began viewing the experience as one she could gain self-knowledge and strength from.

> 'Forgiveness is letting go of the hope that the past can be changed.'
> *Oprah Winfrey*

Self-forgiveness allows us to rebuild the faith in ourselves, and those around us. It helps us realise that we are free from emotional restrictions, so we can once again portray real love. Forgiveness is truly a courageous act and helps liberate the soul. Without forgiveness and acceptance of the past, we remain crippled and unable to run. It will prevent us from ever gaining true happiness or fully respecting the great qualities that reign within us; two major keys to real success. **The deeper your scars, the more room there is to fill them up with love. Don't hate your scars, appreciate their depth.** Free your mind, body and soul.

Task

Write down the answers to these questions:

What are the benefits of me living in regret?

Does it really make me feel better about **myself** to have resentment?

What are the benefits of accepting my past decisions as an opportunity for growth?

Can I gain knowledge from my past that will help shape my current decisions?

What momentum can I build in my life if I make the decision to move forward and never look back?

Using the empowering information and wisdom gained from my old experience, what can I now achieve in my future endeavours?

5. Patience — a master quality

'As you put into practice the qualities of patience, punctuality, sincerity, and solitude, you will have a better opinion of the world around you.'
Greenville Kleiser

Anyone who has created an extraordinary life will agree that patience is definitely at the top of the list. Without the constant use of this quality, it is impossible to create. If you follow any great achiever, someone who has a great relationship, or an individual who would be regarded as a wise mentor, you would see that patience is what keeps that fine line between sane and insane. It enhances the ability to clearly see what is around and make sense of a situation that we would usually get angry with, or not properly assess. Without using this master quality, we will be forced to make irrational decisions that could have a detrimental effect on our life. In business, it could influence us to make decisions that could adversely affect our goals. In relationships it may cause unnecessary difficulties such as stress, lack of trust, paranoia, which would then also result in the deterioration of our health. Impatience will attack every part of your life, especially when in pursuit of your visions. Some people get confused with the whole concept and think that taking action every day towards a vision is being impatient. I would just like to clear up that it's precisely the opposite.

The lack of patience especially takes its toll when on the road to achievement. Most people go for the quick dollar as impatience starts to take over, or will settle for less then the bigger picture they have set up. You will notice that most really successful people struggled drastically in the beginning of their journey, yet they refused to stop pursuing their goal. It wasn't about the wealth right away; it was about getting themselves right first. We must build that inner strength initially. I couldn't tell you how many people have told me they attempted to do something they love, but said after a little while they went back to getting a full time job that they didn't enjoy, just for the short-term satisfaction of having income. They get that money, but are even more unproductive with it because they aren't enjoying their life. A regular income can really benefit you, but not if it takes over your desired passion in life, and is just an excuse to settle or give up. You will never be fulfilled that way. Some powerful achievers have had debts through the roof and been ejected from their houses because they couldn't pay the rent, but they never lost sight of their vision. That persistence always pays off.

In my experience and speaking to many about this topic, I have discovered that impatience is the main factor in what we know as 'quitting'. What we want seems so far away, that it appears easier to stay where we are and just settle. This important question must then follow: **Is it really easier living a life that is less than what you know you deserve?** We will find everything and anything to do besides what we need to do in order to get what we want. We will call multiple friends, think of ten different movies to go and see or go for another coffee; anything to escape the fear of, 'It's just too much to handle'.

Patience is a quality that should be put into practice every day, with every situation. Every time I get impatient, I think back to the life I don't want to submit to and it makes me nearly physically sick. I then visualise my dream life and I am instantly powered with motivation to push forward.

> 'He that can have Patience, can have as he will.'
> *Benjamin Franklin*

I determined that no matter what life threw at me, I was going to do what I had to do. Training yourself to be patient is a great test of strength and something that needs to be done if you want success in any area. It starts in traffic, work, and in your relationships with others. Don't forget, even holding onto rubbish until you find a bin is a great strategy!

We must make changes that will empower our life with patience, even in the simplest of scenarios. Change can really happen in an instant. We all know there have been some defining moments in our lives that have shaped our destiny. Regardless of being a benefit or not, the decision to change can happen quickly, and the results are acutely evident. At times we are not satisfied until we see the end result of our decision. The same goes when we make the decision to practice patience in our daily lives. In business, for example, most will neglect the immediate results of feeding the quality of patience. They will wait for the end result to base their happiness on, for example, the next monthly profits. What they don't realise is that it's a build up of little decisions that cause the end result they desire to become reality. Look at nature: from the growth of a plant, which is the result of a seed, to a collision of clouds, which results in a storm. There is a build up, and things that must take place before a massive result is seen. **The calm before the storm!** If we don't plant the seed and water it, how will it ever blossom? In one moment you can decide that you want change and gather the inner motivation to do it. It is motivation in that instant that gets you started, but it is routine that makes it habit. Think back to the first time you went to the gym, for instance. Because there was too much pain associated with not doing it, and more pleasure in doing it, something switched inside of you. As time went on, you kept the routine and it became a way of life. So, yes, change does happen in an instant, but true results come from repetition, and that takes patience.

> 'Have patience with all things, but chiefly have patience with yourself.'
> *St Francis De Sales*

To master patience is to also have faith in yourself and your creator. I used to fall back on, 'I know why this has all happened'. That was my favourite saying to myself, reassurance of the greater plan that I set for my life. You must build the belief that you know — as surely as you know the back of your hand — that it's going to happen. We have all visualised that great life we aspire to, although impatience plays a major role in stopping us from ever experiencing it. Self-control and remaining strong in the face of impatience are the keys to winning. You are still going to get angry or impatient at times, but battle your hardest not to vent it. **To let out anger is like facing a strong gust of wind and spitting directly in it. You affect yourself the most.** Use all the power you have and focus on making an internal shift. Fight it, overpower your limiting thoughts, and you will win. When faced with a challenging situation, use it as a great time to practise the art of patience. Once mastered, it will help you beat the next one with a little more ease.

Before you know it, patience will be your subconscious reaction, and impatience will quickly result in correcting yourself. Another great tool is to put things into perspective. If you're waiting in traffic, just sit back and think about all those who don't even have food to eat, let alone a car to drive, and you will soon realise that your complaints are very petty. To cut above the rest, you must also use situations like these to your advantage. I've had so many people tell me that they don't have time to themselves to think about bettering their lives, and then I always refer back to the 'stuck in traffic' situation. I'm not sure about you, but I see a lot of time that would be great to really think about making change in your life. **Finding the balance between persistence and patience is the pinnacle when creating something great.** This can only be achieved by constant practice. Without patience, you are likely to give up.

'Patience can't be acquired overnight. It is just like building up a
muscle. Every day you need to work on it.'
Eknath Easwaran

6. The quality of giving — what a gift!

Take a lit candle and light many others with it. Has the flame suffered any loss? And what happens to the flame when you put all those flames together? It gets bigger.

It is the same principle in life. We should always seek to light that flame with an inner peace and self-love from within. Once that has been attained you will be like a light in the world, ready to ignite anyone who crosses your path. People will feel your warmth. There is no greater gift than giving itself.

'It is one of the most beautiful compensations of life, that no man can sincerely try to help another without helping himself.'
Ralph Waldo Emerson

In the car one afternoon with a friend, another realisation dawned on me. He let someone go in front of him, and was waiting for a thank you wave. When he didn't get it, he cursed himself for letting the guy in. It hit me: why expect a wave to determine how you feel about your great action?

By recognising that your feeling should be determined by your own action, not someone else's reaction, your decision to give will not be for any selfish desire of recognition, praise, or for any other reason. It will be purely out of great intention, and that's giving. Things that are done out of pure intent are an amazing gift to all. It is evident that some people only give to obtain something in return. Is that really giving? Even if it is just a thank you that you expect, it takes away the true essence of the act.

You should be proud of yourself, not proud of what others feel and think about you. If you can be really happy in giving, then it's already complete. If you want to be happy for anyone outside of you, be happy for them. Also take note that others' growth is your growth, and vice versa. Contribution is one of only three ways to ever be truly fulfilled

I have heard people say, 'Oh, so I have to give money to charity?' Firstly, you don't have to do anything in life, everything is a choice. Secondly, is that what this world has made us believe, that the only gifts come in a box or a cheque? In saying that, I know most people wouldn't even lose a minute of sleep over kids half way across the world. Surprisingly enough, I don't expect them to yet. We must rediscover and feed our true qualities first. Start with the people around you and begin with things that are basic. What about the gift of love, change, or generosity in everyday life? How about the gift of appreciation, acceptance, gratitude, and communication? Why don't we give ourselves back the gift of life, which so many seem to forget? They are all for free and help you and the people around you. They are far more important than a few cheques a year. In saying that, helping a fellow human in need is the most fulfilling act one could ever perform. As one becomes more self-aware and their heart opens, they will notice the power they have to change someone's life. It will become like an addiction, something you feel you cannot live without.

> 'It is more blessed to give than to receive.'
> *Jesus Christ*

A story that really inspired me and brought me to tears was one that I heard on the radio. It was about a wealthy man who went to Africa to visit a poor village. He met a young boy there who was seven years old and dying of malnutrition. He said the boy's stomach was bloated, his hair was discoloured, and he could hardly stand up. He knelt down and gave the boy an open coconut. He expected the child to eat it immediately, but to his amazement the boy left the fruit by his side. The man walked off puzzled and a few minutes went by. Out of the corner of his eye he saw the boy pick it up and begin to walk. Without hesitation he secretly followed. Pulling back the entrance to the tent where the boy had entered, he saw him kneeling down. Grasped in one hand was a baby, and in the other, the coconut. As the tour guides entered, they told this wealthy man that the baby was the boy's dying brother. The young boy loves his baby brother so much, that any bit of food he gets, he feeds the baby and goes hungry himself. What a moving, touching and inspiring story of human bond. A boy so young, faced with death, is still able to surrender for human love. That really penetrated my soul, as I'm sure it has yours. And just think of how many of us are blessed with so much, yet we give nothing. **One man can save another man's life. That's what one man can do**. There is no greater act than that.

> 'Happiness... consists in giving, and in serving others.'
> *Henry Drummond*

We all have an amazing gift that was given to us. How many times have you had a gift, wrapped up with your name on it, and didn't open it? I'm guessing your answer will probably be never. Well, I have a rude awakening for some: the answer is every day. There is a God-given gift, all wrapped up by the hate, despair, fear, complaining, and all other limitations we let consume our lives. We have the power to perceive things in a different light, however even more importantly, the power to change the way we act.

Sadly, the vast majority of people believe that when they give they are emptying themselves, or are giving something up in the process. In order for them to feel significant, they unconsciously attempt to fill that 'gap' with someone else's approval or praise. When it doesn't happen, they seem to be disappointed. In order to be happy in life, we must recognise that every time we give, we automatically receive. The feeling of giving is the gift! If you focus your energy on the great acts you commit to everyday, you will experience fulfilment.

Real success also thrives on the idea of giving. It helps you to create a stronger passion to not just follow achievement for yourself, but to better everyone around you. I could just imagine how lonely and unfulfilling a life would be if I were to celebrate success on my own. That doesn't merely mean money, but keeping the great qualities you know you have all to yourself. Share them, **allow people to see you for who you really are**, give of yourself and it will come back tenfold. The energy we express with our thoughts, words and actions are the real contribution to the world. It becomes contagious to those around you, because every soul is striving for that fulfilment. Before you know it, it won't feel like a process, but rather a way of life. Then the universe will be happy to welcome you to the never-ending cycle of self-growth.

Gold with Graham…

It takes a simple-minded man to linger around those who are praised, yet a courageous man to pick up those who have fallen.

Walking in the heart of Melbourne city in Australia, I passed a distressed man sitting against a shop front. Near him lay a beanie, a cup, and a dirty backpack. Knees up and head bent, it seemed as if he had given up all hope. I put some coins in his cup, and continued on. As I walked back from the store I went to visit, I decided to sit down on a chair across from him. Watching people walk past, deliberately staying clear and acting is if he were an alien, I couldn't help but get put into a state of compassion. Thinking about what others would think if I sat next to him, I hesitated. I mean, this was the main street in the city, Bourke St Mall to be exact. If you have ever been to Melbourne CBD, you would understand what I'm talking about.

My love for this human was far too great to be held back by what others thought, so I left my fear behind and walked up. I finally realised that it was only when I cared that it seemed others did as well. When I stopped caring what they thought, it seemed they did too. I guess our mind really does create our reality! I knelt down, gave him $10 and said, 'Do you mind if I have a chat with you, sir?' He looked up and said no. I sat right next to him in the same position as he was. It was an eye opener to watch people walk past from down there. I then recognised that this man was disabled. His hands were deformed and he could hardly get the words out to speak. He mumbled that the government had shut down his hospital. He also had a volunteer who used to look after him, but they had also left. I might add this gentleman was one of the nicest individuals I have ever met. He told that me that the previous day he had been spat on and kicked in the face by someone who called him a retard.

What amazed me was his attitude towards life. He said he would help those people if they needed his help, regardless of what they did to him. He even thanked God that he was shown manners as a child. He prays to God every morning and says thank you for being alive. He said that he knows God will watch over him and provide. He hasn't been let down yet and has taken his challenge as a way of life that he must deal with the best way he can. He understands that these people that ridicule him are only affecting themselves and battling their inner turmoil.

As we continued to chat I noticed he sat up and created more energy. I seemed to forget everyone else around while talking until something wonderful happened. People began walking up and dropping money in his cup. Another man brought over food and people were smiling in our direction. I told him to smile back, and he did. This one moment touched my heart and I will never forget it. Graham taught me the power of what one person can do. People will follow your great act.

This man has had so many challenges in his life yet has such a positive outlook. He loves the people that beat him, and has such strong faith. He assured me that he does not beg to people, but has faith God will provide. He said whenever he starts to complain he thinks of all the people that were kicked out of the hospital that were far worse off than him. He is compassionate towards the human race and said his dream is for equality. What a golden moment in my life.

> 'If you can't feed a hundred people, just feed one.'
> *Mother Theresa*

7. Understanding our body of ego

Appreciation, contribution and self-growth are the only ways to true fulfilment. To embrace any one of these, we are required to put down our body of ego. And don't be ashamed of having an ego; it's human nature. Some people just feed theirs so much that it gets in the way of really getting the most out of life.

You are often able to tell if someone is genuine or not as their use of ego is a great indicator. An ego is like a shield that protects us from feeling embarrassed and prevents us from displaying who we really are. We believe if we put it down, others might think we are weird, which makes us feel alienated. Someone with a big ego is generally hiding behind much deeper issues, and they are the people who are unfulfilled in life. They wear a mask their whole life, and when they feel that they are about to be exposed, they lash out and attack your actions, rarely looking at their own. They fear meeting the stranger underneath the mask. They are the same people who usually look at how much they can take rather than what they can give. They are commonly self-centred, their intentions are frequently ill, and their desires are far from contributing. I have also found that those who have a big ego and place themselves above others are insecure. They use their ego as a defensive mechanism to protect much deeper challenges. The sad thing is that even though most are aware of this fact, they still display ego all the time. I guess we just have to learn to direct our ego in a way that actually benefits the world and ourselves. Being human, I still find myself being caught up in ego at times, yet my self-awareness pulls me back into line almost instantly. So if you think you are too cool for school, then think again. **No one escapes the classroom of life; humbly embrace its knowledge or feel its punishment.**

Putting down our ego is not just crucial for lasting happiness, but also in achievement. Self-growth requires us to listen and obtain knowledge from people, which again requires that our ego is put aside. Ego is the number one factor that prevents us from listening, because we remain with the attitude that we don't need help and we can do it on our own.

I was out for coffee with a property investor one afternoon, and he told me a story that Sir Bob Geldof had shared at a seminar. Geldof was telling them about this little chubby kid who would always be hanging around and asking for advice. He later mentioned that he never knew that same kid would grow up to be Bono from U2. Another great story is that of Michael Dell, the creator of Dell computers. He had his first job working in a Chinese restaurant for $2.30 an hour. He would go in early and humbled himself just to listen to the wise owner who spoke about passion and love for the business.

Taking the advice of others and always being willing to take in new information is vital to success. Also, your ego must be down in order for you to listen to the advice your spirit gives you every day. If you have a stubborn mindset that is stuck on one way, you will never be fulfilled. Your spirit is by far your best teacher and guide as it knows all the answers to your questions. That deep voice inside knows what's best and will bump you initially if something doesn't feel right. How many times has your gut feeling been right? How many times have you convinced yourself otherwise and been unhappy? It's usually our mind that gets in the way of listening to our spirit. The key to aligning them both is by separating yourself from your ego. When you unify the power of your thoughts to that wise voice within, your success is self-evident.

If you still feel empty in your life, it is because you are yet to surrender your ego to humbleness.

People will cross our path to help us grow in life, but it's our ego that stops us from noticing this and allows them to slip away. We don't like the way they look, we are judgmental, or we just aren't willing to hear what we know is the truth. Being humble throughout your experiences is a true indicator of whether you are fulfilled or not. If you are not humble, then you'd better start being so, or else you will never find fulfilment, period. Confidence plays a major role in having an outstanding life, but make sure you find the line between confident and cocky. It's a thin line, but you will be aware of which one you are showing.

Task

Do not read on until tomorrow. The qualities we just went through are extremely important to your growth and success. I want you to take it with you for now. The next section we get into is a different topic, so until tomorrow, focus on the qualities that drive success.

16

LIFE'S ULTIMATE DUO — THE SPIRIT AND ITS VISIONS

Passion — the voice of your spirit

'If there is no passion in life, then have you really lived? Find your passion, whatever it may be. Become it, and let it become you and you will find great things happen FOR you, TO you and BECAUSE of you.'

T Alan Armstrong

During a chat with a friend of mine, I was shocked to hear that he wasn't happy after achieving something massive on his 'wants' list. He was an international DJ and radio show host. His songs were making the top of charts and he was playing in the biggest nightclubs in the world. One of his dreams was to play in Europe, which he had just achieved before I saw him. As he walked into the room to greet me, he said, 'It wasn't what I expected'. He told me that he went back to his hotel room after the show and wondered whether he even wanted to pursue a music career. The show went well, the people were great, and everything was in place. So what was happening? After a long conversation, we got to the bottom of it and he walked out with a breakthrough. Throughout his career he had focused on what he thought was his passion: to play music. I asked him this question: 'If I gave you all your equipment on a deserted island, how long do you think you would last playing music all alone?' He replied, 'Probably a few hours'. Then I asked another question: 'But your passion is to play music, isn't it?' He replied, 'Yes, so I don't know why I would only last that long, and I don't know what is making me unhappy'. I turned to him and said, 'Your passion isn't to just play music. **Your true passion is to inspire others with your music**'. Focusing on other people's emotion when they listened to his music, rather than just his own desire was a key turning point in his career.

We all want to know how to add value to this world, the people around us, and ourselves. Doing things for others will always create more meaning in your life. The people who have been the most influential and successful were those who were committed to doing this. A passion is far deeper than materialistic satisfaction; it's that drive within us that sparks the feeling that is far too great to be restricted by words. Even when the thought of it comes to mind it creates that fulfilment. Once you put a lot of energy towards a passionate life you enter the realm of the elite. The thought of it fills you with emotions you have never experienced, keeps you up at night and wakes you up in the morning. It is enforced and embedded so deep within you, that it surely becomes the basis of your decisions. It will guide you over hurdles, find inspiration once gone unnoticed, pick you up when you fall, and be the air you breathe.

You can definitely feel the difference when you enter a room with someone who has passion and someone who doesn't. In whatever area of life, you will notice the ones with a strong passion are those who are running far beyond what others think is the finish line. When everyone else says it's too hard or impossible, they are the ones that prove them wrong.

'If you can imagine it, you can achieve it. If you dream it, you can become it.'
William Arthur Ward

I hear people tell me they have a vision, so I ask what it is and they say things like 'to buy that house'. Now that's great, but what after that? See, a **passion is that invisible force that consumes your whole life and creates vision after vision**. A true passion sees no end, but only everlasting growth. A passion would be to provide for your children, to inspire people to the best they can be, to add value to the world, to help others, to provide a service like no one else, or to do something that you love. Being the best you can be is another great one. If there's any passion that is at the heart of every person, it is to exude that greatness that lies deep within them. We must prove our greatness to ourselves, because if we don't, we are the one who has to answer the question 'Why?'

We all know that we have a lot more to give, but we just need to let that inner person express themself. A great way to drag that spirit out and begin to steer it is to give as many reasons as you can why you want to do something.

We put all these material wants in front of us and call them visions, yet sometimes we struggle to achieve them. The reason is that we forget to build that foundation that is going to hold everything up. We must search deeper, and ask why we want what we do. Is it to provide for your family, to be the best you can be, to inspire or contribute? Whatever it is, you need to build as many reasons as possible why you are doing what you are doing, and let them really align themselves with who you are deep down. That's how you remain at full strength. I personally do not let materialistic things drive me because I know they will flow through my passion. I have a clear indication as to what I want, but then I let my spirit guide me. If we don't do it this way, we get caught up in greed, and we will never be fulfilled. You will notice that you continue to come back to that point of emptiness and then wonder why you even bothered in the first place.

A true passion doesn't just appear bright and strong one day, it evolves over time.

I can't tell you what your passion in life is, as no one but you can do that. This is one of the biggest challenges I see today. It seems when the thought comes up of trying to discover our true passion or calling, it causes us to worry and become stressed. All that does is cloud and suffocate your spirit. As we all know, stress is the biggest killer on the planet and the cause of destruction, so it is definitely not the road to finding your passion. In order to discover the blueprint of our greatness hidden under the collage of social beliefs that become self-beliefs, we must unwrap the paper and then the gift will be displayed. That collage is all the limitations such as hate, fear, self-doubt, judgment, lack of self-love and many more that restrict us from seeing our true path.

Lack of passion in life is truly a grave issue in society. I have coached people searching for their passion in life more than any other challenge. What I am about to tell you will probably change your perception of your passion forever — our whole life we seem to be in search of this 'one passion' that we think will win us fulfilment, and the concept is usually based around a career. We believe that without finding what it is, we are hopeless. Well, guess what: no one who is passionate is only passionate about one thing! I would consider myself a passionate person now, but I didn't wait to find out what career I wanted to do in order to decide that. In all honesty, I don't even consider educating and inspiring people a career, but a passion that flowed on from being passionate first in many other areas of life. I am passionate about being a great person, treating everyone as equals, sustaining the quality of nature, my body, my family, people in general, and so on. I have many passions in life. I didn't just wake up one day knowing what my career was and began being a passionate person, nor did any of the vastly successful people I have met on my journey. If you don't practise being passionate in all the other areas of your life, then you will never discover your true potential.

There is one great thing that all successes in any era have in common. It calls for no debate, it requires unconditional love and is the pinnacle of all emotions, and that is the passion for life itself. When you have passion for every part of your life, things fall into place.

All successful people have one thing in common. They are all addicted to life.

The enormity of visualisation

'Formulate and stamp indelibly on your mind a mental picture of yourself as succeeding. Hold this picture tenaciously. Never permit it to fade. Your mind will seek to develop the picture. Do not build up obstacles in your imagination.'
Norman Vincent Peale

People continually visualise throughout their day. There are very few who embrace the present, but many who envision the past or the future. The issue is that it's of no benefit because those visions usually result in stress or worry. Those same people have no idea how much power those visions have to becoming reality and that they cause them to experience the same emotions they so often complain about. As we previously read about neuroplasticity, constant repetition is effective in shaping who we are becoming. People get all spooked out when they here the word 'meditation', but they are missing out on one of the most powerful gifts mankind has. We are misled to believe that when meditating we are thinking of nothing. Let me assure you, when you are thinking of 'nothing' you are still thinking, because you're 'thinking of nothing'. It's an opportunity to take ourselves away from what we see with our eyes, away from space and time, and start using those thoughts to really create a feeling of success right now.

'Why do we close our eyes when we pray, when we cry, when we kiss, when we dream; because the most beautiful things in our life are not seen but felt only by the heart.'
Unknown

Taking the time out for visualisation is one tool that really successful people have used even if they don't call it that. Meditation, prayer and imagining are all the same thing. They allocate time to completely focus on what they want, not what they don't want. I would get so strongly into visualisation that the hairs on the back of my neck would stand up, because what I saw in my mind was just as real as if I were really there. Sure enough, they do happen.

Dr Andrew Newberg conducted a study to check the neural behaviour and physical responses of meditation by Tibetan monks and prayer by Franciscan nuns. The physiological changes in the brain and discoveries were outstanding.

Dr Newberg found that the front part of the brain, which is usually involved in focusing attention and concentration, is more active during meditation. There was, however, a great decrease in activity in the parietal lobe.

The parietal area of the brain is responsible for giving us a sense of our orientation in space and time. He hypothesised that blocking all sensory and cognitive input into this area during meditation results in the sense of no space and no time. When this part of the brain, which weaves sensory data into a feeling of where the self ends, is deprived of sensory input through the individual's focus on inward concentration, it cannot do it its job of finding the border between the self and the world. Dr Newberg described how this affects consciousness:

'The brain had no choice. It perceived the self to be endless, as one with all of creation. And this felt utterly real. The absorption of the self into something larger is not the result of emotional fabrication or wishful thinking. It springs from neurological events, as when the orientation area goes dark.'

Other experiments have also been performed, including those by Richard Davidson. He is a neuroscientist at the University of Wisconsin, and has led experiments in cooperation with the Dalai Lama on effects of meditation on the brain. His results suggest that long-term or short-term practise of meditation results in different levels of activity in brain regions associated with such qualities as attention, anxiety, depression, fear, anger, the ability of the body to heal itself, and so on. These functional changes may be caused by changes in the physical structure of the brain.

This just goes to show that with enough focus, your mind doesn't know whether what you are thinking about is real right now or not. Who's to say it isn't real, if the same area of the brain is being affected. When we daydream or close our eyes and drift off, we feel the same emotions as if we are actually there. It feels so real, because for that brief moment your mind doesn't know the difference. So if it's true that the more energy we put towards something, the stronger influence it has on our life, then it would have to be the same with what we focus on in our mind.

That's the power of realisation; those very images you choose to see in your mind on a daily basis, be they beneficial or not, are being attracted to your life. That's why things we don't want keep showing up — because we continually think about them! If we direct our mental images to what we want, it causes not just ourselves, but everything else to surrender to manifestation.

'Ordinary people believe only in the possible. Extraordinary people visualize not what is possible or probable, but rather what is impossible. And by visualizing the impossible, they begin to see it as possible.'
Dr Cherie Carter-Scott

I don't care what you want to call it; closing your eyes, directing all your focus to one area as if you are really there, feeling the emotions, and even imagining how you would physically react is going to enhance that area of your life. I just used to sit in my room, close my eyes, and drift off. It would be so real that I would feel the wind on my face, people telling me how much I had helped them, getting that great feeling, having a better relationship with my family, and all kinds of things that have now become reality. I would feel the warmth in a person's hand when they shook mine, or the hug from my nephew, just to inspire my day. I would do it anywhere and anytime I had the chance. **The power of visualisation** also has a weird way of speeding up time towards those things you desire. Things start to happen quicker, and I guess that's how you see the success of some, and wonder how they achieved such things in such a short amount of time. The more you visualise the qualities of life and what you want, the stronger it becomes. It will be a way of life and a means to take the appropriate action.

You can also cut time when something distressing displays itself by simply closing your eyes and drifting away to a better place for that short time. When you start practising this, it might seem difficult to stay focused, but the more energy you put towards it, the better you become at it. Even when you drift off with your eyes closed, it is crucial to redirect towards things you appreciate, or an experience that would immediately make you happy. Have you ever noticed that the trip back from a journey always seems shorter? Why is that? The reason is because we have been there before. If we go somewhere in our mind, feel it, see it, and be it, then we obtain it at a much faster pace. If you don't believe that your mind is the basis of your creations, then ask yourself these questions: Why do we have a mind, and what is its purpose? Use it!

'There are only two ways to live your life. One is as though nothing is a miracle. The other is as though everything is a miracle.'
Albert Einstein

No words I write could amount to the certainty I have in visualisation. It is the key and foundation to all your dreams, and is the basis for your decisions or reactions towards life experiences.

Be different from the rest, and give yourself this wonderful opportunity. When doing this, it is crucial to feel every detail of the image, from the smallest to the largest. Embrace the power and the emotion of it and it will be the foundation of creating that life you desire.

Visualisation experiment

If you have ever played basketball or know a player personally, you would know that many players choke when it's time to take the free throw. Even some of the best basketball players on the planet have this mental block. No one questions their ability to play the game but they have trouble making those shots, and they will be the first to admit it's all in their mind.

Dr Blaslotto at the University of Chicago reported about a study that was conducted to determine the effects of visualisation on the free-throw performance of basketball players.

First, the athletes were tested to determine their free-throw proficiency. They were then randomly assigned to one of three experimental groups. The first went to the gym every day for one hour and practised free throws.

The second group also went to the gym, but instead of physically practising, they were told to lie down and simply visualise themselves successfully shooting.

The third group did nothing. In fact, they were instructed to forget about basketball. At the end of thirty days, the three groups were again tested to determine their free-throw proficiency.

The players who hadn't practised at all showed no improvement in performance; many in that group actually exhibited a drop.

Those who had physically practised one hour each day showed a performance increase of twenty-four per cent. Here's the clincher: the visualisation group, by merely imagining themselves successfully shooting free throws, also improved twenty-four per cent!

It doesn't matter in what area of life you do this, if you run a perfect scenario over and over in your mind with the inclusion of **sight, sound and smell** then it is sure to improve. Visualising and taking the physical action is a duo that is unbeatable.

Training your mind

'Give us clear a vision that we may know where to stand and what to stand for — because unless we stand for something, we shall fall for anything.'
Peter Marshall

Task

Visualise over your updated appreciation list. Be still and make sure you are stationary. Once you fully focus and do it a few times, you won't want to stop. You will discover a shift in focus towards great things in life, rather than things that are of no benefit. The quality of your whole life will improve.

1. Start with focusing on breathing in and out through your nose. From the tip of your nostrils, follow the breath all the way until it flows back out. When you inhale, draw the air down to your stomach, and back out slowly through your nose. You can count up to seven when exhaling to slow down the process. Do this until you feel light and weightless.

2. A euphoric state in your mind should take place; then start visualising. I personally did mine at night when I was relaxed, but still read my list in the morning. This inclusion in your daily ritual will transform your life. But you have to commit to it. Don't just do it for three days, stop, and then email me saying it doesn't work. It's an ongoing process, but results will be measurable immediately, especially in the way you feel.

3. You can also visualise at any time during the day, and listening to music that inspires you is also a great addition.

Your visions will start to play out around you, awareness will rise, and you will notice things that are relevant to your success that once went unnoticed.

Our mind is the canvas on which we create and imagination is its tool. Things once thought of as 'just a dream' will turn into a vision so strong, that your passion will see to it becoming real.

4TH STEP

STEER YOUR RELATION-SHIPS

17

ROCKY, DOCKED, OR SAILING SMOOTH?

'A loving relationship is one in which the loved one is free to be himself — to laugh with me, but never at me; to cry with me, but never because of me; to love life, to love himself, to love being loved. Such a relationship is based upon freedom and can never grow in a jealous heart.'
Leo F Buscaglia

Relationships play such a vital role in our daily life, so it was a topic I couldn't leave unmentioned. I went around to relationship experts, but my main focus was the everyday person. I wanted to know what people are really feeling; those who have overcome relationships that weren't working, couples who have been married for twenty years and are still going strong, and how others found their dream partner. I came to realise that it's in fact just like a ship, it all depends on how it's sailing. You could be on really rocky sea nearly falling off, you could be sailing very smoothly, or on the other hand you might be docked and waiting to be taken out. Let's start with the ones that are…

Rocky

These are the ships that sway from side to side and never seem to settle. I definitely found myself aboard this ship a few times in my life. A lot of it has to do with not being self-aware and not knowing exactly what you want, or knowing, but not taking relevant action.

This one guy in particular, who seemed to be clashing with his girlfriend, asked me what he should do. Now this one is very difficult, because trying to get the real truth out of someone is a battle in itself. Some people will also defend their partner because they don't want to portray them as the villain. Sometimes they don't mention their own faults or they attempt to put *all* the blame on the other person. There seems to be a lot of attacking and defending on either end. It's also hard to get the truth out because it seems so many are pulled into the notion of 'love' and believe that is the sole reason why they should be with their partner. Further to all that, there are always different perceptions. I believe by saying, 'But I love him/her' is not a strong enough reason on its own to stay with someone. I'm sure we are quite aware that we can fall in love many times, and on occasions, with those who aren't right for us. It doesn't mean they're not right as people, it just means they're not right for us. We get sucked in by attraction and other things initially that we allow to get a good hold on us. We then seem to be going on a blind date every time, because we just don't know what is going to happen next.

I sat this guy down and I asked this question:

'What do you love about her and why are you with her?'

This was his answer…

'She makes me laugh, she keeps me on my toes, I'm really attracted to her, she keeps me strong when I feel weak, she gets along well with my family, I love her and I can communicate with her.'

I then went on to ask him what he loves about himself and he gave me only three answers and then struggled. How can we confidently give the best of ourselves if we aren't even sure what we can offer? How can we ever know what we want, when we don't even know who we are? We must be that great person we wish to see in a partner, or else we will sadly never find happiness.

A couple of years ago on Valentine's Day, my mother asked me who I was going out for dinner with. I let her know that I was going by myself, but assured her I wasn't crazy. I wanted to go on a date with me and ask what type of person I am, what I want out of my life, and what's important to me. I'm so thrilled I did, because that night brought up a lot of answers and created many opportunities for change.

In regards to the first question I asked him, 'What do you love about her, and why are you with her?' I explained that every single answer had 'me' or 'I' in it and was nothing short of selfish. It seems that our relationships start to become all about our own wants, rather than being a paired force and helping each other grow. So I said to him, 'Instead of saying "she makes me laugh", how about "her amazing sense of humour". So when she isn't there to make you laugh on a particular occasion, it's okay, because she is still a funny girl and you will always recognise that. **Your partner has her own life as well**. It's not her full time job to fulfil you, that's your own job. Instead of saying "she gets along well with my family", how about "she is family orientated"'. Can you notice the massive difference this small shift of attitude could have on a relationship? You must focus on your partner's qualities, not only what they can offer you.

So many relationships start becoming all about what 'I' want and one person trying to take control of the situation. We have to shift our focus to the other person and why you are really with them, because it's going to make you appreciate them on a completely different level. Acknowledging their great assets is the pillar that will hold you both up when challenges do arise. Let's face it, as long as we are alive there are going to be some cracks, but if it's all about you, then you can bet it's not going to hold up too well.

> 'Consider how hard it is to change yourself and you'll understand what little chance you have in trying to change others.'
> *Unknown*

Another major breaking point I discovered through talking to many people about the topic, and through my own experiences, is that we believe our partner fills gaps within us that we don't believe we can fulfil ourselves. This seems to be the biggest unconscious issue that many face. When that person isn't there to fill that part up for whatever reason, we start fighting, begin to doubt, and things crumble. Being an unconscious issue means we are not really aware that this is the case, but it warrants these deeper questions: Are you really in love with who they are, or are you in love with what you think they fulfil in you that you don't believe you can fulfil yourself? Did you have a clear indication of what you wanted out of a life partner when you met them? Did you really get to know them or did you get sucked in solely by the attraction bug? **At the end of the day, no one can fulfil anything that you don't already have access to.**

When we truly believe that we *need* that person to live, it puts strain on the relationship. We make ourselves believe that if they are not around then we are out of whack, can't function, unable to get by, or do anything in our life. I'm here to tell you now that everything that you think you need you already have — it might just be qualities you are not yet using. Be with someone because you truly want them, not because you feel you need them or have to have them.

An expectation from others can really be an invitation for disappointment. When we expect things to happen and also believe that the other person 'has' to do things, it prevents us appreciating the great things they do for us. Realistically, they don't have to do anything, but if they do, it should be because they want to, not because they feel they have to. If you have to keep asking them to do something and they eventually do it, but you just feel it's not coming from their heart, then it's only because you made them 'have' to do it. No real satisfaction should be drawn from that and, to be honest, maybe that person isn't really your greatest match. If they're right for you, things just happen; you shouldn't feel like you are continually forcing them to. We must be at peace with ourselves and actually want that person for who they really are. You must respect they also have a life that should be lived. A partner's role is to help the other person with their aspirations and add as much value as they possibly can to their life. A healthy relationship is evident because they both seem to bring the best out of each other and seem to shine simultaneously. **A life partner is not about battling each other, but overcoming life's challenges together.** Here are three ways to create a more fulfilling relationship:

- Command your own emotions, **not** your partner's. If you don't do this, your relationship won't stand a chance.

- Set up compelling visions together. If you don't have something to look forward to, you will burn out. Some people are still together, but it doesn't mean their relationship is alive. What do you want your relationship to be like? How can you make it that way? What can you both do to bring that about? What would you like to achieve together?

- Create a strategy plan that you both work through to get those desired visions and outcomes.

If you must, let go

'The jump is so frightening between where I am and where I want to be… because of all I may become, I will close my eyes and leap!'
Mary Anne Radmacher

Our happiness as individuals will almost always be based on the decisions we make, or the ones we want to make, but aren't following through. **People also experience unhappiness because the expectations they have set for their life haven't been met.** This goes for our finances, emotional state and predominantly for our relationships.

It really does come down to what you want out of your life. If you know in your heart that your current relationship is something that you don't wish to participate in any longer, you must feed your truth. There are many people who turn around after leaving their relationship and say, 'I really want it back'. It may be the fifth time they have attempted to end it, but every time the same story is repeated. The question must then be asked, 'Do they want it back, or do they fear the unknown because they haven't yet built the inner strength to let it go?' By probing deeper, the answers I have heard over and over again are that they really want to get far away from the whole situation and have the feeling of being free from it. They just remind themselves of why they can't, not how they can. When they accept that 'can't' is a choice, they automatically realise they can.

My truth was telling me for so long that I didn't want to be in my past relationship, and I would definitely have a lot more money if I saved a dollar for every time I ignored it. I would continually think, 'this person isn't right for me, get out and run'. I would then get down on my knees and say, 'God, just give me a sign'. The funny thing was that asking for a sign was actually the sign in itself! The signs are right there, we see them all day, and that deep voice inside will always be there to remind us. I now believe that if it's an 'I don't know', then it's a 'no'. That goes with business, relationships, and so on. Unless I am absolutely certain, it's a no-go zone. That's not to say I can't make myself certain, but I won't fully commit my life to it until I am.

> 'A sad thing in life is that sometimes you meet someone who means a lot to you only to find out in the end it was never bound to be and you just have to let go.'
> *Unknown*

We are also able to build that certainty when we want to leave a partner. If you have ever been in a relationship where you were not fulfilled and finally gained the courage to leave, you would know that there comes a point where the pain is just too strong, and the grass is too green on the other side. Just like anything in life, a massive shift of emotion caused you to act rapidly and you finally left. You hit that point in your life where you said, 'That's it, I've had enough'. That day came when you refused to continue living someone else's life. I'm sure you also became frustrated with trying to take control over their life, because that's not what it's about. It's not our duty to attempt to turn someone into us, because that will surely create a clash. And essentially, who gives us the right to do that anyway? The reason we become involved with someone is so we can both add different elements to each other's life. Never attempt to make the other person live your life; they should respect yours, and you should respect theirs. Like I said, if they are right for you, then things just happen. You don't continually force them and they don't feel like they 'have' to, they just do it. **When you attempt to control someone else's life, it only reflects the lack of control you have over your own**.

Most of the time we drive ourselves mad in trying to figure out what our partner is thinking. Why did they do that, why did they hurt me, or why are they acting that way? How about you? **In doing this, we neglect to take accountability for our own life and realise it's never what they have done; it's what we allow them to do.** Once we take charge, the decisions to follow will bring the outcome we deeply desire. You must take charge of your own emotions and mental state! They are who they are, but you must be responsible for you and start making decisions accordingly. If they are not willing to make change, then you must.

In determining whether someone is a life partner or not, I think it's crucial that your core values do not clash with their values. At the end of the day, our values are the things we live by. I was speaking to a client of mine who always wanted to travel and eventually have children, but her partner's belief was that travelling was a waste of money and he didn't want to have kids. Obviously not really knowing what she wanted out of a life partner when she met him, she didn't really probe those major details. By the time she found out, she had already built a love for him. He wasn't willing to compromise and didn't want her to travel on her own.

The things this guy valued most in his life were obviously quite different to hers.

So I told this woman to write down everything she wanted to do or accomplish in her life and add up whether his traits would allow them to grow together. After she did the exercise, she discovered that she had put on hold nearly the whole list for him. She needed to take accountability for that and stop blaming him for her inaction.

He wasn't wrong; it's just not what he wanted out of his life. In order for her to live hers, she needed to leave him. After a five-year relationship she ended it. She was hurting for a while, and assured me it wasn't easy, but it was the best decision she ever made. She finally visited her family overseas, and started her own business. She also promised me that she would never be with another guy who didn't want to have children. That has now made the top of her **must** list, otherwise it's an automatic 'no'. She has created clarity and learnt from her past experience, and that's how we grow and attract what we want.

If the things we value most aren't aligned with our partner, how can we ever expect our relationship to be successful?

Any time you have experienced conflict with someone, it's because they have trodden on the things you value most in your life. No one likes the values they live by or what they stand for to be trampled on or questioned. Our values are our life, because we use them as the sole decider of our decisions. If you have ever been uncertain when making a decision, it's because you were still unsure of what you valued most in that situation.

Many people settle for someone who has vastly different values, and who stands for completely different things. The importance of some things is lesser or greater than their partner's. Is it any wonder why these relationships continue to clash? Attraction, wealth, social status, loneliness, and emptiness are just a few factors that will make us hang around. I highly advise putting someone's core values at the top of your list if you want a fulfilling relationship. If you are unhappy in your relationship now because of this clash, and you know the person will never change (not that they have to or even should), then it's time to reassess and make a decision.

Those qualities that we value most, the standards on the top of our list, or the morals that mean the most to us, shape our life. It's true that a lot of people have different values, but we all have the same needs. One of those needs is to be loved for who we really are, not who we pretend to be. We also need someone with similar values to help us grow. If we feel as though someone lives by a different charter of values, we will always have a lack of understanding and frustration towards them. We may even feel that the person is slowing us down. I'm not saying you should not to be with someone who has different traits, because we all do. What I am saying is to look hard at what values that person stands for in their life. That myth of 'never going to find someone again' is just that, a myth. Don't be fooled, in time you will.

Ex partners play a very important role in our destiny; they make us see what we definitely don't want, so what we do want becomes clearer.

I think it's wasting your life being with someone that you don't really want to be with. **We make ourselves believe that it's so hard**

to follow our truth, but I like to see it as being much harder living a lie.

Continually remind yourself of the greater plan, and why you have actually decided to leave. Your mind will play tricks on you, but essentially that deep voice inside will not hesitate to be brutally honest. I personally directed my thoughts and feelings to the notion of being free from the emotional chains that were holding me back, and would visualise about living my own life. The hard reality is that someone usually gets hurt a bit more than the other, but you are not really hurting them in the long run. In time they will know that, because it's far more selfish being with someone that you don't really want anymore, as you know it's putting strain on the relationship. You will be doing both of you a massive favour, and it's okay if they don't see it straight away.

We shouldn't have a partner to fill our emotional gaps with their presence. They should be there to complement the gaps we have already fulfilled, and help us find a way to fill the ones that aren't.

Docked

If you're just waiting to set sail then you are at an absolutely great point. By making the right decisions and taking appropriate action you will attract someone like never before. That dream person won't so much be a fairytale but a reality just waiting to happen. As I mentioned earlier, what you focus on you will be sure to find. If we say, 'I don't want someone who is disrespectful' or 'I don't want someone who is selfish,' for example, then you can bet you are going to notice it everywhere. Remember back in the 'Focus and Find' section where we discussed that reticular activating system in your brain? The RAS is always working, but in order to make it work in your favour you have to direct your focus intelligently. We usually carry luggage from previous experiences that tarnishes any new ones. We will continue to focus all our energy on those particular traits that we now know we definitely don't want, but it still creates a block in front of us. How can we really be hugged if we have our guard up?

Let's give an example... You once had a partner with whom you didn't go too well, hence they have taken on the 'ex' title. Now you are thinking back and believing that all guys/girls are the same and you hold on to that belief. You think about it, dwell on it, but more importantly, you enforce it. You have this unconscious notion always ready to display itself with every person you meet. In truth, what hope do you really give this person if you are going in with that mindset? Regardless of how they might act, it will totally change the way you approach the situation, so the situation will change. Your tone of voice, the types you are attracting, your body language, your quick judgment, all play a vital role. It's as if we wait in anticipation for them to stuff up so we can prove ourselves right. They could say or do something very innocent, but to you it's catastrophic because you will relate anything back to your belief. Then we wonder why the same challenges seem to arise. Have you ever wondered why every person you meet has the same faults?

I don't believe in coincidence — we attract things. However, even if you do believe in it, don't you think it's gone past the point of coincidence? Is there a constant pattern, or are you the one who needs to start making changes? On the flip side, you could shift your mindset. You could acknowledge that your ex wasn't what you wanted so you now know what you don't want in a person, but more importantly you now have clarity on what you do want. If you keep dwelling on what you don't want, then all you do is replay your old relationship over and over again with everyone you meet. Some might even turn sour and cringe at the sight of a loving couple. With that attitude, who would want to be with you, seriously? You need to focus on the things that you want in order to make the changes that will align with your dream partner. When you make change, the vibe you give off will scream, 'I'M READY TO EMBRACE SOMEONE NEW'. In saying that, sometimes we focus on what we want so hard, it shows itself, and then we think it's too good to be true. Opportunities to grasp what you really want display themselves many times in your life; however it is up to you to grasp them. All change starts with you.

Attracting a dream partner

To create something different, you must do something different!

Before we go to the grocery store, we should write down a list of what we want. If we don't, then it seems we just walk around and settle for things that we initially never wanted. We will buy some chocolate, even though we went there to buy broccoli. We will get home, eat it, and then kick ourselves for buying it in the first place. Most importantly, we forgot the broccoli! If you're getting my drift, in order to get what we really want out of a life partner, we must make it real. We must have a clear indication of what we actually want in life to get it. All things manifested begin as a creation in our mind, which we should then seal by writing it down. This will allow you to refer back to that sheet and remind yourself of what you really want. That will enhance the reality due to more visibility. Just keep in mind that we don't always get what we want, but there are certain things we MUST have. Never settle for less than the 'musts', but be lenient with the wants. I wouldn't reject someone because they didn't have the size eight feet I envisioned. And I wouldn't be taking my sheet along to a date. Don't be like a strict schoolteacher marking the sheet with every word they say.

Things don't always turn out exactly the way you create them in your mind, but make sure the fundamentals are in place and you get the same feeling. The present doesn't always come wrapped with a ribbon, but that's your chance to go and put one on, because you're going to help that person grow as well. It shouldn't be so much about what you can take from this person, but what you can give as well. Don't be one of those love hoppers; or that's what I call them anyway. All they do is jump from one person to another just hoping that the right person will pop up one day. I'm sure we all know someone who has barely broken up with one partner and is already with another. But you hear the same story, which is, 'I just can't find the one'. Instead, have faith initially and use your power to be as certain as possible.

Task 1

Clarification of what you want: Write down everything you want and must have in a life partner. Note down everything spiritually, mentally, physically, emotionally and financially. Remember an example would be, 'I want someone who is respectful,' **not**, 'I don't want someone who is disrespectful'. People always seem to write down what they don't want. Make sure you write down what you want.

Now that you have written down your perfect match, ask yourself these questions:

Why would they want to be with me?

What would I have to do in order to attract someone like that?

If I was that exact person on my list and went on a date with me, would I want to go out with myself?

These questions demand that you are completely honest with yourself to get great answers and find areas for growth. If you have written down that you want someone who is fit and healthy, you can bet they are not going to want to be with someone who doesn't look after their body or who eats McDonalds all day. If you are out getting drunk all the time but you have written down that you want someone who is in touch with their spiritual side, then that's a conflicting belief. If you must have someone who is happy, then would they want to be with someone who has a permanent frown and doesn't enjoy life? These are just some examples but I'm sure you get the drift. We try and make ourselves believe that we can get things that we want without making changes first. We must gain the balance of what we want and what we are going to do to get it, because that will ensure our confidence as well.

Task 2

Making change: Go back to your list and note down what you can do in order to attract someone like that. Find what you need to change to align yourself with those attributes on the list. For example, if you want some one who looks fit, but you're obese, then you may have a conflict of interest there. Get into shape!

Task 3

Pick your environment intelligently: I would also take note of the environment in which you wish to meet someone. We must pick our environment intelligently so we can increase the chances of meeting that person on our list. If you want someone who has a lot of mental strength and is family oriented, I don't think you are going to find them at the local sports bet on a Tuesday night. If you want someone who is healthy, your chances are slim of finding them dining in at KFC. You would have a much greater chance at the sandwich bar down the road, but I wouldn't be taking the KFC bag along with you — just a tip. My friend always wanted someone who was spiritual but who liked to party, yet he was going to nightclubs and getting drunk beyond repair every week. He would then ask me why he couldn't find anyone that matched what he wanted. Simple: I told him that if he does go to a nightclub, maybe he shouldn't get drunk and look for a girl who is sober. He should stay sober — that way he won't be attracting the opposite of what he is looking for, and will be a lot more appealing to the girl who is sober. It's quite simple when you think about it, but that's exactly what you have to do: think about it. If you want to find that person, make sure you're looking in the right spots.

The last but not least most important aspect is to be patient. Never just settle because of impatience. That will surely bring unhappiness and isn't fair on the other person. Great things come to those who are great. In order to see something as great, you must understand greatness. Invest in your own growth first and make changes to become great within, and you will attract accordingly.

Fear of getting sea sick

Some people fear getting into a relationship because they believe they will be giving up their 'independence'. We like to think we are independent, which means we don't depend on anyone or anything. Realistically, we are always depending on ourselves, so it means we are dependant creatures. We depend on the grocery store to have our fruit and vegetables, we depend on people to buy our products, we depend on family or friends when we want comfort, we depend on the rain so we can drink — so we are always depending throughout our life. It is okay to depend because we are all in this together. The challenge is finding the balance between your independence and what role it has, and the role of your dependence. This is a common social challenge as more people have the idea that a relationship is restrictive. Again, if you attract what you must have in a person, then you will truly complement each other. **Don't be scared to be dependent, but never base your total happiness on another individual. You alone are the only one who can truly fulfil yourself.**

Sailing smooth

If you are already steady on the ship and have been for quite some time, then I guess just keep doing what you're doing. Maybe you can email me and give me some more pointers; I'm always up for learning. I still know there is always room for growth, so maybe you can still take some great tips and strategies off these vibrant couples I spoke with. If you want your relationship to enter that calm sea then this next part is also for you.

Your average people

Couple 1

I asked this vibrant couple that attended the gym I used to work at if I could sit down and speak to them. They were recently engaged and agreed to take part. I found out that their relationship had been on the rocks, but they were able to save it, and said it was actually stronger now than ever. About one year before we spoke, they were about to separate over a miscommunication. I was surprised to hear that their relationship had nearly come to an end because of how happy they always seemed. The guy had put on about twenty kilograms in a matter of months and she felt as if she was caught in a dilemma. In a way she was, because her physical attraction to him started to decline, and she was concerned about his health. That might seem harsh, but maybe being healthy and fit was something she wanted in her partner, so it's actually not wrong at all. The difference between a friendship and an intimate relationship is **attraction**, so it plays a major role. Looks might not always be the reason someone loses their attraction. It could be a shift of attitude, mood swings, inconsistency or irrational behaviour. She was also attracted to how in control and strong he was in his life, yet that had diminished as well.

'Anger repressed can poison a relationship as surely as the cruelest words.'
Dr Joyce Brothers

One day she decided to tell him that he should start getting healthy and fit again. Taking the advice the wrong way, he began to feel insecure and thought she might cheat on him. He became paranoid and even stopped trusting her to go to the supermarket. She said it was killing her because she loved him to death and never wanted to hurt him, but she told him that she couldn't handle the lack of trust anymore and was close to leaving. Now this caused his pain threshold to hit the maximum, so he decided to finally sit down and face what she had to say. After communicating properly, he said in a sarcastic voice, 'You wouldn't do anything about it'. The next day she went and bought them both a gym membership. Now that's what I call enormous initiative. They began going to gym twice a week and now they are doing five sessions a week. It's a part of their life, and he assured me that he drags her out of bed most times now. They both look great but, most importantly, they feel great. He is soaring with confidence, their business profits have increased, and he told me that if he looked the way he had, he would have left him too!

What a great a way to share time together while also looking after their health. They motivate each other and have fun. They help each other grow, and always try to find a way to push past their limits.

Empowering tip: Always communicate how you feel and exercise together.

Couple 2

This couple was about to get engaged, but had hit a rough patch. Their relationship was built very much on trust, so they would spend a lot of time apart and with their friends. They noticed that their *engagement* between each other had declined, so they decided to sit down and communicate properly. They discovered that they had been seeing each other far less than they had initially, and it seemed that their constant trips away together had been put on hold for quite some time. Both of them decided to get into action. They agreed to cut down on their separate social life and save that money for at least a weekend away every two months. They didn't say, 'we don't have the money', but instead took appropriate action to get the money.

Going on trips with people has been proven to enhance many qualities in relationships and friendships alike. If you have ever been away with close friends, then I'm sure you have experienced the bond that can form. Yes, some people do still clash on holidays — we are human, not perfect — yet overall it does work.

This couple assured me that they would never take each other's presence for granted again, and recognised that their effort did really get the right results. The tip here is to engage more with each other. Don't take the things for granted that once built your bond. Take action and do fun activities together.

This one guy I was coaching in a similar situation with his partner told me that he didn't have the money, and then I found out that he was spending a minimum of $250 on alcohol every week. This is just an example, but seriously, how important is your relationship? If it's not more important than the beer you buy each week, then it's not that important. If you are committed, you will make the money and find the time. **There is always a way.**

Empowering tip: Go away with your partner or take up activities that are new to both of you. Do stuff that is fun and makes you feel great.

Couple 3

We all know that when a woman asks for your opinion on clothing, she is most likely going to do it her way anyway, but it's one of the great things we have to appreciate. When a woman tries on a new outfit that she just bought, and asks her partner what he thinks, he'd better say it looks good, because he probably won't know the difference anyway. She will then ask again, causing her partner to rethink and say, 'Yeah, but I like the other one as well, though'.

Then she will say, 'Why, what's wrong with this one?' with her partner replying, 'Nothing, it's nice, I thought you just wanted my opinion'. Then the final say is, 'Well, I like this one, so I'm going to wear it'. The partner is left bamboozled, and just as they are walking out the door, the question comes, 'Are you sure this one?'

I personally love this, because if women weren't like that, then guys would probably be walking around the streets naked. Women will willingly go shopping alone, but men don't stand a chance. We are too scared to bring something home that our partner doesn't like, because we know we will be going straight back for a refund. Not by force, but because we accept their expertise in the matter, and if they don't like it, then neither do we anymore. All men know they need a great woman, and the saying 'We can't live without them' is definitely a true one.

The last couple I spoke with have been married for eighteen years and are still going strong. They have three kids, and it's hard to see them without a smile. I desperately wanted to know what their secret was, and they willingly agreed to allocate me some of their time, as their motto is, 'If we can, they can'. The first quality that this couple has always been adamant about is the truth.

They also assured me that they try their hardest not to tread on each other's toes, but will always be there to help the other grow. The husband totally respects his wife's role, and the wife respects his expertise in certain areas. Always willing to listen to each other due to their mutual respect, they are helping each other fulfil their dreams. They also let me know that both being highly involved in their children's lives has had a great impact on their marriage. They have never taken each other for granted, and said it was their communication of the truth, no matter how much it could hurt at times, that has given them a long, strong relationship. In order to have a great relationship, it's imperative that we communicate the truth and how we are feeling on a constant basis. Keeping issues to ourself could cause us to act selfishly and irrationally, and that's usually how the battle continues.

Empowering tip: Be honest, communicate properly on a daily basis, appreciate even the smallest things, respect each other's dreams, and always be willing to lend a helping hand. Now that's what I call success.

Summing it up

This is just a few of many couples that all say the same things. So many people attempt to save a relationship by giving materialistic gifts. Your partner might not want a Gucci bag, or a new watch, but instead just a hug. They may not want a holiday, to be taken out for dinner or bought roses. They might want you to actually listen to what they have to say and be present.

I wouldn't go into business with someone who lacks communication, I wouldn't build a friendship with someone who lacks it, and I definitely wouldn't get into a relationship with someone who doesn't have the decency to make the effort to communicate. Why would I? It reflects the lack of respect and structure they have in their own life. To *engage* with your partner is absolutely crucial if you want a fulfilling relationship. If only more people were actually 'engaged' in their relationship before someone gets down on one knee and has to ask for it, there might be fewer break ups.

It's usually the things most take for granted which build a strong relationship. **There is no greater relationship than between those who are self-aware.**

Friendships are such a beautiful thing. It is where one soul trusts another to find comfort and liberation on this journey.

18

THE IMPORTANCE OF PEERS

'Keep away from those who try to belittle your ambitions. Small people always do that, but the really great make you believe that you too can become great.'
Mark Twain

I was in an aquarium to buy my nephew a pet fish, and I explained to the worker that I couldn't have one that grew too large as it was only going in a bowl. He assured me that I had nothing to worry about, because fish will **only grow in proportion to the size of their environment, and then stop!** What a great analogy to the way humans seem to adapt to the people they associate with and the choice of environment they surrounded themselves with on a daily basis. Everything in the world survives by adapting to its environment. The horny lizard in North America is one of many animals that have proven this. It mainly eats ants, and has formed thick scales to prevent being bitten while having its platter of bugs. But the hunter can always be hunted, so when its worst enemy, a coyote, shows up, it needs to protect itself. Through evolution this lizard has developed the ability to shoot blood out of its eye at its attacker. The blood amazingly has canine repellent chemicals in it to irritate the coyote in particular. Humans are no exception in adapting to their environment.

You don't have to be a genius to figure out that you will most likely become like those you associate with, so it means you must pick whom you spend most of your time with intelligently. The reason is that wrong choices of associates could prevent you from growing. What you feed your mind, is what's going to come out of your life. If you feed it garbage all day, what results are you going to get? How are you going to feel? When I was thirteen and getting myself into trouble with some other teens, my grandfather told me, 'When you hang around garbage, you start to smell'. And I'm sure we are all quite aware that some of the actions of man are nothing short of just that: garbage! It was one of the boldest but truest statements I have ever heard.

I'm not telling you to go and dump your buddies, but I would be seeing them in small doses if they contradict what you want to achieve. Some might need to be shown the door if your truth is telling you it's the best option. **If you really want to learn Chinese, but hang around people who speak Spanish all day, which language are you more likely to pick up?**

'There are moments in your life when you must act, even though you cannot carry your best friends with you.'
Mahatma Gandhi

Most times we condition ourselves unconsciously with similar mental, verbal and physical actions as our peers. We also do this to satisfy our urge for social significance and acceptance. Sometimes we feel that if we make massive change, our friends will think we are stupid or crazy. Guess what? Sometimes they do! We then have to ask ourselves: if they are seeing our positive changes that way, are they really reliable friends? Your dearest friends might also ridicule you, but they usually do it out of love. They feel as if they are losing you or, on the other hand, your positive change might make them feel insignificant. By beginning to excel in your life, it may finally show them how unproductive they are being in their own. I understand that no one wants to do that to their friends, but you must acknowledge that it is no reason to stop living the best life you possibly can. At the end of the day, it's their personal issue, and all you can do is communicate properly. Some people find it most difficult to understand in the beginning, but they will eventually, if they are real friends.

I also love when so-called 'friends' throw up the comment, 'You only live once!' People say it in the face of smoking, drugs, or even criminal activity. Really what they should be saying is, 'You only live once, so here, go and kill yourself, start a habit, or do something that could see you spending the next ten years in jail'. I think nearly every time I have given in to that line I have known that it would have been far better to avoid it, and I definitely paid the price.

Do you ever wonder whether these people are using that line for your benefit, or for theirs? Something to think about, isn't it? An intelligent response would be, 'Yes, I only live once, so why wouldn't I live the best way I know how?' Doesn't that just make a bit more sense? You might think that the options are fun in the face of that comment, yet I ask you to have a deeper look and you will realise that what you might think is fun could actually be causing your emotional and mental torment.

I often hear people complaining about being pressured into doing something they didn't want to do. It's quite a pathetic excuse, because they are only attempting to avoid their own lack of responsibility. They should be taking accountability and finding out how to strengthen their mind. You are the one who has to answer to yourself when you lay your head on the pillow. Why haven't I achieved? Why did I do what I did? Why am I in a distressed state right now? No one but you can find answers that will satisfy yourself, so learn to take charge of your life, and ignore outside influences that you know will make you doubt yourself.

'A real friend is one who walks in when everyone else walks out.'
Walter Winchell

Who really cares what the people who are quick to judge the great changes you are making think. I'm sure they are not quick to lend you a helping hand on your journey. The people who ridicule your productivity the most are the ones who are jealous, have no clue about life and, if you look carefully, are the ones living miserably with no sense of direction. Have you ever noticed how negative people spend most of their time with other negative people? Do you want to stop following your dreams and end up like them? I don't think so. Those that don't believe in you just don't believe in themselves. As I mentioned earlier, I was teased, ridiculed, and told I was crazy on a daily basis just for loving life more. They said my ideas would never work, but they were soon to be very surprised. My vision and passion were far too strong to let anyone stand in my way. Yes, it crossed my mind to stop many times, but that's when you must be at your strongest, and when you get past one hurdle, the next one seems that little bit easier. Instead of curling in a ball and giving up, I used it as fuel to drive me even further and create an even deeper hunger. **Sometimes people take the great things you are doing as a personal attack on their own life. Do not let their insecurities dishearten you.**

'Great people construct monuments with the stones critics throw at them.'
Robin Sharma

I discussed my change with a close friend one day and this was his reply: 'I know you are making changes, and I'm happy for you, but I'd prefer if you didn't discuss all this stuff with me. I'm always here for you, though'. I respected that so much, because he is still a friend, and it was his choice not to hear about the lessons that I was discovering with myself. I didn't storm off and get angry, but really appreciated that he was honest, and eventually he did come and ask for advice, and I was more than happy to help. Tell your friends about your change, but don't try to force your beliefs onto others, because that will most likely send them the other way. If you are making great change in your life, then it will be evident to those around you, and they will come and ask you how you did it.

If you have modelled any successful person, you would see that they were always willing to pick their peers carefully. If you want to become a great painter, then you wouldn't hang around someone who is good at the drums and try to speak to them about how to paint. Hang around and get advice from those in the same industry. Don't be shy to go straight to the top, or the best person you know in the field.

A true friend is someone who you can act like a complete idiot in front of and not be the slightest bit embarrassed. Try your hardest to keep this friendship. It is the closest outlet we get to become a child again!

When I was doing personal training, I would notice that, most times, when two overweight people would sign up together they wouldn't last very long. But on the other hand, when I saw someone who was overweight train with someone who was fit, they would soon be looking quite similar. That's not being harsh at all; I am just stating cold hard facts. I got into that industry because I care about people's wellbeing, so the last thing I would do is ridicule someone. It's just the way it is, and if you want to be like it, then you must start associating with it.

If you want to achieve something great, then pick the brains of those who you know have a clear history of achieving. Ask them what their secrets are. When asking, be humble, enthusiastic, and keen to learn. If you go up to those people with a big ego, you can bet they will probably show you the door. Let them know that you are driven and will do anything to learn the traits. Even if you are a millionaire, but having trouble breaking that barrier of hitting your next ten, then ask someone who has. Read up on other success stories. You can bet they were probably in the same predicament at your stage, but found a breakthrough. It doesn't matter how advanced we think we are, there is always someone out there we can learn from. When you associate with people that are great at what they do, then you are forced to step up to the greatness. It's the same as adapting to our environment; we eventually learn to live that particular way to keep up. In business and networking, **be humble, but never gullible!**

Associate yourself with people of good quality, for it is better to be alone than in bad company.
Booker T Washington

5TH STEP

TO A HEALTHY
PHYSICAL EXISTENCE

19

START THAT ENGINE

In order to see how the best of the best perform physically, you have to look at the best. Most top professional athletes have a personal athletic coach as well as a personal mind coach. The ones who don't a have a mind coach do it themselves. But there is one thing for certain: strengthening the mind is unqualified in their success. If these top athletes understand the importance of both mind and body, then why don't we implement this in our physical training every day? This lack is why some cease to continue to exercise or others never begin. People train their body, but they forget to train the powerful force that is driving it. Most people I have trained in my time make one crucial mistake: when they think about the body they want, or a desired level of fitness, they create themselves to feel depressed because they don't have it now. As for the people who actually achieve it, they use those same visions as an empowering motive to get going. Don't be upset when visualising your dream body, embrace it, and feel good because you know you are going to get there.

If you do not respect your body, it will not respect you on your journey through life. Our body is the ship that carries us through this journey, and it must be held in this regard. Would you go and put a hole in the hull of a boat you are travelling on? Of course not, because you will drown. Would you go and destroy a beautifully crafted piece by Leonardo da Vinci? How shocked would you be if you watched on the news that someone had deliberately gone and done this? We may be very moved, yet we will continue to wreck this beautiful piece of artwork called the human body. Our body is us, it is not separate. Our soul is one with our body and mind, so when one is out of balance, it sabotages the other two and something is destined to breakdown.

Wake up and live

Motivation is what gets you started, ritual is what makes it habit.

Our body cries out to us in a number of ways due to lack of exercise or an unhealthy diet. We have aches and pains, feel drained, and get sick on a regular basis. To live that balanced life, our body demands that we respect it. A major challenge in today's society is that even though some people like to train at night, they drag their way through the rest of the day. I would promote exercising in the morning, but if you are a night person, then make sure you're active in the morning. Do you think successful people drag their way out of bed, which drags that uninspired mood throughout the whole day? No way, they jump out of bed without too much deliberation and start instantly.

Have you ever noticed that when you are tired, you stretch and yawn in a slow motion? The reason we do this is because our body temperature is being cooled down. And when our body temperature regulates, our muscles receive messages that tell them 'it's now time to relax and to go to sleep'. When we finish exercising, we should do 'static stretches' to rest our muscles — for example, sitting down and doing a hamstring stretch for fifteen seconds. They are stretches that are done in slow motion. Our muscles need to recover, so static stretches (slow and relaxed) are ideal for this type of rest. So now here are the big questions: why on earth do we do that in the morning when our muscles need to be the most active? And, why are we moving in the same slow motion in the morning as we would before we go to bed or after we train?

Waking up isn't a time to let your body rest, it's the time for it to be active! If you watch any professional sports team nowadays, you will notice that they do very quick movements and fast breathing to warm up their body. This practice is called 'dynamic stretching' and it has now caused all static stretches before games to be abolished. This is because the last thing athletes want is their muscles to rest. If they do, injuries are more likely and they lack in performance. Only after games, once their work is done, are they told to perform static stretches to rest their muscles.

If you think about it logically, you will see it makes far more sense to trigger the muscles you want to use rather than to put them to sleep beforehand. If you want to use your body like the best, then you must model the best. This is what professional athletes do and all top trainers teach around the world. If you want to be wide awake within thirty seconds, this is the key. This one task has never failed me or any client I have ever used it on. I've seen massive results, so I swear by its success.

Wide awake

As soon as you hear that alarm clock go off, jump straight out of bed. Open your eyes as wide as you can and begin doing deep breaths in a quick motion. While breathing, do dynamic stretches — move your body in any way, just make sure you do it fast. An example would be windmills with your arms, star jumps, or trying to touch your toes. If you want you can also take one deep breath in through your nose and exhale three smaller times out through your mouth, while doing sharp movements with your body. You can also add noise for optimal performance. If you're not going to wake anyone up in the process, I recommend doing that as well. If you think this doesn't work, then prove it yourself by trying it the next time you wake up.

Breathing in a quick motion and doing fast bodily movements is scientifically proven to start your engine. It gets your metabolism in gear, triggers your muscles and ignites the cycle of 'energy creating energy'. The only to way to actually produce more energy in your system is to kick start it with energy. If you're being slack, you will feel the lack of energy, so it's self-evident. This takes no more than thirty seconds to be awake, but three to five minutes for max performance. Go have two glasses of water, and read your appreciation list, which takes five minutes. This morning ritual — which doesn't take long — will shift your energy for the whole day. This is also to be done before you train, especially if you feel as if you want to give it a miss for the day. Like the old way of turning on a light bulb, it requires kinetic energy. You must turn that wheel and set it into motion first.

Ten tips to a successful fitness regime

There are some broad keys to success when getting the most out of physical training. Everyone enjoys different things, and you should really mix it up every six to eight weeks anyway to shock your body, but here are things that should be a **must** for every person.

Tip 1: Get started

Get yourself a personal trainer if you can afford one, even for half an hour a week so you can get some idea of how to train properly. Make sure they are good — references are usually the best way to find them. It's a pretty good indication when your friend calls you up puffing and says, 'Phew, they're really good'.

For now, just start being active and take immediate action. Walk, skip, run or hop, I don't care, just do something. Regardless of what you may be thinking, there are no excuses! **Most aches and pains are caused because of people's lack of action, not because of their action.**

Tip 2: Make sure you have fun

Tell your trainer not to get over excited and kill you in the first session. You will get scared off and probably find the energy to run as fast as you can home and never return. Push your body past the limit of the comfort zone, but remember that everything in life is progression.

Tip 3: Music

This is great when training. If classical music usually puts you to sleep than I would advise not to listen to it when training. Listen to something upbeat or that pumps you up.

Tip 4: HIIT

This stands for High Intensity Interval Training. Without getting too technical, this is proven to be the best form of fat burning. An example is running for one minute then power walking for five minutes and repeat for thirty to sixty minutes depending on your fitness.

Tip 5: Tabata training

This form of HIIT is quick, constantly increased in duration and intensity, and produces absolutely amazing results. Most Tabata exercises can even be done at home, so there is no excuse for not doing them. The basis of Tabata training is four minutes of intense interval training/circuit training.

Here is an example:

Get two fairly heavy dumbbells, and something to step up on.

Step up while lifting the dumbbells above your head in one motion. Step down while lowering the dumbbells to your side.

Repeat for twenty seconds, then rest for ten seconds.

Repeat seven more times for a total of eight sets.

So what you have is a total of four minutes of workout time.

Tabata training can be done with a number of different exercises and the idea is to use an exercise that gets the whole body involved, or at least the major muscle groups. Tabata training can be done with barbells, dumbbells, kettle bells or just bodyweight exercises. It would be a little difficult for me to try to explain exactly the different types of Tabata workouts, so I advise going on YouTube or browse the Internet and you will find plenty of visual examples.

Tabata training was developed by Izumi Tabata at the National Institute of Fitness and Sports in Tokyo, Japan. The institute did a study over a six-week period comparing the effects of moderate intensity endurance (aerobics) and high endurance intermittent training (Tabata training intervals) on VO2 max and anaerobic capacity.

To cut to the results of the study: the moderate intensity group training program produced a significant increase in VO2 max of about ten per cent, but had no effect on anaerobic capacity. The high intensity group improved their VO2 max by about fourteen per cent while anaerobic capacity improved by twenty-eight per cent.

Tip 6: Mind on your muscle

If you focus your mind on the particular muscle you are training during the exercise, it is triggered far more effectively, and hence enhances strength. Example: Focusing on your chest muscles when doing bench presses.

Tip 7: Think big

Training time is great to think over your success. In your mind, reenforce empowering statements. During my jog or power walk, I would repeat the words 'I am strong' in my mind the whole way through. When my mind would wander, I would redirect and focus back on that statement.

Tip 8: Straight back

Don't ever sacrifice great posture for heavier weights when lifting of any sort. As soon as you lose your good posture, you lose technique. This means you are not doing the exercise correctly and it increases the chance of injury. This also stands for walking and running. Shoulders should be retracted and chin should be parallel with the ground.

Tip 9: Vision

Set up a compelling vision and don't lose sight of it. See that body, feel being healthy and fit, and consume yourself with its presence right now. Visualise everyday and experience the emotions of its success and it will motivate you like mad. Embrace it as a reality, get excited, and go and get it. Nothing is stopping you but you!

Tip 10: Step it up

When you start feeling too comfortable with the exercises you are doing, push yourself once again. A term that is widely used in the fitness industry for this point is usually a *plateau stage*. It is said that this is a time where people feel as if they are standing still and not reaching new levels. In my experience with clients, this usually happens after eight weeks of repeating the same program. It's essential that we keep the same program for at least six weeks, and then mix it up. This keeps it fun and makes us hit new peaks. When you feel that your program is starting to get a little easy, step up the intensity.

Always combine weight training and cardio exercises in your program, and exercise at least three days a week to start off with. Drink plenty of water and less caffeine (none is ideal). You need to stay hydrated during the day.

Something that is also very beneficial for the function of our body is to get an alkaline enhancer from a health shop. I recommend a product that contains spirulina, chlorella and barley grass, which should also be 100 per cent vegetarian. It usually comes in a powder that you mix with water. Himalayan salt crystal mixed with water works the same way. If you own an aquarium you will know that if you do not get the pH level correct in the water, the fish will die. Well, just a reminder that your body is also made up of water, which also requires you to gain a balanced pH level. This is a process where the acidity and alkalinity in your body reaches 7.35. You can tell what you are currently at by getting a simple mouth swipe from your local pharmacy. Too much acid in your body means your health will suffer, so start balancing.

Task

What beliefs would you have to build about exercise and your diet to live a healthy life?

Why do you want to be healthy and fit?

What does your health mean to you? What is it worth?

Focus on how much you are benefiting from doing this. Never think of the sacrifices, because there are no sacrifices when it comes to getting your health in check, only benefits.

20

MIND AND BODY

'An active mind cannot exist in an inactive body.'
General George S Patton

'My arm's too sore, I'm not feeling well, and my fingernail broke' are only a few of many excuses I've heard in the face of doing something proactive towards people's lives. Nearly everyone has a physical ache of some sort, yet it's those who stop dwelling on it that get the best results.

So many go about complaining about being sick or ill that I've come to the conclusion that occasionally they bring these things upon themselves. The more you surround yourself with illness, the sicker you become. It is estimated that over eighty per cent of all doctors' appointments are made in relation to stress caused illnesses.

I suffer from acute pain, as my ulna no longer joins to my wrist. I broke my arm in three places when I was twenty-one. I wanted to do a personal training course to further my knowledge about living a healthy and fit lifestyle. The specialist told me that I would need to have an operation after the plaster came off because it wasn't healing correctly. The bones were not joining and were way off line. On the previous X-ray, one bone was crossing over the other as it was broken in three places and hadn't healed in twelve long weeks.

The whole time the plaster was on I was certain that my arm would heal in time for me to do the course. No matter what the doctors said, I knew it was going to work out and remained mentally strong. I would visualise being in the course and being healed. The day I went to see the doctor for the final analysis I told him I wanted another X-ray. He looked at me like I was a madman for thinking it would change that much in two weeks and said there was no point. I told him if he wasn't going to give me one, I would go down and get one myself, so he finally agreed. He came back with the results and said, 'I don't know who you believe in, but keep it up'. The arm had straightened and was healed enough not to need an operation.

> 'At every moment, our bodies are continually responding to the messages of our minds.'
> *Unknown*

I once read a story about a young boy who had a chronic illness and didn't have much time to live, according to doctors. His condition was deteriorating at a rapid rate and his mother had noticed that the nurses were using words and body language that would shift his happy mood into a dull one. She decided to secretly go and speak to them. Her request was that every time they went into the room, they should tell him how great he looked, and that he seemed to be making progress. Day by day this boy's condition started to improve due to his new belief. His vitality improved, and his attitude shifted completely. Before long, they were telling him he was really getting better, and he eventually walked out of there. This is only one of thousands of stories I have read and heard about the power of the mind. We are able to prevent and even heal sickness.

Another case I heard was in an interview with Dr Wayne Dyer. He was telling a story about a friend of spiritual giant, Deepak Chopra. Dr Chopra's friend went to get a check-up, only to discover through an X-ray that he had a tumour on his lung. The doctors told him to prepare because he didn't have long before the cancer would take over his body and end his life. It was only a little black spot at the time, but sure enough it spread and he passed away.

After cleaning out his room, family members found an X-ray from fifteen years earlier and decided to check it out. They found that exact same black spot, although because he didn't even know it was there that whole time, he lived a great life. As soon as he found out and was surrounded by everyone else's grief and his own stress, his health declined rapidly.

It is very important that if you know someone who is sick, or maybe even yourself, be aware that the mind is extremely powerful in changing your physiology. Create a happy environment and do not, under any circumstance, make them feel worse than they already might. Don't treat them like little children, speak to them in a depressed tone of voice, or show up with a sad look on your face. They are going to still think you care, but compounding their sickness won't help. Giving off those vibes is in fact selfish and not helping them in any way. Showing your true love would be to make them laugh, tell them how good they are looking, and convince everyone around to do the same. Make the conversations about life, rather than death, and even if they don't live longer, their time remaining will be a lot more enjoyable.

I have come across many sceptics in my life that say 'nothing can be done, once you're sick, you're sick'. Now that's obviously a belief system created by an experience. You must ask questions though:

What was that person like during that experience? How were they before? What was their attitude like? Did they see it as the end? Did they get angry because they felt like the victim?

I can see it's hard to look for another avenue at times, but we must search deeper. My answer is always, 'Okay, so you say there is no other way? Well, has someone in history ever healed themselves before?' The answer is obviously yes, which they soon admit. So then I say, 'Well if someone has done it, there's a way, isn't there?' **If someone else has done it, there's a way!**

Have you ever had an experience where some part of your body is hurting but the pain seems to disappear when you are surrounded by something that makes you laugh? Yet as soon as you become conscious of it again, it starts hurting like mad. That means that of a lot pain and illnesses truly stem from the mind and the attitude we bring to life. I'm sure there are times when you get sick unexpectedly but the way you handle it is up to you.

In my opinion, all healing comes from within and true faith, as well as the combination of contemporary science. Most medication in the world today has been tested against a placebo effect. In medical research, placebos depend on the use of controlled and measured deception. Common placebos are inert tablets, sham surgery and other procedures based on false information. In one common placebo procedure, a patient is given a fake pill, told that it may improve his/her condition, but not told that it is in fact a dud. Such an intervention may cause the patient to **believe** the treatment will change his/her condition, and this belief may produce a subjective perception of a therapeutic effect, causing the patient to feel their condition has improved. A normal study would consist of two groups being tested. Both groups with the same health issue will be told that the pill they are taking is for that particular diagnosis. One group however is given a placebo (blank). Amazingly, most studies have resulted in exactly the same results in both groups. Even more surprisingly, in some cases the placebo effect has had a greater impact on patients. Makes you think, doesn't it?

Neglecting the power of the mind in time of physical challenges is the biggest mistake one can make.

Losing weight versus healthy and fit

If your mind is set on the idea of 'losing weight', it has a negative notion around it and builds a constant fear. As long as you think of wanting to lose weight, that's all you will ever want to keep doing. We are inundated with marketing campaigns that shove such an ideal right in our face. We all know that fear is the number one seller, and what better way to instil it than on appearance.

In the instance of having a 'losing weight' mindset, we surround ourselves with the words 'lose, lose, and lose'. We get into the belief of losing and never seem to be winning, which is why most are never satisfied. The obsession with losing weight becomes a never-ending story.

The majority of 'desirable' people shown in magazines are malnourished, airbrushed or take extreme health risks in the hope of getting work. Having been in the clothing industry, personal training, and now coaching has given me a fair insight into models and other media-related personnel. I have met extraordinarily good-looking people and high profile models throughout my life, yet some of them have the biggest insecurities with the way they look. Believe it or not, some are also the unhappiest and most unfulfilled individuals I have ever met. Don't get me wrong, looking good is great; however **you will never think you look good unless you feel great about your choice of lifestyle**. You go from being happy one day to being upset because you want to lose a little more weight off your right butt cheek, or your right arm is smaller than your other, and this craziness continues on forever. In so many cases it consumes someone's whole life to the point where they forget how to live!

Full focus on feeling (FFF) is the key to success in any aspect. We have to shift our mindset to being healthy and fit. It's about the feeling, not the visual appearance to others. Everyone has different opinions, so you are going to be pretty unsatisfied if you are just doing it for that reason. When you start getting a little wrinkly or your body doesn't seem to keep in shape as well as when you were younger, are you going to hate yourself? That's why this world is filled with appearance challenges, because we believe that feeling great starts with outward appearance. Your body should be loved for the highly technical machine it is. It deserves respect for housing the only thing that is ever permanent: your soul. When we exercise, we **must** amplify the importance of how it's making us feel, because that's what keeps us motivated. Reverse 'looking good, then feeling good' to 'feeling good, then looking good' because that's the truth in remaining happy.

The bathroom scales are something that I believe should be smashed with a baseball bat, as they should not be the measure of your success. First of all, if you are training, you will be building muscle, which weighs more than fat. The scales can definitely screw with your mind, so I suggest you get rid of them. You are not going to see results overnight if you go for looks, but you will immediately notice results when going for the feeling.

A body builder I knew had an amazing physique, but all I would hear him do was complain about his body. To him, there was always something wrong with it and his appearance soon became an obsession. It took control over every area of his life. He saw his relationship diminish, finances go down and his emotional state hit its lowest point ever.

We are all imperfect if you wish to look at it that way, but I like to see it as we are all perfect. Our imperfections make us perfect, because if we were all the same this world would be pretty boring. We all have different perceptions of what we find appealing, but the point of feeling great makes you appealing to everyone. Your glow is contagious, and you will notice when you go for the feeling, the physical shape comes rapidly along with it. I have personally trained hundreds of clients and the ones who go for the looks to make them happy never last, or are unfulfilled. Those who go for the feeling acknowledge that being healthy and fit is a lifestyle to drive them to their peak and help them attain that balance for a great life. **Losing weight is an activity that drives us mad; striving to be healthy and fit is a lifestyle that lasts forever.**

21

INTELLIGENT EATING

What you put in is what you get out

'According to the saying of an ancient philosopher, one should eat to live, and not live to eat.'

Moliere

Did you know that looking fit and feeling healthy is due to only thirty per cent working out, and seventy per cent what you eat? That means you could well be training your guts out, but if you're not eating right, you're not going to feel or look the way you expect. Through my experience of giving nutrition advice, I have found that when people came to me and said 'I don't know what to eat', it was merely an excuse to avoid responsibility. I would then make them write down what they believed was healthy to eat. Most of them wrote down great answers and listed fruits and vegetables, nuts, herbal teas, beans, and even brown rice. I would have done with just rice after seeing the daily intake by some of these people, but they proved they well and truly knew what was going on.

Of course you know, so just do it! I'm sure you are able to notice how you feel once you have devoured a meal like a glutton. When you eat junk, you feel like junk, but when you eat great, you feel great. In all honesty, how much better do you feel about yourself after eating a healthy meal? These are the feelings you must concentrate on when you take empowering action towards a better life. The reason is that it will give you incentive for next time. Also, don't forget to remind yourself of how you feel after you eat junk and what it's doing to your body, because it will surely turn you off. As we discussed earlier, it is imperative that you direct your focus and emotions intelligently. Your food is no exception.

There are all these different 'weight loss solutions' flooding the TV and stores, yet people come back to the same point. Why? The answer is simple to obtaining and maintaining a balanced life: **eat right and exercise regularly! There has never been, and never will be, another way to a healthy lifestyle**. You might lose some weight by taking other products, yet your fat cell receptors are far more prone to storing any food you put in after that. I couldn't tell you how many people have approached me complaining about putting on more weight after they have lost it rapidly. By taking certain 'weight loss' products, they have flawed their metabolism in the process. Once you continually focus on what you are doing to your life through your choice of food your willingness to comply with a healthy lifestyle will happily skyrocket. The obesity issue in western countries is absolutely ridiculous, so don't be part of the epidemic. It is not a complicated problem as most try to make out, it is simply a choice. **Food is for sufficient energy, not to pig out on**.

Here is a great guide of what a lunch and evening meal should be:

- Low in fat (no added butter/oil and lean protein sources).
- Moderate in carbohydrates (pasta/rice/noodles/bread) and protein (meat/chicken/fish/legumes/vegetarian options). Brown carbohydrates mainly.

- High in salad and green vegetables (low in kilojoules but very high in fibre).

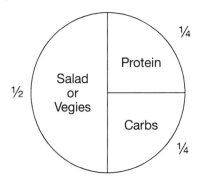

An old method of getting the portion size right is to use your hand:

Palm = protein

Fist = carbohydrates

Handful = salad or vegies (x2)

A morning meal is something that needs to be eaten as a daily ritual. The word breakfast got its name because we have been fasting overnight when we are asleep. Hence we must *break-the-fast*. This helps us to regulate appetite, and provide essential nutrients such as carbohydrates and protein to keep us full and satisfied. It will also prevent cravings later in the day for fatty foods. Cereal and oatmeal in the morning are good. Start your day with two to four glasses of water. I personally have a multivitamin tablet with them as well.

It is absolutely vital that at least most of your meal consists of greens and vegetables to balance out the acidity in your body. It is said that acid build up is directly or indirectly the cause of many diseases we face. Too much acid in the body creates depressed, stressed and sad emotions, which then produce more acid. Meats and poultry are also very acidic to the body. Many believe it is the sugar that eats away at their teeth, yet it is in fact the acid. Have you ever seen what the acid in a fizzy cola drink does to a coin if you leave it in over a few nights? Just imagine what it could be doing to your insides.

If you owned a high performance car that requires optimum fuel, you wouldn't go and put straight gas in there instead, because you know it wouldn't function. We must feed our high performance machine with the essentials it requires in order for it to function at its peak. Without debate, our body demands that we also drink at least 2.5L of water a day. You better get one of those big water bottles and drink like mad. We are also required to **eat six to eight smaller meals throughout our day, rather than three larger ones**. Eating more regularly speeds up our metabolism, which has enormous health and functionality benefits. This is also crucial when training and expending a lot of energy. I advise starting off with one medium sized meal for breakfast, lunch and dinner, and three snack meals in between.

Carbohydrates

Carbohydrates are an ideal source of energy for the body. This is because they can be converted more readily into glucose than proteins or fats can. Glucose is the form of sugar that's transported and used by the body.

But a diet too high in carbohydrates can upset the delicate balance of your body's blood sugar level, resulting in fluctuations in energy and moods that leave you feeling irritated and tired. It is better to balance your intake of carbohydrates with protein, a little good fat and fibre.

There are two types of carbohydrate: complex and simple.

Complex carbohydrates

Complex carbohydrates are often referred to as starch or starchy foods. They are found naturally in foods and also in processed foods.

Complex carbohydrates as natural starches are found in:

- bananas
- barley
- beans
- brown rice
- chickpeas
- lentils
- nuts
- oats
- parsnips
- potatoes
- root vegetables
- sweet corn
- wholegrain cereals
- wholemeal breads
- wholemeal cereals
- wholemeal flour
- wholemeal pasta.

Cut down or abolish the amount of refined white flour products in your diet such as white bread, pizza and white pasta and rice. The refining process produces simple carbohydrates and many vitamins and minerals are lost. Complex carbohydrates as refined starches are found in:

- biscuits, pastries and cakes
- pizzas
- sugary processed breakfast cereals
- white bread
- white flour
- white pasta
- white rice.

Simple carbohydrates

Simple carbohydrates are also known as sugars. They also exist in either a natural or refined form. Natural sugars are found in fruit and vegetables.

Refined sugars are found in:

- biscuits, cakes and pastries
- chocolate
- honey and jams
- jellies
- brown and white cane sugar
- pizzas
- prepared foods and sauces
- soft drinks
- sweets and snack bars.

Complex vs simple carbohydrates

Carbohydrates come in many forms. Complex carbohydrates are generally known as better quality carbohydrates, as they contain other key nutrients like fibre and B vitamins and are very satisfying to eat. On the other hand, simple carbohydrates include sugary and sweet foods. Although they are still classified as carbohydrates because they provide the body with energy, simple carbohydrates rarely provide any other nutrients of benefit to our health, so this is why we should limit their consumption in our diet.

Carbohydrates can also be classified according to the glycemic index (GI): high GI (generally simple carbs) and low GI (mostly high fibre and complex carbohydrates). All carbohydrates form glucose when digested. Glucose is transported around the body via blood and taken into cells to be converted into energy. The pancreas gland in your abdomen secretes the hormone insulin, which controls the uptake of glucose by your cells. If you have any excess glucose, this is converted into glycogen, which is stored in the liver or in fat around the body.

When your body needs more energy, the pancreas secretes a second hormone called glucagon. This converts the glycogen back into glucose, which is then released into your bloodstream for your cells to use. This means the body's glucose (sugar) metabolism is a cycle of glucose, insulin and glucagon reactions. The slower the release of glucose and hormones, the more stable and sustainable the energy levels of the body. The more refined the carbohydrate, the faster the glucose is released into your blood. This can cause peaks and drops in your blood sugar level, and less stable energy levels in the body. Complex carbohydrates provide a slower and more sustained release of energy than simple carbohydrates. In their natural form they contribute to long-term good health, appetite control and sustained energy levels.

Key points

- Carbohydrates are our body's preferred energy source.
- Without adequate carbohydrates in our diet, we can feel tired, lethargic and lack energy.
- Carbohydrates can be simple or complex; complex are best for managing hunger and providing other essential nutrients.
- Eat carbohydrates regularly, at each meal and snack during the day for optimum energy.

Carbohydrates are our body's preferred energy source, meaning that we can most easily convert the energy in carbohydrates into energy that we use each day. Carbohydrates provide 18kj/gram of energy. Our muscles, heart, brain and organs use the energy from carbohydrates to function efficiently. Without adequate carbohydrates in our diet, we can feel tired, lethargic and lacking in energy. One reason for this is that aside from energy, carbohydrates contain B group vitamins, which are essential as enzymes in chemical reactions. Similarly, carbohydrates provide the energy for our muscles and brain to function at their peak.

It is important to eat carbohydrates regularly during the day to ensure consistent energy. Inadequate carbohydrate intake can also lead to sweet cravings. You may be familiar with an afternoon sugar craving? This can often be the result of the body being low in energy from carbohydrate, and the quickest way to boost up the glucose levels is to eat sweet food. However, before you reach for the chocolate bar, complex carbohydrates will soon provide the same energy boost in a slightly longer time frame, but minus the added kilojoules from lots of sugar and fat. So think about the quality of your snack when you feel like an energy boost. Remember that carbohydrates also give you the energy you need for your workout, so be sure to include these in your pre-workout snack.

The easiest way to ensure adequate energy each day is to eat meals that contain some carbs, for example cereal at breakfast, bread for lunch, and some pasta or rice with dinner. Snack on fruit, dry biscuits, yoghurt or rice biscuits. Like all food, it's important not to overeat carbohydrates but make sure that they form part of a well balanced meal that also includes some protein, and lots of salad, vegetables or fruit.

Protein

Protein is the building block of all life and is essential for the growth of cells and tissue repair. All proteins are made up of different combinations of twenty compounds called amino acids. Depending on which amino acids link together, protein molecules form enzymes, hormones, muscles, organs and many other tissues in the body.

There are two types of amino acids:

- **Non-essential amino acids** can be made by the body.
- **Essential amino acids** cannot be made by the body and must be got from food. There are nine essential amino acids.

Animal protein

Animal proteins contain all the essential amino acids. This type of protein is found in:

- meat
- poultry
- fish
- eggs
- dairy products.

Oily fish (salmon, sardines, trout, tuna) is a good source of protein. It has the added advantage of being high in types of fatty acids that provide protection against heart disease and to some extent stroke.

Oily fish contains up to eight times as much omega-3 and omega-6 fatty acids as lean fish (cod, haddock, skate).

Plant protein

Plant protein contains many amino acids, but no single source contains all of the essential amino acids. This type of protein is found in:

- legumes (peas, green beans)
- cereals
- beans
- pulses
- grains
- nuts
- seeds

- soya products
- vegetable protein foods such as Quorn or veggie mince.

You need to combine different plant proteins to make up the complete range of amino acids needed by your body. In practice this is achieved without any special effort, for example by eating baked beans with bread (toast) or using milk on cereal. **Aim to eat more plant protein than animal protein**.

Amount of protein in foods

Nutrition labels list protein content. Here are some examples:

- One skinless chicken breast (130g): 41g protein.
- One small fillet steak (200g): 52g protein.
- One beef burger or pork sausage: 8g protein.
- One portion of poached skinless cod fillet (150g): 32g protein.
- Half a can of tuna: 19g protein.
- One portion of cheese (50g): 12g protein.
- One medium egg: 6g protein.
- 150ml glass of milk: 5g protein.
- One tablespoon of boiled red lentils (40g): 3g protein.
- One portion of tofu (125g): 15g protein.
- One medium slice wholemeal bread: 4g protein.
- One medium slice white bread: 3g protein.

We should aim to have 90g of protein for men and 70g of protein for women daily. If you are training hard, then this could be increased. You might have to check with a nutritionist or a doctor beforehand just to get the all clear.

Healthy protein tips

- If you decide to eat meat, include fish in your diet at least twice a week.
- Snack on seeds and unsalted nuts. Try sunflower, pumpkin or sesame seeds and brazils, cashews, walnuts, hazelnuts or water soaked almonds.
- Look at using pulses as an alternative source of protein. They include chickpeas, a wide range of lentils, split peas and a vast range of beans from the black-eyed to the broad, butter and kidney beans.
- Have at least one to two vegetarian days each week.

If you are a meat eater take these precautions:

- Use lean cuts of meat and poultry.
- Trim off any fat, e.g. the skin on chicken breasts and the rind on bacon.
- Choose smaller portions.
- Reduce the frequency of meat-based meals.
- Pay particular attention to how you cook meat.

Fats and cholesterol

Fat in our diet is essential for our health but which type we consume is important. Fat provides more kilojoules per gram than protein and carbohydrates so it means we must minimise its consumption. To be exact, it provides 38kJ/gram, unlike protein, which is 17kJ and carbs at 18kJ.

There are four kinds of fats:

Saturated fats are solid at room temperature and include animal fats such as the fat found on meat, in chicken skin, and butter.

Other foods that may contain significant amounts of saturated fat include takeaway foods, snack foods like biscuits and cakes, sausages, salami, and cream. Eating greater amounts of saturated fats is associated with an **increase** in heart disease risk.

Polyunsaturated fats are more commonly known as omega-6 and omega-3 fats. Omega-6 polyunsaturated fats are found in the oils of sunflowers, soybeans, and grape seeds, as well as nuts and seeds. Omega-3s are also polyunsaturated fats and are known as 'fish oils' as they are found only in deep-sea fish. Polyunsaturated fats are known to **decrease** heart disease risk when they replace saturated fats in the diet.

Mono-saturated fats are found in canola and olive oils, some margarines, nuts, seeds, avocadoes and olives. Mono-saturated fats have been found to **decrease** levels of bad cholesterol when they replace saturated fats in the diet.

Trans fats are the newest addition of dietary fats and are found in some oils, margarines and processed foods. Trans fats can **increase** heart disease risk, like saturated fats.

Cholesterol is a type of fat in the blood. It has many important functions in the body such as hormone development and cell structure; however having high levels of cholesterol in the blood increases the risk of developing heart disease.

A number of factors may increase the tendency to develop high blood cholesterol levels. These include eating foods high in saturated fats, having a family history of high cholesterol, and being overweight. People with high cholesterol in the blood may be able to reduce it by limiting foods with a high amount of saturated fats, eating some unsaturated fats, eating more fruit and vegetables, and grainy breads and cereals (a high-fibre diet can assist with reducing cholesterol).

When you make a promise to yourself, you must keep it. Usually the promises we make to ourselves are the ones that will really fill the gap between where we are, and where we want to be.

6TH STEP

AWAKEN YOUR MIND, UNCHAIN YOUR HEART

22

THE INFINITE HUMAN SPIRIT

*There's more to you than meets the eye; it's your soul. I can't see it,
neither can you, but we can feel it.*

Your greatness lies in the spirit that waits patiently within your
being. If you are yet to tap into it or listen carefully to what it tells
you in the face of decisions, then that's the reason your dreams
seem so far from ever coming into existence.

I've had many people tell me they don't know if they have a soul,
and others who think they might, but have no real grounds for
their belief. I would just like to sum it up the best way I can.
We see our human body like a machine. The brain thinks and
visualises through chemical responses, the heart pumps blood
and our lungs help us breathe. Looking at it from the outside it
appears very technical, scientific and easy to explain our physical
existence. However, have you ever wondered who is observing the
surroundings you see with your eyes? **Who is controlling your
machine (body)?** Who's aware that you're thinking? Look around
the room, and think about who is actually directing that focus?
We cannot just get up off the chair and walk automatically; we are
obviously being commanded by something. Who calculates what
you are going to say before you say it? Most would answer these
questions with 'I am' with a bit of confusion, and that's exactly
right. 'Me' is only your physical existence; however 'I' is your spirit

that is in control. We can't see it, but we can feel it everyday, and it's the voice we are in constant conversation with. I guess that's why when our soul passes on from this earth we are no longer able to control our body.

'Man struggles to find life outside himself, unaware that the life he is seeking is within him.'
Kahlil Gibran

Once you let that conscious voice take over your life, that deep wisdom that is quite aware and knows what's right for you, then you will discover your greatness. It's that invisible force that lies deep within you, the person you know you really are. It is the person that most of us never let other people see. We become too caught up with reacting to our environment or fulfilling what we believe other people expect. One of the most popular quotes in history was when Jesus Christ states 'I AM who I AM', meaning the complete full spirit of God. A great spirit lies within all of us and that's why many men and women have defied the odds throughout history. Every single person has a great calling and purpose in life that no one else is called to do. We are all designed to fill our spot that no one else can fill. When every person realises that, then they live the life of their dreams, but more importantly the world will truly be united. As long as those spots continue to be ignored, it leaves big holes, which I guess is the reason so many fall through the cracks.

The human spirit is so fascinating and infinite that it overcomes what many in society would regard as 'impossible'. We have seen it throughout history. One man can change the course of the whole world and implement a revolution; we can survive under the most horrific situations, or create what would have once been perceived as unbelievable.

I find inspiration in men who have the courage to walk the path of truth. One man in particular is Nelson Mandela — a great example that man's will is far greater than all the odds put against him. He created a passion so strong that he was able to successfully rally for peace and equal rights, which was a major part of the fall of Apartheid in South Africa. Mandela grew up in a small village with hardly any of the resources we have today, and was repressed by white supremacists. Because of his vision to help his people he was jailed for twenty-seven years in total. Now how many of us would have given up on our dream after six months, one year, and we don't have half the challenges such a man does? His greatest pleasure and most private moment is watching the sun set with the music of Handel or Tchaikovsky playing. That was denied him in prison and he noted that simple moment in life was one thing he missed the most.

Three years after being released from jail, Mandela was elected president of South Africa. This is one story of many about how human spirit is used to utmost glory. We seem to forget that we are human and have that same spirit within us. When one has a compelling vision, determination to overcome any obstacles, but most importantly the passion for life, the possibilities are endless.

'There is no passion to be found playing small — in settling for a life that is less than the one you are capable of living.'
Nelson Mandela

23

A SPIRITUAL JOURNEY THROUGH THAILAND

'If we are facing in the right direction, all we have to do is keep on walking.'
Buddhist Proverb

As I was beginning to write this book, I had been thinking about going to Asia to talk to a Buddhist monk. I knew I had found an inner peace here in the west, but was always interested in how at peace they were. I wanted to get away from the west to do it, because I wanted to see if someone from the east with a completely different religious and cultural background, social status, and environment, could have similarities to what I had found within myself. I declared that before I finished my book I would go and feature that part in it. I remember discussing this topic with my mother. I had no money or job at the time, but I knew it was going to happen. I wasn't really concerned with how or when; I just knew I was going to make it happen before I finished the book.

About three weeks later while writing by the beach, I received a text message from one of my friends. Katie, who is in the travel industry, and whom I hadn't known for long, told me that work was sending her to Bangkok, Thailand. She was going to inspect hotels over there, and asked if I would like to go. It was for one week and everything was paid for. I instantly got goosebumps all over my body. I asked her why she offered to take me. Her explanation was that she felt a great energy, and even though she hadn't known me for long, felt a very friendly connection and trusted me.

A question then dawned on me: Was it that mysterious what had happened, or was there more of an explanation? A 'light bulb' moment arose once again. I knew that the only reason this happened was because of my change. If I had met Katie through my previous thoughts and actions, this opportunity would have never come up. People told me that I was lucky, but I was quick to remind them that I created it far before it had even happened. I had been there in my mind! She also had no idea that I even had the thought of going to Asia, so I decided to leave that detail out. It crossed my mind that she would think I was crazy and take back the offer.

When you act great, you get great experiences. Great experiences create extraordinary opportunities, while extraordinary opportunities create great experiences.

I thought it was now time to step it up, so off I went on the Internet to track down a monk I could meet with. Not just any monk, mind you; I wanted a master, and I knew it was going to happen no matter what. That's why this opportunity arose, to fulfil what I already knew. I emailed many people but got no reply. I didn't let it faze me, and kept on persisting. I had seen on the net that people had gone and had a quick chat with some monks while visiting the Royal Temples in Bangkok. It was now a week before the trip, and Katie had sent through the week's plan to see if I wanted to change anything. This is how it read:

Day 1: Arrive in Bangkok, dinner at PP hotel

Day 2: Shopping at MBK, lunch etc.

Day 3: Breakfast, Siam Paragon, etc.

Day 4: **Royal Temple Tour with English speaking guide**.

Bingo! Again I was overwhelmed: it sealed it one more time. This was happening to fulfil my vision. I was a co-creator in all of this, and at that moment, I remember just knowing I had found the key to life — **the ultimate power between Mind and Matter**. I got down on my knees in my bedroom, and screamed out, 'Thank you!' This all started with a strong vision, and it was beginning to play out around me.

After seeing the email, I decided to call Katie and let her know what was going on. She was pretty amazed, and told me that she would contact her connection, Panja, in Thailand to see if he could arrange a monk to meet with me.

We met with Panja for dinner the night before the tour. I had told him about my situation, and we began to get into a pretty deep discussion. Panja opened up and told me about his life. We became friends instantly. He said he was shocked to see a young guy from the west think and talk so deeply to him. He also mentioned that I didn't look like the type to embrace life in such a manner. After having laughed it off, he told me he learnt not to judge a book by its cover; how ironic.

After seeing my genuine feelings on the topic, Panja told me he would try his hardest to make the experience with the monk a great one. We also spoke about Panja's remarkable story, which he gave me permission to share. If you want to hear about persistence and someone who chased for his dream then this story is it.

One of my favourites

'A man with many riches and no inner peace, is like a man in a river,
dying of thirst.'
Yogananda

Panja grew up in a small village in the south of Thailand with
twelve siblings and his parents. Living in an area where money
didn't have a major role, they lived off the land. We in the west
would class this as poor, but to most of the people that live there,
this is a rich lifestyle that they wouldn't give up for the big city life.
As a child, Panja would catch fish with a bamboo stick so they
were able to eat. They didn't have a clock to tell the time, so every
day Panja was sent outside to watch for the one airplane that used
to fly over, because they knew it left around the same time each
day.

He told me that through it all, he believed he wasn't meant to stay
there. He wanted to go to Bangkok to study, but Panja's parents
had a misconception of city life and didn't want him to leave. He
would be the first family member to ever leave the village. With
this playing on his mind, he decided to head for the city to pursue
his dream. When he arrived he had no money, nowhere to live and
his village background had not equipped him to get a city job. So
Panja became a temple boy for four years just so he could be fed
and sheltered while he studied. His duties were to be of service
to the monks, gardening, cleaning, preparing food and doing
anything else that needed to be done. He told me that people were
compassionate towards him when he told them he was from the
south, and he would quickly assure them that his people were
happier than anyone he had met in the city. When he was unhappy

about the smallest things, he would instantly remind himself that at least he had food to eat.

After finishing studying, he got a job in the travel industry. He later became the head of World Travel Thailand and lives what he classes as a great lifestyle. When he visited his village years later, his father was worried and asked where he had been, as the last train arrived at 9a.m. and Panja hadn't shown up until 12p.m. He told his family that he had flown there and they were overwhelmed that he had been in an airplane.

Another thing about Panja's story is that as a child looking up at the plane to tell the time, he would envision himself sitting in one. His job now sends him all over the world, and most of the year he is in a plane, travelling. To top it off, he is one of the most humble gentlemen I have met. A great man that contributes to the world, acknowledges he had success far before his achievements, and is grateful for his life when he was a temple boy struggling to get by.

How we take things for granted sometimes amazes me. I think of this story when I find myself complaining about the most insignificant things. So many of us let opportunities pass by or cease to create them because we waste our life whining. A story like this really makes you want to start living the best possible life you can, doesn't it?

Another step forward

'To the mind that is still, the whole universe surrenders.'
Lao Tzu

The day of the temple tour arrived and our guide Sam greeted us. The funny thing about this situation is that Sam had just found out he was taking us for the tour the day before. He has a 'brother' in one of the temples that we were set to visit. After speaking to Panja, he had tried to organise a meeting for me with one of the most respected monks in all of Thailand who was stationed at that same temple. The monk had just returned from giving seminars overseas, and had arrived only the day before. He was an extremely busy man and getting him to have a one-on-one wasn't going to be easy. Sam continued to remind me that he was waiting for a phone call to see if it was going to go ahead. I assured him that it would, I just knew it. I was creating this, and this was the reason I was there. Ten minutes before we were to visit the last temple for the day, he got the call, so off we went.

I knew that it would work out. I had declared that I would meet a monk that was a master, and he was. Dr P Boondham, a PhD in Philosophy with multiple other Masters awards to his name. As well, he is the teacher to all other monks. He is on TV, radio, and travels the world, including to the USA, to give seminars about the power of the mind and inner peace. The doctor also has his signature quotes printed on key rings. He represents Thailand at a number of world peace summits and is well known by country leaders. He told me he had met the prime minister of my birth country, Australia, only a few weeks earlier. Above all, I wanted the meeting to be in private, with no one else around.

After being told that he was a busy man and would only have about half an hour, I tried my hardest to think through what I was going to say to him, as I knew I needed longer. I decided to walk in with all restrictions aside. We ended up speaking for over two hours, and he invited me back two days later. We spoke for another few hours, exchanged gifts, contact details and became 'brothers'.

In my explanation of the meetings I have preserved exactly what was said. Dr Boondham has broken English, but I am transposing straight from the text I wrote in the original exercise book so I don't mix up the genuine meaning of his message.

Master of the mind — day 1

'Minds are like parachutes. They only function when they are open.'
Sir James Dewar

When I walked into the temple, excited but a little nervous, I was greeted by a frail older man whose presence blew me away. I was told to sit down in front of him. Another humble monk came in to give us both some water, and we continued. Just being in his presence I could feel his calm nature and inner peace. I couldn't help but be rapt by every word he uttered, as his demeanour was nothing like I had ever come across in the west.

First we went through some basic ritual explanation of Buddhism, with the lighting of candles, incense and so forth. At no time was he trying to convert me to his religion or sell it to me; he spoke from the heart about all mankind, which gained my full respect.

The words were subtle yet every one powerful and full of meaning.

Here is some of my unedited transcript of his words that I would like to share:

A person should not believe blindly. No superstition.

You should be able to properly reason with your belief.

True happiness only comes from within.

If you do not train your mind, it becomes weak.

The correct way is the way for everyone, peace and love. This is the only way you will find happiness.

Next was Eight-fold Path:

Right understanding

Right thought

Right action

Right speech

Right effort

Right livelihood

Right mindfulness

Right concentration.

Right understanding

Understand the things happening correctly, not just how they appear in an instant.

Maintain right understanding at all times.

If you love yourself, you love others because you understand more.

We are human beings, we are feeling the same. Right understanding creates you to act correctly.

Right thinking

When you think, you have to think correctly. Not out of hate, but love, no matter which situation, to stay strong.

Right action

Physical

Help only in truth, good intent, act correctly.

Verbal

Talk the truth, not lies and deceit. Talk properly, no cursing to others or yourself.

Mental

Purified mental state.

Mind is controlled by the anger, ill passion (greed, envy, resentment), and ill power. Must eliminate these.

Man becomes slave to materialism. The mind of man is not free this way.

Liberated by only controlling the mind, meditate, make strong.

Right effort

Maintain legally, morally for money, the right way.

Right livelihood

When you maintain family life, you must do it correctly, rightly. Not against the law of rules and regulation of society. No breaking the law. Not breaking the law of that good society.

Right mindfulness

Must maintain and train the mind.

Control the mind with mindfulness, wisdom. When you're feeling trouble, you try to maintain mindfulness.

Focus the mind.

Concentration of the mind. Mind should always be strong, feeling normally.

Mindfulness and wisdom, strength should be maintained.

Right concentration

When your mind is not happy, your mind is in trouble. You should concentrate by maintaining meditation.

Follow Anapanasatie — breathing in and out through nose, sit to control the mind. Concentrate on breathing and thinking of only that.

I just want to highlight the end notes he told me for day 1:

We are feeling only from the matter of the mind. Nothing externally.

Mind is the master of body, mind is the master of action, mind is the master of life.

Man gives in to lies — ill passion, greed, anger, hate, sadness. Try to destroy these things.

At the end of our talk we exchanged contact details, and I was glad to hear that Dr Boondham was interested in having another chat a few days later.

Master of the mind — day 2

Being self-aware is not the absence of mistakes, but the ability to learn and correct them.

When I arrived in the temple at about 1:30p.m. I was nodded and smiled at by all the monks that had seen me there the few days before. I'm not sure what Dr Boondham had told them, yet they all seemed so friendly, and it was quite breathtaking. To have these humble men get me water and sit me down, it was totally different to anything I had experienced. I felt so much tranquillity, peace and love in the temple garden; the energy was quite astonishing. It was 40°C on the day so it was scorching hot, yet the humility I was surrounded with made me forget the temperature. A monk took me into the temple where the doctor was sitting in the same spot. He was underneath the shrine with his legs crossed, and wearing an orange robe. As I sat down, he got off his thin cushion and came right up in front of me, sat on the hard surface as I was, and began speaking.

Giving correctly

If a man comes up and asks you for fish to eat, do not just give the fish. If you do this, the man will continue to come back for more, again and again. When you give the fish, you must teach him how to catch the fish, so he can depend on himself, learn, catch many fish, and teach others.

Lead by example

A learned man may teach and write many books, but never put into action. Do not be this man who just lives a life of 'serving spoon'. Spoon serves apple, spoon serves banana, spoon serves orange, but the spoon never tastes the fruits of life. The life of man should not be serving spoon.

We get the knowledge, a concept, then must bring it to action.

A man knows a lot of things but never put into positive action.

Learning by doing.

Some things are not easy to understand, you have the right to criticise to get the truth. Believe the things which are wisdom.

Man's action by right or wrong, depends on the action of man.

When a man acts wrongly they don't ever fully accept inwardly what they have done, unless spiritually liberated.

Happiness

Momentary happiness — eating something nice, sit on a comfortable chair.

Access happiness — buy a new watch, nice clothes, good car, family member make you happy.

Attained happiness — from within, awakened, must be concentrated. This is true happiness.

- *Materialistic convenience is not real happiness*

- *We must get the mind right, clean and purified. The less angry someone is, less greed and ill passion. We must always control our passion with thoughts and action, don't let passion control you.*

- *When you lose something, illusion starts to take over, and you begin to worry.*

- *We never came with a watch, and we don't take it when we die. We do not need the watch, so it can never make us fully happy and should never make us sad.*

Everyone needs peace, in and out. External peace is easy, new car can make you feel happy only temporarily. This is easy to duplicate. Inner peace is hard to attain. Only with mind fullness can you sustain happiness

We must all get mind fullness first, which is training mental strength in all situations and use our wisdom as guide. Someone who gives into anger has no mind fullness, no strength.

Dr Boondham then went on to explain how youth in south Thailand are taught a moral subject at school. After monitoring them, he said it has had a fundamental impact on their growth and learning. It was quite surprising that he brought this up, as this has been one of my visions to implement in the west for a long time. We began speaking about youth and other daily affairs such as news and the amount of negative energy that is being portrayed on a daily basis only to generate fear in people. This is all contributing to the destruction of people and this world.

It came up that parents, older siblings, and many others teach youth about their belief systems, yet it is quite evident that they don't even help themselves. Will people listen, especially kids, when you say one thing yet they see you act in a contradictory manner? They will do as you do, not as you say. Teaching peace for humanity is the approach the world is taking.

Until recent times, it was thought that war was a way of gaining prosperity for a nation. Now, it is undeniably true that peace is the only way for everyone to prosper. We have even managed to come together as one world and create the Global Peace Index (GPI). GPI is used to monitor how peaceful each country is. It shows that the more peaceful the country, the more productive it is. With this information, strategists have discovered that peace and prosperity go together. The world is now focused on bringing peace, because once that is achieved we can focus more intelligently on bigger issues. Curing disease, maintaining nature's essence so that we can live in better conditions, harvesting crops so more people can eat, regulating the world's temperature, and advancing in technology needs far more energy than wasting it on a ridiculous war created by egotistical men and women. We all play a major part in bringing peace to this earth and setting up an environment that is worth our children living in.

I went back to the hotel that night after spending the day with Dr Boondham and I was staring out the window. I was looking over the lit up city of Bangkok and had a feeling of absolute comfort. I sat there and really embraced what had just happened, and the questions that were answered on this day. They would definitely affect my life forever. I found what I was looking for, and that's the same love that dwells within all mankind. It doesn't matter where you are in the world, what your religious background, or any other social limitation, the truth remains the same for all. We are all human beings, and have the same feelings and emotions.

I found it amazing that someone from the east, a Buddhist monk probably triple my age, had the same feelings as a young man from the west. I have had completely different experiences throughout my life, I come from a different religious background and social tag, yet the human love was so strong that we created a bond and mutual respect. When you open your eyes and let your ego fall asleep, you discover the connection that makes us all one, and the power that could turn this world forever. I always used to think, 'what can one man do?' Yet I now realise that this was affecting my own life in the process. Imagine if everyone had that thought — the world would be finished.

I guess I was just looking on the outside to try and comfort the inner. I finally noticed that the opposite way around really opens the door to life.

24

IT'S NOT JUST YOUR LIFE

Life starts with you, anywhere, anytime

*Living in someone else's dream is like being a bird with clipped wings.
It looks up to witness freedom, but can only tiredly walk around and
attempt to fly. To its anguish, it is picked up by its owner and placed
back in its cage. Live YOUR life!*

There is this notion that we have to hit 'rock bottom' to ever see the other side of our life. Maybe this is true to an extent, but only because we keep on believing it is. In feeding such an idea, does it mean that someone who doesn't think they have been as low as others cannot progress and be awakened to their greatness? I hear it all the time, and that's why I had to add this part in.

This one guy said, 'I haven't been through half the stuff you have; maybe if I do I will realise it then'. He is only one of many, and I couldn't think of anything further from the truth. Some people will even reassure me that I must have been through a lot of 'life experience' to obtain the knowledge I teach. Who hasn't, though? I just decide to probe my experience until I am inundated with answers that I can grow from.

It's sad that some of us have to wait to hit that 'low point' in order for us to wake up. We have all had our individual experiences, and I'm sure there have been times in your life where you have felt lost and confused. It may be that way now. The reason I know it's not a must to hit 'rock bottom' is because one of my best friends discovered his greatness and he said his life was pretty enjoyable before he decided to go deeper.

Yes, it rocked him a bit when he would ask questions and certain beliefs would be tested, but it helped him grow. He would text me at 3a.m. sometimes because he questioned himself so deeply that he needed a second opinion on the answer. I always replied with, **'If it seems that it can enhance your life, regardless of how much it tests your old belief, if it is reasonable, makes proper sense to you, helps you to display a more loving nature to everyone and everything, then yes, go for it'.**

Just by opening up his mind, letting down limitations and gathering knowledge from other sources he was able to find his truth. As we have discovered, 'rock bottom' is only a perception, so I choose to see it is a POA (point of awareness).

Everyone has wants, and the only way they are accessible is if the changes start with the individual. To be awakened to your power within is a personal choice. Even when faced with really difficult challenges through life experience, it is up to you to grow in those times. That's why when people tell me about their 'problems', I reply with, 'Problem or choice?' Think about it: are they really problems, or do we have a vast array of choices to make in those times? The word 'problem' is far too restrictive. We are always faced with numerous options to direct our focus. Next time you say 'I have a problem' change it to 'I have a choice', and see how different you feel.

That kid!

'I've learned that people will forget what you said, people will forget what you did, but people will never forget how you made them feel.'
Maya Angelou

One unexpected event can really shake you, although at the same time, remind you that you are just as equally on the right path. When you start to feel more love on the inside and that starts to project outwardly, the truth of who you really are begins to display itself. We are tested, but not in a way that sets us up to feel failure, but instead to the point of recognition and growth. Your views become stronger, they advance, and certain things start to cement that. One of those situations took place on a rainy night only to help shape my destiny once again.

The supermarket became a place for yet another awakening. As I was entering I saw a child no older than ten. He was alone at 11p.m. and smoking a cigarette. It was evident that he was limited by social beliefs, and had no real sense of direction even at such a young age. I noticed about four people walk past him, and ignore a conversation that he tried to start. He was very polite in his approach, but no one seemed to take notice of him, or they were just too busy feeding their egos.

I believe we can learn a lot from children. As we grow older, we like to believe we are getting wiser. I have found with children that when they burn their hand on something hot, they know never to touch it again. How often do we adults get burnt, yet continue to act in the same way, and get the same results? I think we can all take a page out of a child's book in this instance.

As I was leaving, the boy asked me if I played soccer. I replied that I didn't but played other sports. I had a strong urge to talk to him. I wanted to explain that love is within him always, and that he had an important role in the world, that he was special, and no matter what anyone believed of him, all he had to do was believe in himself and he could do anything. All these thoughts were flowing through me, but I got in my car and drove off. As I was driving, the thoughts became stronger and the feeling was overwhelming. I turned my car around and went back to look for him. He was gone.

The instant feeling of neglect I felt towards this child put me in such a state that I had to hold back the tears. The powerful message this event taught me was that that kid might never hear that again. My simple words may have had the power to ultimately change his life forever. Just through that short message, who knows where he might have ended up?

I'm sure those other people had a preconception of where that would be and so they ignored him. Instead of showing him that he was a human being they contributed to another possibly sad story. I realised that boy could turn to drugs next, having no guidance, and by a few words could have been saved. That's the power of it.

'Courage is what it takes to stand up and speak; courage is also what it takes to sit down and listen.'
Winston Churchill

I was disappointed until I realised the change that I am able to make. I gathered a great purpose and empowering direction. I'm not going to let these limitations hold me back. When I feel the urge to help, it's the world telling me to step up to the plate. It's an opportunity to allow us to see who we really are, and the only way to gain fulfilment. We must be the change we wish to see in the world, and **we are just as much the things we don't do, as the things we do**.

Are those people failures for just walking past? Of course not, but we must acknowledge that that type of energy being displayed towards one person all contributes to their innner turmoil. If we realise this, and are able to make a difference, then we are not just saving those around us, but ourselves as well. We are on a journey of getting to know ourselves, and such acts will help you. People who use their intelligence identify that helping others is actually helping themselves.

Set up youth for real success

'Children need models rather than critics.'
Joseph Joubert

It is quite clear that the youth are in desperate need of proper guidance. Our generations revolve around teaching kids how we think they should react to things, or our own individual beliefs. As we have already discussed, some beliefs we have are not always the truth, so how do we know we are teaching them correctly? Just because we are adults doesn't mean we haven't been negatively influenced and are passing that down to the younger generation.

There are some children that won't hold back on telling us when we are taking a turn for the worse. My sister has no shortage of lectures from her four year old for smoking; sometimes kids know better. But the majority of times, we are the role models, so here are a few tips on how we can monitor whether we are teaching them things that will empower their lives. The first point is that we must be able to make sure that what we are teaching them is aiming towards a true love. We must also question what we are teaching them, and ask how this could benefit others or affect their lives. **'If I do teach them about love and real success, do I practise what I preach? What detrimental effect could this particular belief have on their wellbeing when they have to be out on their own? Is it leading them towards more hatred and believing in failure rather than enhancing and enriching the quality of their lives? How has this belief negatively affected my life? Are they in fact limiting beliefs?'** This all goes back to really looking deeper into what you find with your own beliefs that will help you empower youth and set them up for a quality life. While doing this, you will equally enhance your own.

So often we teach children our own individual belief systems, which are evidentially different to what they might see on TV, from their friends, or what they hear at school. I don't think I have ever been bombarded with as many crime shows on TV than in the last few years. And they're making primetime more often! In all seriousness, what is the world coming to? Is it that exciting to watch the slaying of people? Even if they catch the 'bad guy' in the end, it doesn't alter the rest of the garbage kids are subjected to in the rest of the show. Not to mention the absolute crap that some music has in it. Some rap songs or dark music only talk about sex, selling drugs, killing and torturing people, disrespecting the world, and so on. Obviously these people are in desperate need of having to fill up their ego because they don't have any fulfilment in their lives. Surely, only someone who is deeply unfulfilled would look up to someone who sings about how many people they had to sell drugs to or kill to get their gold chain!

With all this confusion going on, can we ever change the course of the world? It is increasingly crucial to believe there is a common way for all mankind. I think we are neglecting the greatest lesson at school and at home, which is one on love, respect, appreciation and abundance for all people; a subject that teaches our children there are limitations from hate, disrespect, judgement on people's looks, social status, and religious background; a subject that teaches we are all part of the same team, and promotes a common reverence for all fellow humans. They must be made aware of how those things drastically affect their own lives.

As an adult, it is your duty to make sure that teaching about love and kindness is at the top of your list. But, more importantly, you must practise what you preach.

Regardless of cultural differences, imagine if someone asked what we are, and we all answered with, 'human'. That one word has the power to change the world. Rather than separating ourselves, could you picture what a difference it would make in the world just by that one word answer? Being a black belt and state gold medallist in taekwondo, Bruce Lee was always one of my inspirations when I was growing up. In an interview I saw, he was asked if he classed himself as Chinese or North American. His reply was, 'You know what; I want to think of myself as a human being, under the sky, under the heavens, like one family'. If we could prepare ourselves and our youth for the challenges that we face on a day-to-day basis, then the results would be astounding. We must teach them a universal respect for all things and allow them to see that they are part of this world, and that the world is a part of them.

I was inspired to write about this topic when I witnessed a child accidentally hit his head on a seat at a local mall. He began crying, and his mother called it a stupid chair and told him to hit it back. Once the child started striking back, he stopped crying and smiled. There were people around laughing because they thought the situation was cute. I would like to think that what this child has been taught has done nothing but satisfy his mother's selfish desires. She just didn't want to be embarrassed anymore by his wailing. Although this might seem a trivial incident, that child will grow up to believe that when he is faced with physical or emotional hurt, revenge is the best option. That will be his subconscious reaction. What a misconception and a lie. This is why I repeat, **it is absolutely crucial what we teach the next generation**, as belief systems create us to make decisions, and hence sculpt our life accordingly.

Proper education is the only way to enhance the quality of people's lives, and that's why I say you don't have to hit 'rock bottom' to make change. We can make subtle changes and educate children on fulfilment and love, rather than wait for them to be taught through life experience. They will definitely have challenges along the way, as we all do, but proper education for you and them, will set us all up for real success.

25

THE MYSTERY OF LIFE

When you really think about this infinite galaxy, and this sphere you are walking on, it really makes you wonder about the mystery that surrounds us. Trying to figure out all the answers would drive us insane, and stop us from really embracing what we know as life. Through my journey, I have come to some awakenings that I would like to share, which I believe are very important to understanding and enriching our life.

Past present future

'What we are today comes from our thoughts of yesterday, and our present thoughts build our life of tomorrow: Our life is the creation of our mind.'
The Buddha

In order to experience wholeness, we must conclude that the present moment is the only thing that is ever real, and therefore, complete. Have you ever wondered where yesterday went? Take a look around — can you grab it? It didn't just disappear, as we know nothing in life ever does. How does a part of the world leave the world? It ultimately can't. So if your experience still exists somewhere, then where is it? Only in your mind! It is yet another thing stored in the vast and infinite realm of your consciousness. That means it's accessible, recreatable, and believable, just like the thoughts we have of our future. We become so entrenched in the notion of past or future, that we forget the most important time of all: now. And even when a thought about the past comes into reality again, or a thought about a future desire comes about for the first time, we are still experiencing it in the now, aren't we?

An example of a past thought being recreated would be to organise a family dinner similar to one you had a month ago where everyone thoroughly enjoyed themselves. A future one would be to create an experience you have never had. But how often do we get the experience we desire, yet not appreciate it enough because our mind is too busy wandering, rather then ever being present in that moment? That's a life that is far too common for most.

There are certain people who try to hold onto their past or a happy experience they once had and base their fulfilment on that. This could be a good tool to get some quick satisfaction, but the only way of being truly fulfilled is to embrace the beauty of now. No matter what challenge I am faced with, I always fall back into 'right now', and a sudden peace manifests itself. I do this to clear my mind at the times when it feels like it is racing around or wandering. Once that is done, you will be in a prime position to put something that will benefit you in its place.

And seeing that all experience is in the mind means we have control over it. I'm certain there have been times where you have looked back and shifted your mindset over an experience. The experience itself then seems to change all together. Those times when you have looked at something that you initially took as being bad, yet after further assessment, the same experience seemed great. We must be aware that the situation was always up for that other perception, as the situation itself has not changed. But it was your choice to attach a different mindset to it and draw a benefit. This can be done from any situation or experience if we focus on looking for one.

Living in the moment is not the absence of care for the future; it's to actually create the future with awareness.

People often talk about a 'past' and a 'future'. **The 'past' is only a mental image, just as the 'future' is; however, they are pictures that affect how we act in the present**. You are the editor of the photo album in your mind. Would you repeatedly look over a photo album that brought up shocking emotions? Then why do you do it in your mind? If we acknowledge this control, then it allows us to really embrace our decisions right now, as we know nothing else is essentially real. Let me put it to you more simply. Most go about their day worrying about something that has happened, or stressing over something that hasn't even happened yet. It's a ridiculous and insane thing to do. They are literally creating imaginary scenarios in their mind and killing themselves in the process. It affects what they are creating and attracting in their life, because they make it a priority. The funny thing is, they never needed to worry or stress, because neither of those events are real, but by continually thinking about them, they make them a part of their reality in the present.

As we have been told by many great people in history, our thoughts become real.

I have a little exercise for you to do. **Right now take one of your hands off this book and repeatedly move your fingers up and**

down. Watch them closely and concentrate on their movements for about thirty seconds. Do this now.

Now look at your whole hand. Touch it, embrace it. **You are in the now.** Did you think of anything that made you worry while you were doing that exercise? Of course you didn't, because you were focusing on the present moment. You came back to reality. Where are the things you once stressed about? Take a look around. Exactly — it is only a story that you are replaying in your mind.

Being one with your mind means you have the power to manipulate it any way you like. Who's in control of your thoughts? You are. Truly successful people have a strategy with this knowledge. By acknowledging they are the only ones that have the power to create scenarios or stories in their mind, they think of ones that are of benefit to them. The other stories that have a detrimental effect are quickly attacked and overpowered. This is one secret fulfilled people know.

I once read that a good way of finding the 'now' is too look up at the clouds. When you see it as just a cloud, you are in the now. But as soon as you start seeing faces or shapes in the clouds, you know your mind has wandered. Now we can't always stay in the now. Our mind will certainly wander, but by knowing you have the ability to fall back into 'right now' to clear your head when something is affecting your life, that is power. At most times, our mind should wander only to make sense of past experiences, or create an empowering path for our future. When it's not doing either of these, find comfort in the 'now'.

'The art of life is to live in the present moment, and to make that moment as perfect as we can by the realization that we are the instruments and expression of God Himself.'

Emmet Fox

Predominantly, whatever we choose to think about now, whether it's an unpleasurable experience or that great life we envision, will certainly have an effect on what we do next. This acknowledgement really altered the way I approached my life, as I began really embracing the moment and using my time that was 'real' as productive. It stopped me from procrastinating, because I became aware of the enormous power that my present thoughts, words and physical actions have in creating my life. **Every new moment creates new opportunities. A fresh slate offered by life**. You can think what you want, feel what you want, and create what you want. The next time you find yourself fixated on a past experience or a 'what if' scenario that is negatively affecting your state, ask yourself these three questions:

What do I want to think?

What do I want to feel?

What do I want to create?

Who's in control of how you think? Who's in control of how you feel? Who's in control of what you create? These three important aspects to life are solely your choice in every moment. You are in control of all of them, so choose intelligently.

To create things that are worthy of looking back on, you have to change your decisions in the present. The scenarios you replay over in your mind and the stories you tell yourself shape your life.

Your gift to create

'Whether you think you can, or think you can't, either way you are
right.'
Henry Ford

This life is a plane of endless possibilities, and what you choose
to do now is a creation of what will be next. It starts with our
thoughts, comes out of our mouth, and then reflects through
our physical actions. **Manifesting our visions into reality is just
like a puzzle. First we take a good look at a picture of the end
result, hold onto it, and then set out to fit together the pieces.**
We have also been given the gift of freewill, so what you decide
to create next is entirely up to you. If you decide to think and
believe strongly about something, whatever it may be, you will
create it. Everything that exists in this world is someone's creation.
It began as a mental image, a strong vision, followed by a passion
that caused action to create. A table, a bridge, a book, or a painting
all follow the same principles in order to be created.

It's also evident that we manifest most things throughout our
day. The mind is so powerful that we are able to narrow down to
one thing and make it real among so much choice. Let's say you
choose to go to a store at 8a.m. to buy that new outfit you have
been waiting for. It began as a thought, you told people where
you were going and you created the scenario in your mind. It was
your vision, but you had already been there in your mind. Now
even though it was only in your mind at the time, you knew that's
where you were going to go. You planned to wake up at 7a.m.
to get ready and took the appropriate steps to manifesting it into
reality. It then became your creation.

You automatically deviate from the mass by merely realising your power to create.

On the other hand, if you decided not to go to that shop, then it would never have become real, and what you chose to do instead would have taken its place, right? Does that mean your ability to create going down to the shop didn't exist? No, it did exist — you just chose not to go. It existed as a realistic option you may have taken. Your consciousness offers you have a vast array of possibilities in all moments. You could have washed your car in that time, watched TV, read a book, or begun working. And if that were the case, going down to the local shop would have never been a creation in your reality. **It's quite fascinating how most of our life is created by our choices!**

Every moment we are creating our life. We create as we go.

Destiny — the choice is yours

'Shallow men believe in luck, strong men believe in cause and effect.'
Ralph Waldo Emerson

Most people live their whole lives believing that their experiences were due to a mysterious luck that circles the universe, and just oddly chooses random people to have certain experiences. If we know anything about how the world and nature operate, it's that everything has its place. Too regularly, people use the concept of 'luck' to escape accountability for their own actions. This universe and everything in it has been proven to be a wonderful energy that connects us all. All the experiences that have recently happened in my life, and to others around me, have made me throw out that limiting belief in luck.

If you do believe in coincidence, then explain it. If you believe that things just happen out of luck or coincidence, then what is the basis on which you allocate experience? It's absurd to pick and choose what you think is luck, and if you do, then what's the reason behind all the other experiences? See, if we believe in luck or mysterious coincidence then it must hold up for every single thing that happens in our lives, and we all know to believe that is just a cop out for not taking responsibility. It would mean we have absolutely no control over our life, which is a lie. It's not okay to say something is luck to suit yourself, but not say it about everything. That would mean even waking up in the morning and not getting hit by a car on the way to work is 'good luck'. Dropping a pen would be 'bad luck'. If you get my drift, in order to believe in luck, you must adapt it to every little thing that happens. We all know that we are in far more control than that.

Reason cancels out coincidence. Cause and effect cancels out luck. If you want control over your life, look to cancel both of them out with those substitutions.

People want to believe that things just happen for an unknown reason because they don't want to believe they had any control over the outcome. Most times we say something was 'bad luck' because of a failure to see that opportunity as one for growth and a means to act differently. We may not see the reason or the cause instantly, but with enough thought, we will in fact see that every experience has meaning and is a basis for learning. I'm not sure about you, but I find it hard to believe that there is a man up in the sky rolling dice on our life. Everything that happens in nature is due to cause and effect and we are no exception. This is a hard concept for some to grasp, because our ego stands in the way of taking responsibility for our life.

We all hold the paintbrush to our lives. It's not until we truly understand and take hold of this that we are able to make clear decisions. It all depends on how you look at your experience. If you refer to it just being luck or coincidence then the true meaning of the experience seems to go past with no benefit. Taking accountability and gathering knowledge from an experience that can benefit your life also helps the whole world. We are not in this alone, and if everyone took accountability then this world would be a much better place. If someone slips on a banana peel on the floor and breaks their back, would that be bad luck? I would have to say that it was due to the inconsiderate and stupid act of another person who dropped the peel, and also due to others acknowledging that it could be dangerous and walking straight past it. **Luck has no grounds for growth or action; accountability does**.

'Nothing happens by chance, my friend…No such thing as luck. A meaning behind every little thing, and such a meaning behind this. Part for you, part for me, may not see it real clear right now, but we will, before long.'
Richard Bach

There is a God-given path for all of us, and it's the path of love, which opens up all the doors to our life; but then again, it's still our choice whether we wish to walk it.

We attract what we focus on. I am a massive fan in the old saying 'everything happens for a reason', yet most times I couldn't put my finger on what the reason was. It would confuse me even more until another similar event would take place. When I really started questioning everything about my life, I came to a rude awakening about that saying. The deeper I went looking for those reasons, while trying to be honest with myself in the process, I found that the reasons were all pointing to me.

I definitely had to let my ego down when doing this, because that's the only way the truth seems to arise. We become confused always looking on the outside to try and find a meaning, unaware the answer is actually right here, within us. Was it me that was attracting these things in my life? Was I the reason they were happening? The answer would keep falling back on me. I would calculate the way I had been thinking, and it was quite true. I was attracting these things in my life through the attitude I was taking to it everyday. The way I thought, the words I spoke, and the physical actions I took were all contributing to my downfall. I would try to believe that things 'just happened' but that belief leads to no benefit. So do we really believe that, or are we just scared to face the truth? When a certain situation arises, are we taking any accountability? I also discovered that the reason something happens is subject to whatever we wish that reason to be. If things happen for a reason, then make sure you make the reason an empowering one that you can grow and learn from. **An experience means whatever you want it to mean**.

It wasn't until I began really taking control over my life that I became aware of the power I had to shape my destiny. It was in fact me the whole time; and it makes sense, considering I've been given freewill. Funny that it took that many experiences to finally have a light bulb moment on the matter. As I began taking sole accountability for the position I was in, it turned around radically. Doing this is the only way you are ever going to gain that control, and make everlasting change. As long as we blame everything and everyone else for the position we are in or the experiences that arise, we cannot excel. Don't get me wrong, **we definitely can't control everything outside, but we can control what significance it has on our life or how we react to it**.

'Destiny is no matter of chance. It is a matter of choice: It is not a thing to be waited for, it is a thing to be achieved.'
William Jennings Bryan

One of the greatest examples of this was from a young woman named Bethany Hamilton who had her arm bitten off by a shark when she and her friends were night surfing. She was an aspiring professional surfer at the time, and even through such a challenging experience she decided to pursue her dream and won many titles. She has inspired millions of people around the world with her book and movie *Soul Surfer*, which features actors such as Helen Hunt. Bethany is definitely someone who sees her experience as a means to teach others — not as bad luck. She said she would not take back what happened to her, and regrets nothing.

Our truth will always display itself throughout our life, but given freewill, we have a chance to grasp it or live a life far from it. We know if we are not following our true path, it is usually indicated by the emptiness we regularly feel. Taking accountability and relating your current thoughts, words and actions to what position you are in is crucial in allowing your spirit to tell you the truth. You will be shocked at times, but the deeper you search, the closer you get to that gift in every experience.

Uncertainty versus certainty

There are times in our life where we seem so certain about something, but it soon becomes obvious that life has something else in store for that moment. Thinking about it, though, its life's uncertainty that makes it worth living. If we knew all the answers, there would literally be no point, and it would take away any experience or emotion. There would be no thrill, challenge, love or appreciation. It's like when we go and watch a movie with a friend who has already seen that same film. We read up on it, we get a fair idea of what's it's about, and we go to experience the rest. How annoying is it when your friend starts telling you what happens? You're like, 'Shut up, I came to watch it'. We don't want to know all the answers; if we did, life wouldn't be worth living.

Don't think about life's uncertainty until it shows itself, and then deal with it intelligently. When uncertainty shows itself, I still make certainty out of it. Until it's displayed, just be certain, because there is no reason to be otherwise. What chance do you give yourself if you're reminding yourself of uncertainty before it's even happened? Even when it comes to the smallest things in life, I find people are so uncertain. It's no wonder their goals seem unreachable. We say things like, 'I might', 'I'll try' or 'maybe'. With that attitude nothing is ever going to get done. When you make the decision to actually do it you will always find a way. We just need to make the decision. We say things like, 'What if...' or create scenarios that aren't real and tarnish our decisions right now, usually resulting in attracting those very things we tried to avoid in the first place. Acknowledge that life has its uncertainties so you won't be shocked when they arise. In the meantime, focus on creating certainty and eliminate all barriers in your mind.

We are one

'If we have no peace, it is because we have forgotten that we belong to each other.'
Mother Teresa

Humans don't know all the answers. Throughout history we have tried to find out what the truth is, but everyone will have something different to say. Various religious sectors, scientists, and even the guy at the local convenience store all claim that they have the truth. Among all the religions in the world, there are more that **45,000** different factions. It's bad enough to be fighting against other religions, but many even manage to fight within their own religion. Christians versus Christians, Muslims against Muslims, and Hindus with Hindus. In all seriousness, what on earth is going on? Where is the basic human respect? Was that really God's plan — to give certain people permission to destroy something he had created out of love? I don't think so; sounds more like a selfish human act, don't you think?

Ultimately, there can only ever be one truth, because it would mean that everything else is essentially a lie. So who's right and who's wrong? There has to be a truth that everyone can accept. Once a mind is fully awakened and a heart unchained, that truth becomes clearer. It has no limitations or restrictions. It's not a matter of gaining any selfish satisfaction of ego, like 'I'm right and you're wrong'; it's just the truth. I would have to say that ego sums up the notion of 'evil' as it is truly the cause of separation in the world.

What is it going to take for the world to see that happiness, peace, appreciation, unity, fulfilment and real success stem from the ultimate truth: **love**? That's the special feeling. The truth is your truth, that deep voice inside that always displays a way of demonstrating more love. Some believe that voice will give them nothing but disappointment, but those who are truly rich in life know that it's that exact voice that creates their dreams to come true. It is the one we rarely dare to reason with because we will be exposed to lying to ourselves on so many occasions.

Love is the essence of all creation and that is the truth. All great leaders who have led their nation out of suppression and into liberation did it through love. Nelson Mandela, Mahatma Gandhi, Martin Luther King Jr and Mother Theresa are great examples. Their message was clear and concise; put down your arms and give love — and it worked! The same goes with finding liberation in our daily lives. Apply it and you will prove it to yourself.

We were never meant to separate ourselves from any part of creation, but I guess that was the human pride factor. The 'I'm this' and 'you're that' notion has been in the foreground of every war or obscenity in history. Love is pure and is not prideful. And it definitely does not wish to be separated from anything that it dwells in. That is why the great teachers never asked for a religion to be based around them. Others did that on their own accord. All these masters came to do was teach about love for all creation. I am a major believer in God, but I don't believe the higher power is separate from me or any part of creation. If I stuck to that concept, I would never be able to understand or feel the creator's presence. I know this because I used to claim I believed, but never acted as if I did. Further to that, my inner self was not at peace, and that is a sign that we have not yet grasped the true nature of the higher power which exists in everything.

As we are all one, the universe and everything in it is at the mercy of our actions. We affect everything, and create anything!

If you believe that the creator is separate to you, then I ask, 'Where is God?' Is he really up there? Where's up there? Up there is infinite! If you are able to feel the higher power (love) within you, then doesn't that mean that power exists in you? If God is all, doesn't that mean we are one with all creation? If we feel emotions that are so far from explanation, and understand there is a much deeper level to life than what surrounds us with our eyes, then it seems it is within. We are not separate from anything, or anyone. If we were, it would mean we wouldn't have the ability to affect it, and we all know that is untrue. Everything exists within our own conscious realm, even the very concept of God. Hence, we have the ability to influence or affect everything, even if it's only through perception.

Where did consciousness originate? No one knows, and I guess that's why most of the world's population acknowledges that there must be something greater. There's a simple reason in which I have no choice but to really believe that all this was created. **I can't come to terms with how something could come from nothing.** If you ever find the answer I would like you to email me instantly. But then I'd reply with the question, 'Then where did that come from?'

Scientists say it was the big bang theory; well what created the big bang? Then they will come up with another answer, but then what created that, then what created that. It's a never-ending cycle, and if you attempt to comprehend it, you will realise there is actually no reasonable explanation to ever figuring it out. It's like asking

'What came first, the chicken or the egg?' The human mind is clearly incapable of discovering such a finding. If you don't believe we have a creator, then all I will ask you to do is **think of what created thought!**

Most people wait in anticipation for a miracle to happen in their life, unaware that the miracle is actually life itself.

I'm sure it is quite obvious that when something is created, it has a part of its creator in it? We can all at least comprehend that much. So that means if all this started from something — and it had to because something definitely doesn't come from nothing — there is a part of our creator within all of us. Call it God, higher power, Allah, Yahweh, ether, plasma; it doesn't really make a difference. It's still within you and it's the same for all. Just like a painter and his painting or a sculptor and his statue. A part of the painter or sculptor remains in their creation forever. It starts with passion, love, but most importantly it is a means of expression. Those attributes will be evident for eternity. Don't you have your mother's DNA within you? Of course, because she took part in creating you; a part of her has to be in you. As far the connection between each other, well that's just evident in everyday life. Take a good look at just how much other people affect how you act in one day, and they don't even have to say anything half the time.

Science has proven that everything in the universe comes from the same source and is made up of the same compounds. *Matter* exists in everything! The common definition of 'matter' is anything that has both *mass* and *volume* (occupies *space*). For example, a table would be said to be made of matter, as it occupies space, and has mass.

Matter consists of protons, neutrons and electrons. **Electrons** are tiny, very light particles that have a negative electrical charge. **Protons** are much larger and heavier than electrons and have a positive charge. **Neutrons** are large and heavy like protons, but have no electrical charge. What I find fascinating is that our positive charge is larger than our negative. I wonder if that has anything to do with hearing that **love conquers all**, light will put out the darkness or happiness will win over sadness?

You are made up of this matter, along with your TV, car, the tree on the front lawn, and the guy in Africa. The world and everything in it truly does come from the same source. Isn't everything created from the earth? Take a look around? From dust we came, to dust our bodies return. We will be entangled with everyone and everything forever because everything is held together by a common element. Even the events that take place in outer space influence everything that happens on planet earth. If one thing did not play its part for one moment, nothing could survive.

Most major religions also state that God is above everything else. Well, is there something that exists in everything? Yes: energy. And if God is greater than this, then it means that our creator too exists in everything and more, right? Being one with all means we have the power to influence everything.

'So powerful is the light of unity that it can illuminate the whole earth.'
Baha'u'llah

You might be thinking, 'Well what is the creator and what shape or form does it have?' It's ultimately unknown. It's like asking the same question about consciousness; no one can answer that, and even quantum physicists are stating that it's easier to do work leaving it as the unknown. The most intelligent people in history have tried to figure it out and failed miserably. We will never get to the bottom of it as humans, because like I said before, there is NO bottom. That's how you know there is a greater meaning to life. But how do you truly embrace such a mystery? You consume yourself with it every time you project love. It's evident when you have that person that you really love next to you, in a mode of total appreciation, or those overwhelming emotions when contributing. The best way to know our creator is to understand the creation. Once you understand yourself and the world, its magnificence will show itself.

We know there is definitely a mystery to life because we don't know all the answers. We look up in the sky; there's a sun, moon, all these planets, this galaxy. We have all wondered what it's all about, and what it all means. We are as tiny as a speck of dust in the universe, so there's more to life than the petty complaints we surround ourselves with on a daily basis. Life is to be enjoyed.

We have a tendency to bog ourselves down with all these things that we will never find out. It then seems all too much, we begin to doubt, and forget the most important thing — to **live**! Some will attempt to know all the answers and will put limitations on the unknown. They consume themselves with 'past lives', or the 'afterlife', yet neglect the most precious time of all: right now. I have found a new comfort in not knowing exactly where I will be next, or what I was before, but I know I am getting closer to love in this, and that will carry on and on to whatever the next holds. Understanding there is more to you than meets the eye, and realising there is a major purpose to this mystery we call life is extremely important to your happiness. It allows you to search deeper, accept your greatness, and use the once-slumbering power within you. This will ultimately help us defeat what society has branded us as being and prevent us falling back into insignificance. It's also very important to not get caught wandering in a daze all day about these mysteries. You may just bump yourself on things nearby, and it's going to hurt! Searching for more is great, but make sure you always remain conscious of the reality of the present moment.

Realistically, all you have to do is ask the question 'What am I doing here?' and you are thrown into this massive realm of possibility that is far greater than you alone. Do you really think that whatever it was that created this world only did so to obtain praise? Isn't that selfish? I think it's an insult to believe that a God that dwells in all things would need anything from us. Life is our gift; it is not meant to be lived in fear of something that is love. A recent study showed that eighty-eight per cent of the world's population do believe in something. This figure is higher in the US, where it is estimated that ninety-five per cent of the population do. We understand that there are lots of questions we don't have answers to and that there is a far greater meaning to life, which is why I think so many do believe. We want to continue to have hope and faith, because we know it has seen us through on so many occasions. We just need to learn how to really amplify those qualities of the creator that dwell within us.

'A wise man sees himself in everyone and everyone in himself.'
The Buddha

Finding the connection…

The wind that circulates through the world is the same air we breathe. The sun is what gives us energy. The planet we live on is mostly water. What is your body mostly made up of? When we go and blow on a leaf, it has the same effect as when the wind hits it. The water that drops out of the sky is the same water we drink to stay alive. It's so amazing that I can walk into an old building and literally feel its history and the energy in the room. You don't have to be an Einstein to figure out that we are all interconnected and one in essence. I feel people's pain and I don't even have to see them. I would also like to note that whichever man or woman created the word 'universe' was definitely inspired by collective consciousness. 'Universe' is Latin for **one version**.

In being one with this endless universe, we are built with infinite intelligence and have a higher power that most have yet to tap into. This is why there are individuals that seem to be on a completely different level to others. They have discovered a hidden source. There's a great mystery going on in the world, but we seem to be blinded to this phenomenon. The most important aspect to this realisation is that God has always been with you, yet on occasions we choose not to listen to that wise voice that lies deep within our heart. If you fight the thought that the qualities of a higher power reign with you, you will never discover the essence of life. You will also not express the one love for all creation and therefore will never be at peace.

'You menace others with your deadly fangs. But in tormenting them, you are only torturing yourselves.'
Milarepa

This next acknowledgment that I discovered was basically the foreground of my change forever. How does being connected with the world and everything in it affect my life? Well, **if I harm you, I'm only harming myself in the process.** By harming myself, I'm harming you and this world. If I disrespect the environment, I'm only doing it to myself and it will distance me from ever discovering my greatness.

If we do ill things, or act with negative intent, the world will answer back ferociously. Some people like to think they can get away with treating others poorly but the effects are immediate in their own life. Every time they do, it penetrates their soul, and an inner peace becomes harder to grasp. They will battle their inner demons until the day they die unless their actions are liberated. On the other hand, if you are pure, respectful, loving and give of your true self, the world will answer accordingly.

Those who bully and tease others are a great example. How do you think they feel? Short-term satisfaction is no means of gaining true happiness. They are scared because they haven't yet discovered their greatness because of their constant decisions that go against reason and truth. When they go home and lay their head on their pillow with no one to bully, they realise they are empty. Others usually submit to their energy, which then affects their own life and the people around them. It's like the continuous ripples caused by dropping a pebble in water. We are never going to eliminate such people or situations in our lifetime, but it is our choice about what significance they have on our life. If you hate back, are you any different? But if you feel compassionate to these people and realise that they are unaware of how their actions are affecting their own life, then you will be able to interrupt the energy pattern.

The lack of understanding that we are all one is what separates us.

All giants that have come before us have spoken clearly about this unity in the world and the effect it has. In Hinduism and Buddhism, karma is held in extremely high importance. The core meaning of **karma** is **action**. Karma is the direct effect your actions have on your own life. As soon as you commit an action with a certain intention, you are immediately affected. Whether that's in a positive or negative way depends on the action and the intention you choose. Dr Wayne Dyer summed it up beautifully when he said, 'How people treat you is their karma; how you react is yours'. Even in the Bible it states, 'Each one should test his own actions, then he can take pride in himself, without comparing himself to somebody else, for each one should carry his own load... A man reaps what he sows... Let us not become weary in doing good, for at the proper time we will reap a harvest if we do not give up' (Gal 6:9). Clearly this is not just talking about what is to come, but this life, and right now. The message is quite clear I think; **the energy you give off is the energy you get back**. Everything you do emanates energy, including your thoughts. If you doubt this notion, then just review previous actions you have taken, and see if your attitude (energy) has anything to do with the experiences you have had. In relation to that, notice how those actions made you feel? Even if some brought short-term satisfaction, did they really fulfil your life and purpose, or create a deep inner peace? The way we feel after we take action is usually the best indicator.

Don't just treat others how you would like to be treated; treat yourself how you would like to be treated.

The challenge I frequently hear is when people tell me they have tried being nice and loving, but they feel that if they continue they will be taken advantage of. If that is your motto in life, then you are actually only giving to obtain something in return. No one can walk all over you unless you let them, so the giving of your true qualities should require nothing in return. If you give only to receive then you have given nothing. When you emit love and kindness to everyone and do not expect a response externally, the reward is apparent. Do not wait to fill yourself up with their gratitude, but embrace the fulfilling feeling you attain from giving. If you are faced with this challenge you will realise they are trampling themselves for having a heart that is not yet filled with love. Be compassionate in this situation, but be even more grateful and proud of your choice of action. **No one can take your happiness unless you let them**.

The greatest thing that inspires me to push my vision forward and enhance the power of my passion is when I hear people talk poorly about life. I know from experience how sad it is to resist life. We will never reach our full potential, nor will we live the life we envision with that mindset. Most times all it takes is to shift your focus onto something that you love, and you will see how easy it is to free yourself from that imprisoning thought or emotion. This leads to the great question, **'Are we slowly dying, or are we beginning to live?'** It seems the world has been caught up in trying to find a cure for death, which is inevitable. We are blinded by the fact that the only cure for death is life, so we'd better start living. You really live when you truly live as you are; not how you think you have to live.

Hard to grasp notions

'And we have come to know and to believe the love that God has in us. God is love, and the one who resides in love resides in God, and God resides in him.'
1 John 4:16

While beginning to comprehend that we are all one, it also brings into question other notions about the source from which we originate. A common one is the word 'he' that gets used to replace God. I believe if it's used to narrow the higher power down to something that is absent from this world, then I disagree. Most people take the word 'he' literally, even though when you ask them, they reject that it's a 'he' or a singular, separate entity. This is due to not being able to ultimately explain what God is.

The concept of God is used by many people as a tool to separate from each other. It's a contradiction, considering all major religions claim to be followers of love. In my opinion, using the word 'God' to separate from each other is the greatest blasphemy. It honestly doesn't matter what religion you are, there is no excuse for treating another human like garbage, or believing yourself superior to them. If you follow beliefs that enforce those notions, then you have been sadly deceived and will never experience true fulfilment.

I know many spiritual people who say, 'I'm not religious, because that is separation from the world'. I am quick to remind them that categorising themselves as 'spiritual' is equally separating. When you think you are superior to someone else, and use religion as an excuse for your ego, you actually contradict the very religion you claim to protect. Was the true message to ever separate ourselves from the world or place ourselves on a higher pedestal than others? Doesn't that display a form of hatred? I'm sure these great teachers just came to teach love, but some people use the grand message as a means to fulfil their own selfish desires and emotional gaps.

When people ask what I am and are getting ready to throw me in a category like a piece of meat, I always answer with, 'I Am who I Am'. When they ask what organisation I am part of, I answer with, 'Life. My religion is Love'. Yes, some people do think I'm crazy but I get a good laugh out of seeing the expression on their faces.

Many people have built a concept of fear around God. I truly believe to fear God is the biggest insult. When you fear your human father, you may do things that he wants, but not because you truly want to. It's not coming from your heart because you feel as if you have to, right? So in fact, no satisfaction should come to your father, and if he were intelligent, he would not want you to continue to feel that way towards him. But when your father shows you love, and you have that same love for him, you will do things from your heart. And that's where meaning and depth come into an action.

At times we get down on our knees and call out to God for something. I know I have done this one many times myself. Some are bought up to believe that asking is enough. We say things like, 'God, can **you** please comfort my aunty at this time,' or 'Please give me more money'. It's as if we deliberately ignore the resources we have within us that have the ability to answer our own prayers. We then never get what we want and doubt that there is a God. Have you ever heard that voice telling you that you can have everything you have ever wanted if you are able to work for it with the qualities you know you already have? Those moments when something tells you to 'get up and go for it'. Now how many times have you ignored that voice in the hope that it will magically appear by getting on your knees and asking for it? Well, God is that voice telling you that you can have it all, but you must use what you have to get it. **Underachievers are too busy asking, while the great achievers are doing**. I wonder if it's ever occurred to people that everything they have ever wanted or desired will come about from their own actions; that in fact we are here to create with the gifts that have all ready been given. We must take accountability and responsibility for our life.

We have been socially conditioned to think humans as being incapable of godly acts. We are co-creators in all of this. After asking for money, opportunities, happiness, and so on, we suddenly realise that living a successful life doesn't happen that easily. Is there really nothing you can do to enhance the chance of fulfilling your prayers or your dreams? I remember watching an inspirational interview one night in which John Conteh, a former world boxing champion, discussed the spiritual aspect to his success. He mentioned that once he realised that **God helps those who help themselves**, his attitude in life and commitment towards his dreams were never the same. For a brief moment, I want you to think about how you pray or even converse with yourself in one day. Ask yourself this question, 'How many times do I say please, rather than thank you?'

Every key to our life has been given, the master key being love. In prayer we must have faith that the gifts are already there, like wisdom, power, energy, love, respect, happiness, patience and fulfilment. It's not like we can really go to the local supermarket and buy these qualities off the shelf. We must unwrap everything that is stopping us from expressing these qualities. We must rejoice that our inner voice will really light up the path, and trust that the events that take place are the result of our creations. They may not always be controlled physically, but we can control what certain events mean in our life. Situations take place to help us harness learning and growth, especially those that you think are the lowest points of your life. Have faith in yourself, but above all be thankful in prayer and meditation.

And in recognising that the point of life is to learn, it brings to light the stereotypical notion of heaven and hell. I couldn't imagine a god that is 'unconditionally loving' damning us to hell for eternity. Have humans interpreted this notion of their own accord? Has anyone been to hell or heaven and back to tell us what it is like? I know one thing, and that is we experience hell on earth when we don't tap into our awareness and fail to experience more love. That's all I can really understand in this human body, so that's what I'm going to work with.

I don't believe God is something to be feared, but to be embraced as love. When you fear God, you fear yourself, and that is no way to live. When you do something that is considered a sin, you run and hide, scared that the ground is going to open up and swallow you. That's not life. We are human, and this is a journey of self-discovery. We must take those events as learning, and use fear the best way we can, as a chance for new action.

'Such love has no fear, because perfect love expels all fear. If we are afraid, it is for fear of punishment, and this shows that we have not fully experienced perfect love.'

1 John 4:18

Then there is the thought that God chooses individual people to do his work. But if God chose that person and broke their freewill, then why didn't he choose everyone and we could all live happily ever after? Well, that's the whole point: everyone is chosen because the qualities are already there; most just choose not to use them. God doesn't choose or want certain individuals, he does not favour some and not the rest, **God already is**. So does that mean God created us with a want, as if he needs something from us? Does that mean God has ego? What does God look like? God doesn't choose and shouldn't be limited to our human concepts of wanting or characterising. It's an insult in its truest form, as God does not need anything from us.

You don't have to go and be a speaker on a world scale, an author, or what others deem as appropriate. In your daily affairs just show love and let your truth guide you, because you will get it back, and that's contributing. It's even funny what a smile can do. When you see people in the supermarket or wherever you are, just smile and be extremely nice and you will notice this power. You may get the odd person who doesn't appreciate it, but don't stress about those guys, it's just that they don't appreciate life themselves. You are the decider of how your life is created, and essentially we are our own judges. But remember, the great gifts reign within you, and they have always been there.

People say that we must believe in God, yet what most forget is that God also believes in us. The only way you can believe in God is if you believe in yourself. I don't believe that God is loving; I believe that God is love. They should never be separated. When we feel love in our heart, that is God. **God** is **love** and love is life. That's what unites the world and helps us to discover our greatness. Love (higher power) cannot be seen or limited, it has no shape or form, it dwells in all things, it is forever in existence, complete fullness, and the ultimate truth, but above all, it's that special feeling.

'For beautiful eyes, look for the good in others; for beautiful lips, speak only words of kindness; and for poise, walk with the knowledge that you are never alone.'
Audrey Hepburn

7TH STEP

FINDING FULFILMENT:
A REAL SUCCESS

26

A TRUE HAPPINESS

'If an Arab in the desert were suddenly to discover a spring in his tent, and so would always be able to have water in abundance, how fortunate he would consider himself — so too when a man, who as a physical being is always turned towards the outside, thinking that his happiness lies outside him, finally turns inward and discovers that the source is within.'
Soren Kierkegaard

There is one certain myth when it comes to happiness and it leads to confusion and disappointment for all who embrace it. It causes us to become confused, continually question who we are, and sends us around in a circle never finding an everlasting happiness. These points in our life derive from the notion that true happiness can be *obtained*.

Have you ever bought a new car or a watch and then after a month or so you realise that it's **just** a car, or a watch? Those materialistic purchases only seem to bring short-term satisfaction and do nothing but send us mad trying to figure out how we are going to get the next fix. We go on a holiday to make us happy, find a partner, eat some food that we like, sit on a comfortable chair, or go and make some more money. When we spend the money, come back from the holiday or eat that food, it seems we are unhappy once again. All these external aspects of life have restrictions of other people's behaviour, environment, social status, time, appearance, and so on. With so many limitations, is it any wonder that your so-called happiness seems to come to a halt on a regular basis? Shift your focus towards things that really matter in life and you will notice your power to create a true happiness.

While I was in Thailand I met a multimillionaire who had twelve strong businesses over a few countries. He was also the owner of a number of suit shops there and I bumped into him while he was on holiday checking up on the stores. If you have ever been to Thailand, you will know what I'm talking about when I say that the guys at the suit shops are pretty hard to get away from. But it was all in good fun, because I ended up liking them and buying three.

I was discussing true happiness with one of the workers there, and he said, 'That's what makes you happy,' pointing at a screen saver of a Lamborghini on the store laptop. The other guy, who I didn't know was the owner of the store, and of that very Lamborghini, said, 'That hasn't made me happy'. We began chatting and he offered to take me to lunch.

I found out that this great achiever who had millions of dollars was one of the unhappiest people I had ever met. I discovered that this man had been chasing what he thought was happiness his whole life to be faced with nothing but emptiness. No matter what he obtained, it never fulfilled him. I totally shifted his focus to allow him to see that happiness was right there within him the whole time. That same attitude he takes when going to buy a new car should be the same one he takes out to life everyday. I'm glad to hear that his progress is outstanding and that he is contributing to his country for the first time in his life.

Thinking about it, this makes sense when we hear about millionaires being addicted to drugs, while poor kids in Asia are doing the same thing. What's the difference? There is none, because they are both sectioning off their happiness. When it comes to finding happiness in addiction, it is important to realise that in doing it you will not find happiness, and in not doing it you might also not find happiness. Sounds a bit tricky, but by not doing it, you might also find that you are still unhappy. This is due to, again, believing that your happiness lies in something outside of you, and not a choice within that you are able to produce at any time.

The only way to true happiness is to recognise that it has always been *attained*. It was never those particular things that made you happy; it was always your choice of attitude in the face of them. If you believe that your happiness lies in certain circumstances or 'things', then how could it be if they also bring you pain? We hear a strange noise coming from the car engine, scratch the new watch or the food isn't as we expected, and all of a sudden our outlook changes instantly.

The greatest gift a person can discover within is to acknowledge that they have always had the power to produce whichever emotion they like, including happiness. Let's take going away on a holiday, for example. We plan it, we tell people about it, and we get absolutely excited about what's to come. The funny thing is that you are actually not on the holiday yet, so your happiness cannot be the holiday itself. Even a month leading up to it we seem to be much happier throughout our day. Workdays don't seem all too hard anymore; we ignore insignificant hiccups and choose not to focus on the worst in life, because WE ARE GOING

ON A HOLIDAY! **Create a vision, a projection into the future, or something to look forward to. It will also increase your willingness to keep that same feeling and use it to overcome and create a different outlook on challenges along the way.**

'A happy person is not a person in a certain set of circumstances, but rather a person with a certain set of attitudes.'
Hugh Downs

Once we finally go on the holiday, everything just seems amazing. The people are the nicest you have met, the buildings are extraordinarily beautiful, and you even seem to appreciate things that you once would have tried to avoid back home. In reality they were just buildings and people like anywhere else. The reason they look like the 'best' bluestones you have seen is because your attitude towards life is different.

You then come back home and meet a tourist in your town. They begin to tell you how amazing your city is, but you can't figure out what all the fuss is about. The truth is that when you shifted how you felt about life internally, it created everything outside to shift with you. Without argument, we will always see on the outside how we choose to feel on the inside. This means your happiness was always attained, and is accessible anywhere at anytime. Just like the holiday, I urge you to walk around your town with that same enthusiasm and happy feeling, and you will see it reflect instantly. Even if I told you right now to close your eyes, drift away and imagine a time where you were at your happiest, you would be able to feel those same emotions. Are you really there? I don't know, open up your eyes and tell me. The point is that no matter where you are or what situation you are at in life, a sad or happy feeling has always been there for you to grasp.

I would personally close my eyes in the times that I felt were about to shift my happy mood and go to that place or envision that special something that I love. **If we shift our focus towards happiness, our energy will flow in that direction.**

If you decide to look at the worst things in life, you are choosing to be unhappy. If you command your focus towards what's great in life, even in the face of challenges, you will produce emotions accordingly. As time goes on and the more you do this, the stronger and more emotionally intelligent you become. However, as we all know, this is life, and it's just not that easy at times. My theory about happiness is simple: **I am content with knowing that I will not always be happy. That is my happiness!**

I have come to accept that life is not made up of the stereotypical happiness that society has created. To reach the pedestal that social happiness is put on, it must mean we are in that bubbly, enthusiastic mood — or that's the common notion, anyway. And if we are not, then it means we are sad. Nothing is further from the truth. How about when you are in a mood of complete concentration and don't want anyone to interrupt you? Would you say you are not happy then? I wouldn't, because life has never been just two emotions: happy or unhappy. It even gets to the point where friends and family will ask you what's wrong when you are just sitting there. Do I have to be sad or there is something wrong to just sit on my own for five minutes? You must eliminate the concept that society has created about 'happiness' and accept all emotions as a part of life.

Our main mission in life is not to try and hold onto the concept of 'happiness', but rather to pursue and discover a self-worth. Embedded deep in every soul a thirst of self-love waits to be quenched. Once the source is found it can never be abolished, even in times of unhappiness.

27

TO FIND A HEART FILLED WITH LOVE

Love gives naught but itself and takes naught but from itself. Love possesses not nor would it be possessed; for love is sufficient unto love. When you love you should not say, 'God is in my heart,' but rather, 'I am in the heart of God.' And think not you can direct the course of love, for love, if it finds you worthy, directs your course.

Kahlil Gibran

First we are awakened through the power of change, and then enlightenment of love comes knocking on the door. I highly advise you to open and embrace it, as it's true life in the purest of forms. As you have probably already noticed, at the start of your awakening (self-discovery) you are not judging others on a social level, but on a consciousness level. The reason this happens is because you are starting to live life as an observer of cause and effect. I know you have probably heard the words 'conscious awakening' before, but it is just referring to the **self-awareness** which finally allows you to discover the massive impact **you** actually have on your own life, and the world at large.

If you are fan of the *Oprah* show, I'm sure you will remember the segment when her crew went to assist the Hawk family, who were all heroin addicts. The two sons, the father and the mother were all addicted, not to mention they had a baby who they were desperately trying to look after. Mike Hawk, the father, was separated from his family during rehab. The follow-up show months later revealed some astounding changes. I saw a man who was enlightened with an inner peace that was truly breathtaking. He spoke like a true master and someone who had been like this his whole life. But he wasn't — it had only been a few months! So many of the things he spoke about were the same exercises we have completed throughout this book. His inner journey completed his outside world. He even deliberately walks past the drug dealers that he once 'scored off' in the streets to prove his strength. By adding meaning and purpose to his life again, he was able to create the life he so often dreamt about. If a man who was a heroin addict for years turned his whole life around in a few months, then anyone can. Being consciously awakened to your true potential is the only way to ever be spiritually free and experience a true fulfilment.

Going through my own journey, I would describe it as like having a bucket of water thrown over me and waking up after years of sleepwalking. I stopped looking at the world through a cylinder. My mind was opened, which allowed me to finally discover the meaning in every experience. Every time I left my phone at home and had to go back and get it, all the times I tripped over, all the 'missed' opportunities, the bad times and the great times, all led me up to this point, right now. I began to fit together all the pieces of the puzzle, and it was all making sense.

After you experience such a realisation, you feel as if you need to go and shake everyone into it, and that's caused by the love that is starting to emanate from you. As time goes on, if you choose to go deeper, you are enlightened. You will notice that you appreciate other people's differences as judgement fades. Instead of feeling on a higher level to the rest, you bring everyone around up with you. I guess that's why it's so infectious. It sets you free from the mental, physical, and emotional chains that enslaved your heart for many years. The beauty of it lies in the one love you attain for all creation. Your heart knows how to free itself from resentment and hate, and you will finally see life as it was intended to be.

Once I was awakened, I realised I had an option of stopping there. Being awakened to who you really are allows for a good life to be lived, although nothing is more fulfilling than being enlightened by that master key that opens up all the doors to our life: love.

I went so deep that I questioned and challenged everything about my life. It went on for months, and there were nights when I felt as if I was in the dark. Everything about your reality starts to shift. When you decide to fully jump into the ocean of love its ferocious tide will rock your whole world. It will force you to shift beliefs you had forever, cry about things you once laughed at, and become a true child of life itself. Your heart is not weighed down, and your mind not surrounded by darkness. As the sea starts to calm, your heart fills with love's light and free flowing water, which is one that makes you never thirst again. As it fills up and starts to overflow, it radiates to everything and everyone around. You will notice that same love that dwells within you is in all creation, and you finally realise you are a part of it, and it is a part of you.

'Love is patient, love is kind. It does not envy, it does not boast, it is not proud. It is not rude, it is not self-seeking, it is not easily angered, it keeps no record of wrongs. Love does not delight in evil but rejoices with the truth. It always protects, always trusts, always hopes, always perseveres. Love never fails.'
I Corinthians 13:4-8

Surprisingly, I would wake up day after day to mysteriously find new answers and create more strength. My inner peace became overpowering and my whole attitude towards life had changed. I discovered my connection with this world, and aligned with my spirit to be the greatest person I knew how. The process was so intriguing, tireless, and fascinating, that the deeper I went, the more I was overwhelmed with awe. After a while of monitoring your thoughts, and directing them back to love, it seems new growth happens constantly. You are always reaching new levels.

Many people in history have died trying to find the 'Tree of life' hidden by God in the Bible. They thought it was an actual tree and to their constant disappointment they never found it. What they were oblivious to was that the tree of life is within all of us, but is hidden due to our separation from love and unity with the creator. It is truly to discover the unity between your soul and God, and the ego and higher self.

Discovering the essence of your being, and using it with the intent for the good of the world has been called many names in history. It's been called such things as the 'Great Work' and even saints such as St Frances of Assisi, Teresa of Avilla, and St Augustine have spoken about this phenomenon. Mahatma Gandhi, Mother Teresa, Orison Swett Marden, Albert Einstein, Martin Luther King Jr and nearly every other influential person spoke about our higher powers. It is also the core message of every major religion. It is a truly rare gem to find, but if you don't stop on your quest of self-awareness you will be aligned with new answers.

At one stage as I was going along my journey of self-discovery I was curious to know if I was the only one experiencing this. I felt alienated from the rest of the world. It was playing on my mind one day, and as I was walking down my corridor, I looked up to where the set of encyclopaedias was. I hadn't looked up there in years but my attention was drawn on this day. I saw a little white book in between all the other large ones. It was the only book that wasn't in the set and it was no bigger than my hand. It had no pictures on the front or a big title, just a plain and simple white book. I opened it up and had to immediately sit down from being so overwhelmed. It was a book on those saints and other people in history who had experienced this connection with their soul. It mentioned how some were persecuted and killed because they couldn't explain in words what it was exactly. I totally understood their situation and couldn't help but sympathise with their predicament. It's one that cannot be explained in words as it's far too great to be restricted. A love so pure is a feeling that is not bounded by finite words. It is to see the world in the eyes of God, and be surrounded by beauty.

As we begin to understand ourselves more — and I'm sure you have made some great progress after completing the tasks in this book — we enter the never-ending cycle of self-growth. With it, we spiral upwards, and find ourselves in love's direction.

When you can close your eyes and fall back into love anytime you like, even at the times that seem the most distressing, then open them up and see the world that way, its enormous power is displayed.

I'm only really in love with one thing. I'm in love with the feeling of love. I have felt that love in everything.

28

THE BEGINNING

'The ideals which have lighted my way, and time after time have given me new courage to face life, have been kindness, beauty and truth.'
Albert Einstein

After so many years, I finally began to live. I discovered that I was actually slowly dying before. Most people believe they are getting closer to death by physically growing. They feel aches and pains; they fear the number of their years as they start to increase. They think that every year passed is another step to leaving this earth, and they get depressed. But why would you be depressed about leaving when you don't even make the most of it when you're alive? When you are self-aware of your actions, it is the complete opposite. You acknowledge that every year that passes is another year you have learnt how to live!

We surround ourselves with stress, worry, selfishness, sadness, hate and every other feeling that kills us. Not just physically, but mentally, financially, and spiritually. It attacks every part of our life, directly or indirectly, and affects most people around us. Seeing you only have one shot at this life, why on earth wouldn't you give it the best shot you possibly can and be the greatest person you know how to be? Don't just live because you were born, embrace that you were actually born to live. Just because you are alive, it doesn't mean you are living. This is why it seems so many only begin to live when they finally stare death in the face.

I have come to a point in my life where I appreciate every part of its existence. The joy, the sorrow, the uncertainty, the laughter, the crying and the love all have equal respect and importance. It didn't take long to condition this embracing of life, which truly changed every aspect of its direction. I know I must show as many people as I can for as long as I can, because it truly does open up all the doors to life.

The explanations I have given in this book were the best way my spirit could pour out the strategies to find an ultimate fulfilment. It is still a journey, but I have faith that you will persevere. I trust that by doing these tasks you have had a pretty good taste of the other side, which I call life. The ultimate advantage of success is success itself, and to find fulfilment as you are now. An inner peace must come first, so complete this book ten times if you have to. Use it as your guide and not a 'read and put down' story, because that's not what it's about.

Never give up on that life that flashes before your mind, as that is the true path the creator had intended for you. We are meant to be great, experience emotions like never before, and continue to grow through any challenge. We were built with the gift to create our own life any way we choose and have a source of infinite intelligence to gather from.

Love yourself, love others, love life, and the world is yours.

Follow these tasks and let them consume every part of your life. Let your mind work overtime on your success instead of working on your disappointment. I'm not sure about you, but I am not, under any circumstances, throwing life away on being the victim. I will not waste it on hating, judgement, or selfishness. I want to win for myself, for everybody around me, and the world. Take the leap of faith, push yourself, and live the life you dare to dream. Feel those same emotions and attitude that you know you will have when you obtain that money, be able to share love with that person, or attain that inner peace, and it will happen.

The choice has always, is always, and will always be yours. Be true to yourself and persist for those visions, no matter what. You will make mistakes, but get on with life and it will become your cause.

Acknowledge that some experiences in life happen without us ever really knowing why. Why are there earthquakes that kill thousands of people? Why does someone get stabbed to death while trying to help someone else? Or why does a baby have a deformity from birth? These are the events in life that make us search deeper. If anything, they should make us want to strive to be a better person.

See, in life we get thrown curve balls, but it's not how quickly we can move out of their way, it's how well we learn how to hit that home run that counts. Experiences are there to shape who we are, even though at times they seem too much to bear. Isn't it true that some of your hardest experiences taught you the most? In time we may know why certain things happen, but even if we never do, it is no excuse for not being the best person you can be.

I don't care how much I think someone has mistreated me; I have come to appreciate the massive role they played in my life. For that I do not hate them, but love them.

In order to create an outstanding life you must have two things: a great SOM (state of mind) and the ability to command your own emotions.

This book offers you insight into both these aspects, yet your individual and unique journey will go on. The blueprint of your greatness is just like your fingerprint — it is one of a kind.

In conclusion, I really hope you enjoyed walking this self-journey and sharing it with me. I was inspired to write this book because of so many people displaying their confusion on how to actually go on a self-journey. Most wouldn't even know where to start, so I thought this would be a guide.

Congratulations on completing this book (empowering way of life), as it is a massive accomplishment. But do not stop here. You have many experiences and challenges to come. I really hope one day we can meet and exchange stories. I thank you humbly for allowing me to share your emotions, your mind, and your life through this journey. I know it's been a rollercoaster of emotions through this book, because I have felt it too. I consider us friends, wherever you are on this earth. And friends help each other spread their great message! It gives me great pleasure to know that we have connected. Funnily enough, even though we have never met, I feel as if I know you personally, and I'm sure you feel the same about me. Until we connect again, dream big, act extraordinarily, and live with purpose.

I find myself asking the same questions I did at the start of my journey:

Looking up high I wonder, what is all of this? What does this all mean? What am I doing here? A new comfort seems to arise now, which puts me at the essence of all creation. I am a part of it all, and it is a part of me. I guess the best answer is,

LIFE IS TRULY WHAT YOU MAKE IT.

It would be great to hear from you. Send me your feedback, your story or just to connect again. You can contact me at:

www.danielchidiac.com

info@danielchidiac.com